VALOUR ROAD

ALSO BY JOHN NADLER

Searching for Sofia

A Perfect Hell

VALOUR ROAD

JOHN NADLER

VIKING

VIKING
an imprint of Penguin Canada Books Inc., a Penguin Random House Company

Published by the Penguin Group
Penguin Canada Books Inc., 90 Eglinton Avenue East, Suite 700, Toronto, Ontario, Canada M4P 2Y3

Penguin Group (USA) LLC, 375 Hudson Street, New York, New York 10014, U.S.A.
Penguin Books Ltd, 80 Strand, London WC2R 0RL, England
Penguin Ireland, 25 St Stephen's Green, Dublin 2, Ireland (a division of Penguin Books Ltd)
Penguin Group (Australia), 707 Collins Street, Melbourne, Victoria 3008, Australia
(a division of Pearson Australia Group Pty Ltd)
Penguin Books India Pvt Ltd, 11 Community Centre, Panchsheel Park, New Delhi – 110 017, India
Penguin Group (NZ), 67 Apollo Drive, Rosedale, Auckland 0632, New Zealand
(a division of Pearson New Zealand Ltd)
Penguin Books (South Africa) (Pty) Ltd, 24 Sturdee Avenue, Rosebank, Johannesburg 2196, South Africa

Penguin Books Ltd, Registered Offices: 80 Strand, London WC2R 0RL, England

First published 2014

1 2 3 4 5 6 7 8 9 10 (RRD)

LIBRARY AND ARCHIVES CANADA CATALOGUING IN PUBLICATION

Nadler, John, author /–B)
Valour Road / John Nadler.

Includes bibliographical references and index.
ISBN 978-0-670-06821-0 (bound)

1. Clarke, Leo. 2. Shankland, Robert. 3. Hall, Fred. 4. World War,
1914–1918—Manitoba—Winnipeg. 5. Victoria Cross—Biography. 6. Soldiers–
Manitoba—Winnipeg—Biography. 7. Winnipeg (Man.)—Biography.
8. World War, 1914–1918. I. Title.

FC3396.25.N33 2014   971.27'43020922   C2014-902776-1

eBook ISBN 978-0-14-319314-2

Visit the Penguin Canada website at **www.penguin.ca**

Special and corporate bulk purchase rates available; please see
www.penguin.ca/corporatesales or call 1-800-810-3104.

For the Valour Road Children—
Gail Cargo, Leo Clarke Jr., Richard Clarke,
and Joan Hall Paulseth

CONTENTS

PROLOGUE

Winnipeg, November 2012

November 11, 2012, should have been a fine autumn day—
comfortably cool, the air tinged with the smell of burning
leaves, and elm trees bearing the fall colours of orange and amber.
But the day that dawned was extraordinary. During the previous
night, an early winter storm had descended on the city. By daybreak,
temperatures had toppled to eight below zero, and twenty centi-
metres of ice and snow blanketed the ground. The severity of the
storm stunned even lifelong residents of "Winterpeg," a community infamous for its frigid climate. And on that morning, many
in this city of 730,018 people could be forgiven for peeking at
the polar wasteland outside their windows and choosing to remain
indoors, instead of attending the ceremonies scheduled at the
convention centre, the legislative building, McGregor Armoury,
Minto Amoury, and Vimy Ridge Memorial Park, among other
venues.

November 11, of course, is Remembrance Day, a day when
Canadians reflect on the men and women who serve and have

served in the nation's armed forces. For most, it is a time to remember those who fought and, in too many cases, died in the two world wars of the last century. Indeed, the first of these global conflicts, the Great War, which ended on November 11, 1918, gave rise to Remembrance Day. But as important as this day is to Winnipeggers, the storm of November 2012 threatened to trap patriots in their homes.

However, there was one gathering where no amount of ice or snow could keep people away. That morning, a disparate band of Winnipeggers, representing all walks of life, bundled up and trudged to the memorial that stands in a plaza at the corner of Sargent Avenue and a lane originally known as Pine Street, in the city's West End. Some were soldiers: cadets, reservists, and active-service personnel from the locally based Thirty-Eighth Canadian Brigade Group. Most of the active soldiers wore dress uniforms, and a few revealed the family nature of this gathering by holding children in their arms. Some were veterans, the aged warriors of the Second World War, who shivered in the plaza alongside much younger survivors of Canada's more recent conflict in Afghanistan.

Neighbours from the West End were also present. They included teachers, blue-collar workers, homemakers, retirees, and children. And everyone—soldier and civilian alike—was solemn. They knew that they stood upon hallowed ground. This memorial celebrated the heroism of three men, Leo Clarke, Robert Shankland, and Frederick Hall, who in 1914 lived on Pine Street, a short distance away. When the Great War broke out in August that year, these men answered the call and marched off in the name of Canada and the Empire. In different battles at different times, Clarke, Shankland, and Hall faced horrific and daunting challenges, and met them with such heroism that each man was awarded the Victoria Cross.

Not every Canadian now understands the significance of the VC. It's a medal, but not an especially fancy one. One Canadian radio commentator admitted that the "Victoria Cross isn't really much to look at."

> There's the bit of dark red ribbon and the small, bronze
> cross—not gleaming gold as you'd think, but quite black.
> You can just make out the royal crest in the centre, and
> underneath, the scroll with the words "For Valour."

But ever since Queen Victoria presented the first VC in 1856, it has been the most prestigious battlefield decoration of Britain and those Commonwealth countries fighting under the Union Jack. Today, Canada issues its own version of the VC. In the past, deserving Canadian soldiers were eligible—but only the most deserving. Just ninety-six Canadians have ever been given this honour, and, incredibly, three of these men—Clarke, Shankland, and Hall—lived as neighbours on a single Winnipeg street intersecting the plaza where this Remembrance Day service was taking place.

Gathering in this neighbourhood on Remembrance Day to honour these three men had become tradition in Winnipeg. But for eighty-four-year-old Leo Clarke Jr., nephew of one of the heroes, it was much more than that. Leo Jr. was re-enacting a ritual that his family had been observing for eighty-seven years, ever since the first neighbourhood memorial went up in 1925.

When Leo Jr.'s father, Charles, was alive, his family's observance of Remembrance Day began in the basement of their old family house, located a short distance away. Father and son polished medals, and then cleaned a Colt service revolver that had last been fired at the Battle of the Somme. During these moments, the

Clarkes said little, but their thoughts revolved around the original Leo Clarke. For the father, Leo was a lost brother. For the son, he was a namesake and an uncle he never knew. On Remembrance Day, the Clarkes would take part in a neighbourhood service. With each year, this local observance expanded until it had become an event that drew patriots and pilgrims from across the city and country.

On November 11, 2012, as the hour of 11 A.M. approached, Leo Clarke Jr. and his family, which included his wife of almost sixty years as well as grandchildren, nieces, and nephews, stood front and centre before the memorial—a statue of three soldiers in silhouette. Everyone watched as Leo's son Paul took his place behind a microphone. Bareheaded in the cold, Paul Clarke read the official citation for the Victoria Cross given to his great uncle. It told the story of a violent skirmish in France in 1916, and an astonishing act of heroism that won the day.

When Paul finished, others stepped forward and read out the citations for Frederick Hall and Robert Shankland. As with Leo Clarke, these official records were eloquent and short. They told how Fred Hall had defied enemy fire and the poisonous air of Ypres to save the life of a comrade, and how Robert Shankland had almost single-handedly turned defeat near the ravaged Belgian village of Passchendaele into a stunning victory.

After the citations were read, the clock struck the hour, and the crowd fell silent. Some in attendance imagined these men, and wondered how they had lived and fought. Others turned their thoughts to other soldiers in other wars. A few, no doubt, remembered relatives who had served their country. But some who had listened to the stories of Clarke, Shankland, and Hall must have wondered what more was known about these men. What forces had formed and driven them to their prodigious feats?

Theirs was and is an epic saga about young men caught up in a monstrous clash between nations. But at heart, it is a simple tale—one of neighbours, friends, and brothers, and it all began on an ordinary street on the edge of this city nearly one hundred years ago.

A CITY ON THE EDGE
OF THE WORLD

Winnipeg, August 1914

On August 4, 1914, Paul's great grandfather Henry Trevelyan "Harry" Clarke and his large family lived in a tall wind-beaten house on Pine Street, a short distance away from where the memorial plaza would stand a century later. Harry had heard that Great Britain had declared war. And not only was Britain at war, the Empire—and Canada—was at war as well. As Harry Clarke considered this sobering news, he might have wondered how it was possible. How could such a conflict have found him and his family in this remote city perched on the edge of the world? For years, Harry, his wife, Rosetta, and his six children had lived quietly and happily in their home, largely unmolested by the machinations of the larger world.

The Clarkes first arrived in this neighbourhood on the western outskirts of Winnipeg exactly nine years before, when a horse-drawn wagon carried the family and all their worldly posses-sions along a muddy trail that had already been christened Pine Street, and stopped in front of their newly built—and not quite completed—house. Born and raised in England, Harry Clarke had just brought his family to Winnipeg and now they were settling into a permanent family home. Harry Clarke was a quintessential Brit of that era, possessing both physical toughness and gentleman-like dignity. Tall and wiry, his heavy moustache seemed to cleave his thin face. He was a striking figure when wearing a jacket, high starched collar, and homburg hat. But despite his gentlemanly appearance, Harry Clarke possessed a thick vein of frontiersman, which may have been why the West End of town appealed to him. Harry hailed from a family of British soldiers who combined their zeal for adventure with a devotion to God and academia. Harry's distant ancestors included eminent clerics, such as the chancellor to Chichester Cathedral and rector in Buxted, Sussex. Harry's grand-father Edward Daniel Clarke had been a celebrated Cambridge scholar of mineralogy and chemistry who travelled extensively around the known world, and brought back rare manuscripts and artifacts. Harry's father, Beaumaurice Stracey Clarke, had been a British army chaplain during the Crimean War and in the 1857 Indian mutiny where he earned the moniker "the Fighting Parson." Beaumaurice Clarke eventually gave up campaigning, and retired with his wife to a small parish in Billericay, Essex, where he sired eighteen children, including Harry.

Harry didn't seek a life in the Church, but he inherited the Clarke penchant for travelling the world. He went to sea as a cabin boy, but ultimately chose trading over the navy. He joined the Imperial British East Africa Company, and, among other tasks, worked with labour crews of mainly freed slaves on a railroad between Mombasa and Lake Victoria in what is now Kenya. True to his ancestors, Harry's moral compass never wavered. Slaving was still big business, and Harry did everything he could to foil the flesh merchants whenever he encountered them. Once, according to his telling, he commandeered a slave barge and freed its captives. Like other men of his generation, he relished the role of African explorer, even guiding the famed traveller Henry Stanley during one of his later expeditions. After Africa, Harry journeyed down the Amazon, mined diamonds, and almost died from beriberi. Somehow, amid all this activity, he found the time to court and marry another parson's child, Rosetta Caroline Bodily, and together they moved to Canada and started a family. In 1892, the newlyweds had their first child, a boy they named Lionel Beaumaurice, or Leo for short.

Leo Clarke was born in a small town on Lake Ontario when Harry was working nearby as a farm hand. But the Clarkes did not remain for long in the New World. They returned to Essex, and added four more children to the brood before Harry again contemplated the stars, and decided that North America was, after all, where the future lay. In 1903, the Clarkes arrived by rail at the Winnipeg station. They had come to the Manitoba capital for the same reason that thousands of others were arriving on a weekly, if not daily basis—"Prosperity" and "Progress," the two words emblazoned on the city's welcoming arches. Poised at the fork of the Assiniboine and Red Rivers, Winnipeg sat on land where a century before frontiersmen had made fortunes trading beaver furs and buffalo hides. By the time the Clarkes arrived, grain powered the prairie economy, and Winnipeg was the epicentre of the action—a major rail terminus and home to over 42,000 people. By 1914, the city had more than tripled in size (according to the 1911 national census, Winnipeg's population was 136,000, although the city fathers put the figure at 166,000), and the *Chicago Record-Herald* declared it "one of the greatest distributing and commercial centers of the continent." Clearly, Winnipeg was a place any family could forge a new future.

The Clarkes arrived without a penny. Harry had lost his wallet to either a thief or bad luck, and the lack of shelter in the bustling boom town meant that their first dwelling was a tent on Henry Avenue, just off the rail yards. But the frontier was good to Harry Clarke. He found a job as superintendent of the local office of Metropolitan Life Insurance Company, and within two years he moved his family to their new home on Pine Street: a two-storey, whitewashed structure with an open veranda. The house was unfinished, lacking both glass in the windows and a staircase to connect the ground floor to the bedrooms above. And although it sat in a new suburb of the city, the Clarkes might have been forgiven for thinking they had moved to the country. Their new home in lot 785 faced west across a great field of wild grass that ran up against two railway lines running north–south. Somewhere beyond these lines stood the city of St. James and the Assiniboine farming district, and beyond that the western plains unfolded like the ocean, stretching for nine hundred miles before reaching the Rocky Mountains. The Clarkes' closest neighbour was an elderly lady in "a tar paper shack" whose only companion was a cow she kept "tethered out back." As Charlie Clarke later wrote of this time: "Pine Street had no road, nor sidewalks, nor sewer or water or light, just swamp and open fields…. But we made do."

By 1914, the inhabitants of Pine Street were no longer just making do. Harry and Rosetta thrived, adding a sixth child to the family, and the city's amenities had reached them too. Running seven blocks from Portage Avenue along the Assiniboine to Notre Dame Avenue in the north, Pine Street now boasted boardwalks, a graded dirt road, and a sewer line to replace the backhouses that once squatted behind every dwelling. Scores of Winnipeg homes, even in the western neighbourhoods, had been wired for electricity, powered by the Pinawa and Pointe du Bois hydroelectric dams.

Sturdy, wooden houses now lined both sides of Pine. They were all roughly the same: solid and unpretentious with sloped roofs and wide verandas where their people reclined on warm summer evenings, buffeted by a prairie breeze.

Like most in the West End, the folks who lived on Pine Street were working-class, and mainly from Great Britain. On Sundays, they likely met for worship in St. Patrick's Anglican Church on the corner of Pine and Ellice, and the music would spill into the street from St. Patrick's choir, with its soprano section of fourteen boys and three women and its tenor ensemble of six local men. Descended from generations of Church of England ministers, the Clarkes numbered among St. Patrick's most devout parishioners.

Theirs had been a relatively settled life. But on the morning of August 4, 1914, Harry Clarke and his neighbours had worries as dire as any other subject in the broad British Empire. On the local front, the *Winnipeg Tribune* warned that thundershowers were coming. But in Europe, of course, storms of another kind were raging. War had erupted between France and Russia on one side, and Imperial Germany and Austria-Hungary on the other. Germany had declared hostilities on August 1, and when news reached Winnipeg, Harry could only have been shocked. There had not been a war in Europe between the great powers since Napoleon's armies fell at Waterloo in 1815. The ensuing century had not been without bloodshed. The battle scars that Harry's father, the Fighting Parson, carried from the Crimea and India proved this. But apart from brief wars in 1866 and 1870, all the conflicts of the past one hundred years were colonial affairs, fought on the periphery of the so-called civilized world. Indeed, a later historian would call the period between Waterloo and the summer of 1914 "the most peaceful century in European history." But peace reigned no longer.

Truly baffling was how suddenly this amity had died. There had been rumours of war all summer, but they concerned the threat of violence in Ireland after Britain's passage of the Home Rule bill. So obsessed were Brits with fears of civil war at home that few took seriously the bullet from the assassin's gun that killed the heir to the Austro-Hungarian Empire that controlled much of central and southern Europe. In addition to Archduke Franz Ferdinand, the heir's wife, the Duchess Sophie, was murdered in the ambush in Sarajevo, capital of the empire's possession, Bosnia and Herzegovina.

The killing sparked widespread tension. The assassin had been an ethnic Serb, and Vienna suspected that the killer had been sponsored by the nearby state of Serbia, which had its own designs on Bosnia. "Feeling Against Servia Is Strong," declared the Manitoba *Free Press* on July 1. "Emperor Francis Joseph continues to bear up bravely under his bereavement." Shortly after the murders, Austria-Hungary, headed by the royal Hapsburg family, issued a diplomatic note to Serbia with a list of demands. Among other things, Vienna insisted that Serbia allow Austrian officials to conduct an investigation into the assassination within its borders. If these demands were not met, Vienna threatened violence. The demands did not necessarily presage a continental war. There had been southern European dust-ups in 1912 and 1913—the First and Second Balkan Wars—and not much had come from them. But for prescient observers, the 1914 Balkan crisis was different because Russia, which claimed patronage over the Slavic states of central Europe, encouraged Belgrade to be defiant. It was also different because Austria-Hungary immediately secured Imperial Germany's support for any action. Suddenly, this minor crisis on Europe's periphery involved two additional powers: Russia and Germany. And this was potentially explosive because of the network of military alliances that both connected and divided the continent. The Triple Entente linked France, Britain, and Russia in a military pact. This 1907 treaty had been sealed mainly to resolve colonial disputes, but in Europe it pitted these three Allies against the other great power block—Germany, Italy, and Austria-Hungary. Ergo the great peril: if Austria-Hungary were to attack Serbia over the killing of the royal couple, Russia might join the war, thus dragging the other powers into the crisis.

Sadly, there were other factors at play. As the great Prussian General Helmuth von Moltke noted, the Balkans by 1914 had become a tense and highly militarized "powder keg." That fateful summer four million men—virtually every able-bodied male of fighting age on the continent—was either in uniform or a reservist with a regiment. Given the time it took to move large armies in the event of war, Europe's leaders were poised to act on a moment's notice, fearful that rivals mobilizing before them would enjoy an incalculable advantage. Generals didn't fear war declarations; they feared mobilization orders. And this fear had become terror in Germany, which believed it could only win a war against Russia on its eastern border, and France in the west, by defeating France first with lightning speed, and then wheeling its forces around to face the armies of Czar Nicholas II. Germany's "Schlieffen Plan," named after the chief of staff who had authored it, would prove hopelessly flawed, but its warped logic ruled the day. On July 28, Austria-Hungary declared war on Serbia. On July 29, Russia ordered "partial mobilization" of its forces, and on August 1, Germany officially went to war with Russia and France.

On the morning of August 4, Harry Clarke and thousands of other Winnipeggers awoke with one thought on their minds: would Great Britain actually go to war? Britain had not leaped into the fray immediately. The Triple Entente did not compel it to defend its allies any more than its treaty with Belgium—whose borders Germany planned to breach in order to attack France—required it to fight. Both commitments were optional. In the hours and days before August 4, British leaders, including Prime Minister Herbert Asquith and First Lord of the Admiralty Winston Churchill, gazed across the English Channel, considered the competing and clashing new world orders, and struggled to decide which course most benefited the Empire. Did Britain want continental Europe controlled by arriviste Imperial Germany, with France and her colonies as vassals? Or did it prefer the status quo—Britain's old foe France, independent and ascendant, and the colonial world left largely intact?

Ultimately, Britain sided with the devil it knew. Days earlier, Imperial Germany, determined to take the most direct and unguarded route into France, demanded free passage through Belgium for its armies. Brussels refused, and Britain declared its support of the Treaty of London's 1839 convention that guaranteed Belgium's neutrality. On the morning of August 4, German forces marched west, and laid siege to the city of Liège. That night, after Germany dismissed a British ultimatum, the Asquith cabinet issued a statement declaring that "a state of war exists between Great Britain and Germany as from 11 P.M."

Britain had declared war. And Canada, as a member of the Empire, was also in the fight. Winnipeg received the news at about 8 P.M. local time. If Harry Clarke was among the crowds gathered in front of the newspaper offices of the *Free Press* on Carlton Street or the *Telegram* on Albert, he would have heard the news immediately. Had he been reclining on his veranda at home, the sun falling into the horizon ahead of him, he might have heard throngs of patriotic Canadians taking to the streets and singing "Rule, Britannia!" and "God Save the King." Even if he retired early that Tuesday in August, some neighbour would have carried the news to Pine Street.

As the newspapers had promised, a summer storm descended on the city. Winnipeg was going to war, and judging by the fever gripping its citizens, nothing ever would be the same. As one Winnipeg minister declared: "the old world had passed away."

The declaration of war sparked a plethora of responses. "When news of the war came," admitted Winnipeg mother, writer, and suffragette Nellie McClung, "we did not really believe it." McClung and her family had been ensconced in their cabin at Winnipeg Beach on the shores of Lake Winnipeg, fifty miles away from the city, when word came by the 9:40 morning train on August 5. The news stunned her.

"War!" thought McClung, as she commiserated with teary and frightened neighbours in adjoining cabins. "That was over! There had been war, of course, but that had been long ago, in the dark ages, before the days of free schools and peace conferences and missionary conventions and labor unions!" Even the rumour of war began to exact casualties. "Someone should be made to pay dear for this," declared a doctor's wife, who lived beside McClung. "This is very bad for nervous women." It was bad for men too. When Winnipeg minister Reverend Charles Gordon, rusticating at his summer house at Lake of the Woods, was handed an August 5 newspaper, he went off alone to make sense of its contents and "consider what it had to do with me. With me and my wife and my children. I was thinking of them," he later wrote, "more than of the great world outside."

Prime Minister Robert Borden, leader of Canada's three-year-old Conservative government, had been in Ontario's Muskoka region, attending its annual regatta, and looking forward to a day of golf when he was recalled to deal with the crisis. The German kaiser and key French and British diplomats had also been vacationing as events spun out of control. The "World Conflagration"—as Reverend Gordon of Winnipeg called the conflict—grew from inattention as much as anything else.

But for everyone who was shocked or made thoughtful by the war, there were others who were carried away by patriotic fervour. Back in Winnipeg, the crowds that gathered in front of the newspaper offices quickly grew. "[F]illed with the war spirit," euphoric mobs marched down streets in the centre of the town, waving the Union Jack and—in sympathy with France—the tricolour, and belting out patriotic hymns, including Canada's de facto anthem, "The Maple Leaf Forever," and the French "La Marseillaise." In some quarters of the city the mood turned ugly. One throng stormed down Heaton Avenue in the north of the city and smashed the windows of the German Club, an old-country society of German immigrants. The mob didn't seem to care that members of this association were naturalized citizens, committed to organizing nothing more insidious than picnics, socials, and cultural events.

The strangely bellicose euphoria inspired a good many men to enlist. In 1914, two pillars held up Canada's young military establishment—a permanent force of three thousand professional soldiers and the volunteer militias. The latter were privately funded regiments, which had been raised over the years to face enemies such as marauding Irishmen, or Fenians, attacking from the United States; Metis rebels led by the agitator Louis Riel; and more recently the Boers in South Africa. There were some fifty-nine thousand part-time soldiers in militia ranks, in one hundred eighty regiments. Winnipeg's militias included the One Hundredth Winnipeg Grenadiers, the Seventy-Ninth Cameron Highlanders, and the Ninetieth Winnipeg Rifles, the oldest of the city's militias, whose dark-hued uniform gave rise to their description as "little black devils" in the 1885 uprising.

The Borden government initially planned to send a token battalion to Europe. But Britain requested a division, and two days after war was declared the Canadian cabinet authorized the raising of a contingent of twenty-five thousand men. The warlord in charge of this mobilization was Minister of Militia and Defence Sam Hughes, a flawed, temperamental, and ambitious politician who held firmly to eccentric ideas about how Canada should fight this war. He had a low opinion of Canada's professional army, seeing it as a backwater of bureaucracy and sloth. So he chose to build the Canadian Expeditionary Force (CEF) from the country's citizen soldiers, instead—men who he considered to be business minded, freethinkers, and innovators. On August 6, he dispatched 226 telegrams to militia colonels across the land, informing each to "buckle on his harness and get busy." The twenty-five thousand men of the CEF would come from these regiments. The decision to tap the militias instead of the army was fateful. Not only was Hughes discarding the experience of Canada's professionals; he was defining Canada's war as a people's war—a crusade of the common man.

Inspired by headlines such as "Canada Ready to Strike Blow" and militia recruitment drives of "parades, martial music, and flags," all manner of common men stepped forward. "Every mother's son is spoiling for a fight," declared the Winnipeg *Tribune*. And so it appeared. Seventeen-year-old boys and seventy-year-old grand-fathers joined the lines outside the gates of the Winnipeg Rifles picket-fenced Drill Hall on the corner of Broadway and Osborne and the armoury of the One Hundredth Winnipeg Grenadiers located on Main Street near the intersection of York Avenue. But because the contingent needed only twenty-five thousand men,

17

recruiters imposed strict criteria for selection. Soldiers were to be young (under forty-five years), fit, tall, and reasonably literate. Only the cream of western Canadian manhood, wrote one journalist, would have the privilege of fighting for their country. In fact, many of the recruits weren't born in Canada. The majority of the volunteers—like a good many Canadians—were Brits who had come to Canada seeking fortune, adventure, or a new life. These men were inordinately tough. Many had fought before in the British colonies and were eager to fight again. "He would go," lamented the wife of one British volunteer in Winnipeg. "He loves a fight—he went through the South African War, and 'e's never been happy since."

Men enlisted for a variety of reasons. Many were inspired by simple patriotism. Some were inflamed by sensational newspaper reports of atrocities supposedly committed by the Germans in Belgium. Peer pressure was often a factor. Some men yearned for adventure and, in the words of one western Canadian recruit, "a desire to see the world." And still others were lured by the romance of service. "I was proud of my battalion," wrote Winnipeg's Reverend Gordon, also the militia chaplain with the Seventy-Ninth Cameron Highlanders. "I had loved the splendid, historic, romantic glory of the kilted Highlanders."

Amid the excitement and optimism, a few insightful lads saw impending disaster. "Nations can't go to war now," declared a labourer on a crew working along the Columbia River. "It would be suicide, with all the modern methods of destruction." A member of Prime Minister Borden's cabinet agreed, calling the newly declared war "the suicide of civilization." But even those with no idea of what the future would bring knew one thing. "The world is changed," one vacationer muttered as he hurriedly left his cabin at Lake of the Woods. "Everything is changed and we must meet that change."

In Winnipeg's West End, the changing world touched the people of Pine Street. As it had elsewhere, the news had swept through the neighbourhood. Along its roughly seven blocks, Pine was home to many Brits and sons of the Empire of fighting age. Devonshire-born Charles Hutchings, who lived with his wife at 939 Pine, was just over thirty years of age; Alexander Burnett at 872 was a Scot and a pre-war militiaman with the Seventy-Ninth Camerons; the three Ritchie brothers, George, William, and John, from Ayr, Scotland, lived at 733 Pine; and thirty-one-year-old William Gaunt was the head of the household at 772. Although Harry Clarke at forty-five years was too old to enlist, he had three boys of military age—Leo, Harry Jr., and Charlie.

For years, the crowded Clarke household had raged like a happy army barracks. With five sons and a daughter, there were more children than rooms, which may have been why Harry's oldest sons had chosen to sleep on the veranda in the summer instead of in the single room the boys shared. But Harry's oldest sons now were young men, and two of them, twenty-one-year-old Leo and eighteen-year-old Charlie, had gone west to work. They were far away from the war fever gripping Winnipeg, although Harry had no way of knowing what the mood was like in north Saskatchewan where Leo surveyed for the railroad, or in Edmonton where Charlie laboured in a store. The father had no fear that Harry Jr. would enlist. Harry's second-born son had a weak leg that made him ineligible for service. For the present, no Clarke boys would be lining up in front of militia halls, and although he was the patriotic son of a soldier of the Empire, Harry Clarke could only have been relieved.

THE PINE STREET BOYS

Winnipeg, 1914

THE MUSICIAN

If Harry Clarke was in no hurry for his sons to go to war, other young men on Pine Street wasted no time in enlisting. In an upstairs bedroom at 772 lived a twenty-nine-year-old shipping clerk, Frederick William Hall. Although he was just a lodger in this house and had been in Canada for only a year, Fred Hall was well known in the neighbourhood. He was a musician who played trombone for the militia band of the Seventy-Ninth Cameron Highlanders. Before a parade or concert, Fred was occasionally spotted in the full Highland dress: a glengarry angled daringly on the side of his head and a plaid hanging from his right shoulder. The uniform also included a woollen doublet with shell epaulets on the shoulders, a kilt, and sporrans, which hung down from his waist like twin horses' tails. In his broad left hand, Fred would grip his trombone with the ease of a rifleman holding a musket.

Fred Hall's comfort in uniform betrayed his background, as did his bayonet-straight posture that made him look taller than his five feet eight inches. He was new to the Seventy-Ninth Camerons, but not new to the military. Before coming to Winnipeg in August of 1913, he had spent the last dozen years of his life with the famed Lanark-based Scottish Rifles, the first and perhaps the greatest of Scotland's regiments, then better known as the First Cameronians. Fred had entered service as a seventeen-year-old. In the early twentieth century, boys graduated to manhood early, and it was normal for a young man to enter a profession in his mid-teens.

Fred Hall was particularly ambitious. He had excelled in school and apprenticed as a lawyer for two years before choosing the army as his vocation. His family—parents and six siblings—were not surprised by his decision. Ever since his birth in Belfast in 1885, Fred Hall had been imbued with army customs and traditions. His father, Frederick Matticott Hall, also had enlisted as a boy, in his case in the Border Regiment, propelled by a financial setback that had left his family in the poorhouse. Because of his extreme youth, Fred Hall's father may have been slated as a bugler or drummer, which was fortuitous. The bugle introduced Fred's father to one of his great passions—music. Expert at the coronet (and eventually an array of instruments including violin), the elder Hall rose to the rank of bandmaster, and was noted for his exceptional talent.

Frederick senior's other passion was his family. He was stationed in Belfast when he noticed a petite and coy soldier's daughter drop her Bible during church service. Frederick Matticott stooped to pick it up, certainly knowing that in their reserved world such an accident was an invitation. He accepted the invitation and, in due course, took Mary Finn as his wife. His devotion to Mary and his children was probably why he left the Border Regiment in 1888. Army life entailed long absences policing the periphery of the Empire. He took up the job as bandmaster for the Second Volunteer Battalion South Lancashire Regiment, the British equivalent of a militia, and set his family up in a grand house in St. Helens, just outside of Liverpool. There he worked furiously and happily, leading a local orchestra that became a popular "feature at social functions across the district." He took students and scoured pawnshops for quality instruments, which he resold. Respected and well off, the Hall family prospered until tragedy struck. Frederick Matticott died of "a painful internal complaint" after a short illness, leaving his widow and younger children without a provider.

Mary Hall struggled to keep the family afloat after her husband's passing. She worried especially about her youngest, Henry Cecil, "Harry" for short, who was ten years old when her husband died. Mary Hall and the family launched various ventures. Her daughters May and Ada, gifted musicians as their father had been, taught piano and voice. The family moved to London and ran a "high-class" boarding house for a time in West Kensington, which even took in German army officers who came to Britain to learn English. But stability eluded the family, and in 1913 Mary Hall and three of her children moved to western Canada, in search of a new life.

Fred Hall junior arranged the family's shift to Winnipeg. Posted with the Scottish Rifles in India, Fred wrote to an old comrade, Peter Stanton, a former drummer in the regiment, who had relocated there. Thanks to Fred's arrangements, Stanton was waiting at the Winnipeg station when Mary and children Ada, May, and Harry arrived in early summer 1913. Stanton brought them home and set them up, which was a godsend, given that the Halls had only ten dollars to their names.

Three months later, when Fred's twelve-year hitch with the Cameronians ended, he left the army and joined his family in Winnipeg, finding them in a rented house at 179 Spence Street, located downtown near the corner of Broadway. Mary was overjoyed to see her "Freddie," and to have more of the family near. But Mary knew he had made a significant sacrifice to be by her side. "He gave up the prospect of a good future to come out and give me help," she would later say. She may have been correct. His father's son, Fred Hall was so talented a musician he had been accepted into the Royal Military School of Music in Twickenham, West London, where he had studied "conducting, arranging, harmony." If he had remained in the army, he might one day have become a legendary bandmaster like his father. But if Fred Hall regretted abandoning the Cameronians, he didn't let on. It was clear, however, that he cared for his mother. After securing a job as a shipping clerk in the Winnipeg plant of the cattle company Gordon, Ironsides & Fares, he gave her forty dollars a month from his salary. It also was clear that he pined for army life. Soon after his arrival, he sought out Winnipeg's only kilted militia, the Seventy-Ninth Cameron Highlanders, and volunteered for their band.

By the end of summer 1913, Fred was settled. He had a job. He was reunited with his blood family. And he had been adopted by an army family as well, one filled with Scots from the old country just like the men he had once served with. As for a home, he opted not to live with his mother and siblings in their crowded Spence Street house, where his sisters tutored students in the parlour. Fred had been independent too long to live under his mother's roof. Besides, his siblings were strangers in many ways. His brother Harry, nine years his junior, had been raised very differently. While Fred had been a soldier's son, Harry grew up the offspring of a successful St. Helens musician. In the last years of the elder Hall's life, the family had lived in a great house and enjoyed the community's respect. Harry recognized how different he was from his brother. "I respected and admired Fred," he later said, "but he was inclined to be too strict and took life too seriously...." Not that Harry lacked seriousness; he had excelled in school in St. Helens. But Harry possessed a fun-loving streak that put him at odds with his brother Percy, who had also come to Canada and was homesteading in Saskatchewan. Of all his brothers, Harry related best to Edmund and "Ted" shared his mischievous nature. Six years older than Harry, Ted had also become a bandsman for the First Cameronians, and as far as the family knew, he was posted in Malta. As for Harry Hall, his father's early death had steeled him. Although his mother fretted over and pampered him, Harry, who turned nineteen when the family arrived in Canada, had become a fiercely independent young man who likely saw in this new world the chance of adventure and opportunity.

The prospect of adventure in a rough and prosperous corner of the Empire probably enticed Fred as well. Fred found a room in a house on the western edge of the city. Pine Street was made up of people much like him—transplanted Brits who were either fleeing an old life or searching for a new one. The Canadian prairie and the Manitoba sky must have been greater and vaster than he imagined, but he couldn't have been too surprised. As a soldier, Fred had seen enough of the world to understand and appreciate the vast Canadian West. A special type of person was drawn to land like this, an immense frontier both wild and liberating. Pine Street stood on a kind of precipice, with the security and modernity of a city on one side, and wide-open spaces on the other.

It is not surprising that Fred found a home in such a place. Nor is it surprising that he would renew his ties to the military. Once, at a family gathering, the conversation turned to the greatest disaster of their generation—the 1912 sinking of the RMS *Titanic*. When someone mentioned what a fearful death drowning would be, Fred turned to Mary and said: "Mother, I always had the feeling that I would die on the battlefield." His family had laughed and "ridiculed" him. Was there anywhere in the world farther away from a battlefield than the Canadian West?

But a mere year after Fred Hall's arrival, rumblings in Europe rocked even Canada. On August 7, only days after war was declared, Fred Hall donned kilt and doublet, took up his trombone, and joined the Cameron's band as it took to the streets to lead the militia on a parade through the city. In a grand show of patriotism and a lure for volunteers, the five-hundred-man militia marched from downtown to the village of St. Boniface on the east side of the Red River, propelled forward by the cheers of an astonishing fifty thousand Winnipeggers who lined the streets. As they paraded, the band played the militia's official ballad, "March of the Cameron Men," music Fred Hall would have known as intimately as his own name:

> *There's many a man of the Cameron clan,*
> *That has followed his chief to the field:*
> *He has sworn to support him or die by his side,*
> *For a Cameron never can yield.*

Fred Hall would not yield. He immediately enlisted, but not with the popular Seventy-Ninth Camerons, which may have been filled to capacity. Instead, Fred joined the 106th Light Infantry, a relatively new local militia authorized in 1912, which probably had spaces available and a need for experienced men.

On August 15, Winnipeg's first contingent of volunteers left the city by train. They were two hundred local members of the Princess Patricia's Canadian Light Infantry, an outfit formed and funded by a rich Montrealer and named for the daughter of Canada's Governor General. Friends, family, and fellow soldiers gave the boys a raucous and emotional goodbye, which included, wrote one local historian, "a boozy celebration in the Army and Navy Club" the night before. On August 24, a much greater send-off took place. The lion's share of Winnipeg's volunteers, a complement of 2,447 men, marched to the CPR station for deployment. They included members of the Seventy-Ninth Cameron Highlanders, the Ninetieth Winnipeg Rifles, the 106th Light Infantry and two members of Mary Hall's family. Both Fred Hall and his youngest brother Harry, who had also signed up with the 106th regiment, bade their teary mother and sisters goodbye before boarding a train headed east to the Canadian contingent's training camp at Valcartier, Quebec. This camp, wholly conceived by Sam Hughes, existed at that time as little more than farmers' fields, a short distance from Quebec City and the St. Lawrence River. But it would be home for Mary Hall's sons for the foreseeable future, and she was distraught. As difficult as it was to see her oldest son march to war, there was one consolation: Fred Hall was an experienced soldier. Although a former bandsman, he had been trained and certified in martial skills ranging from musketry to telegraph operations. Mary was more fearful for her youngest, Harry, whom she had doted on since her husband's death. As the train pulled away, Mary and the hundreds of other mothers surrounding her wept with good reason. Most of these first-wave volunteers would be killed or wounded within a year. Of the two sons Mary Hall said goodbye to at the Winnipeg Station, one would never return.

When the Winnipeg contingent arrived at Valcartier, they were dumped unceremoniously into a tent city that would soon hold 30,617 men. At Valcartier, the Halls and their comrades marched, drilled, and learned the rudiments of soldiering. The newly minted riflemen then were organized into battalions, and the battalions organized into brigades. On October 3, 1914, the Canadian First Division of the CEF boarded ocean liners, and set sail for Great Britain. Ten days later, they arrived in Plymouth on England's south coast to great fanfare. Every ship in the harbour welcomed them. "There was the screaming of sirens and the tooting of many whistles," one soldier remembered, and sailors lined the rails and huzzaed. The soldiers were received just as enthusiastically onshore, and then they were sent by rail to a camp on the Salisbury Plain near Stonehenge, where they would train and endure one of the wettest and muddiest winters on record.

And while they languished, the Great War unfolded on the continent into a very different war from the kind that the Hall boys might have imagined. On the Eastern Front, the Serbs had initial success in fending off the armies of old Austria-Hungary. But in the west, Germany loosed six hundred thousand troops on Belgium and northern France, ushering in a war of unprecedented size and violence. In France's first engagements with the Germans, a series of clashes in Lorraine later remembered as the Battles of the Frontiers, two hundred fifty thousand Frenchmen perished. In late August, Britain's small highly trained professional army, known on the continent as the British Expeditionary Force (BEF), met the Germans near the Belgian city of Mons, and suffered one thousand six hundred casualties. Overwhelmed, the BEF fought a long rearguard action as the German army struggled to reach Paris and conquer France so that it would be free to turn its armies east against Russia. A desperate last-ditch effort by the British and French checked the German juggernaut near the Marne Valley and foiled Germany's plans for a rapid end to the war in the west. The fighting continued as the two enemies flanked, clashed, and flanked again, edging sideways like clawing beasts northwards toward the sea. Once in Belgian Flanders, near the medieval city of Ypres (pronounced EE-pray), the battered and weary enemies dug in and resumed the war from the cover of shallow trenches cut into the alluvial polders.

The French and British had won the day by stopping the German march on Paris, but their victory only brought more murder on an industrial scale. By the time the snows fell in Winnipeg, the news from the Old World was bad. The *Tribune* headline on December 1 declared, "The Enemy Renews Struggle With Mass Attack on Yser Canal," and the *Free Press* ran a lengthy British casualty list. The loss of life beggared understanding. In just five months of conflict, eight hundred thousand Frenchmen and sixty-four thousand British had been killed or wounded. And when 1915 dawned, the war and its bloodshed showed no sign of abating.

THE WEE SCOT

Fred Hall was one of the first men from Pine Street to be deployed with the CEF, but he was not the only man to step forward that summer. Another was the lodger at 773 Pine Street, Robert Shankland.

Bob Shankland shared a house with a family of four siblings named Ritchie, who—like Bob—came from Ayr, Scotland, a western coastal city immortalized by the poet Robbie Burns as: "Auld Ayr, wham ne'er a town surpasses, / For honest men and bonnie lasses." The leader of the Ritchie clan was the eldest brother, George. When and how George Ritchie and Bob Shankland met is not clear. But they hatched a plan to travel to Canada and then on to Winnipeg, where they landed in 1911. Nine years older, George Ritchie may have been the mentor in this partnership, and based on Bob's later instructions to forward part of his army pay to George's work address, he may have lent Bob money for the transatlantic passage. In short order, they both secured work at the Winnipeg dairy, Crescent Creamery, a growing concern about to expand into a new $350,000 plant.

Once settled, George sent for his siblings. The youngest, John, and the oldest, Annie, arrived the following year. Brother William came in 1913, and by the terrible summer of 1914, they all were ensconced in the simple A-frame house with a squat veranda that stuck out like a pregnant woman's belly. The Ritchies would have been well known on Pine. But their friend and lodger Bob Shankland was another story.

Described as "quiet and retiring," Bob attracted little attention. Perhaps it was his diminutive height. He stood a touch over five feet four inches tall with the bland porridge-white complexion of a true Scot that an army doctor would later characterize as "sallow." Perhaps Bob was too busy to be noticed. On weekday mornings, Bob trundled to the dairy, where he worked as assistant cashier. In the evenings and on weekends, he might have been on his way to play soccer for the Crescent Creamery's football team, which competed in the city's eighteen-club Mercantile League. Bob also had tried his hand at the New World sport of baseball.

Even as a boy growing up in Ayr, Bob was known as a young man in a hurry. His father, William, and mother, Jane, both laboured as railroad porters, jobs that provided adequately, but not munificently, for Bob and his older sister, Janet. Bob Shankland clearly wanted more. Attending school at Smith's Institution (later known as Holmston School), he won academic honours every year. In his spare time, he was a soldier of the Lord with the Ayr Parish

Church's Boys' Brigade, a Scottish Presbyterian version of the Boy Scouts, although its organizers resented overt military comparisons. Like the Scouts, the Boys' Brigade attempted to instill in its charges good personal habits, piety, and, according to the Brigade's motto, a "Sure & Steadfast" nature. Declared one Ayr Brigade camp song, "Our object still remains the same, towards Christian manliness." Even among these young manly Christians, wee Bob Shankland stood out. One Ayr native said of him: "He was aye a game yin." He was game for anything. A childhood spent watching his parents strain under the weight of other people's luggage may have inspired him to achieve greater things. However, ferocity was in his blood. As a lowland town, Ayr may have lacked the rawness of the highlands, but the area's legacy was one of defiance. Scottish folk hero and true believer Richard Cameron, leader of the Covenanters, the seventeenth-century holy warriors who resisted English attempts to subvert the Church of Scotland, had died in battle at Ayrs Moss, a short distance away. There, Cameron and his men were said to have fought like "madmen." If childhood is a type of battle, Bob Shankland fought the good fight, graduating from Smith's Institution with the Dux Medal for being the top scholar and athlete of his graduating class.

Bob trained as an accountant with a firm on Ayr's Newmarket Street and ultimately found a bookkeeping job in the Townhead Station of the Glasgow and South Western Railway. It might have been a proud moment for Bob's father, William, who after years of toil saw his son accept an office job with the railroad. But Bob was not satisfied. He and George Ritchie somehow met and plotted their great life-changing move to North America.

For ambitious young men, the Canadian West was heaven. When Bob Shankland arrived, Winnipeg stood at the peak of its growth and promise. Opportunities seemed as innumerable as the men rushing along its streets. And Pine Street was very different from Church Street in Ayr, with its crowded brick houses and coal smoke–tainted air, where Bob had lived. Pine's wind-beaten houses, rough-hewn boardwalk, and open yards gave off a tentative quality, as if the prairie were always encroaching and the street might at any moment be overwhelmed. But for men like Bob Shankland (as for Fred Hall), this rawness signified new beginnings. For men bent on reinvention, there was no better place to be.

When Bob Shankland made the decision to go to war, he sought out the Seventy-Ninth Cameron Highlanders, the one militia where he was certain to feel at home. But like Fred Hall, Bob had no chance of finding a place among the 10 officers and 247 men of the Highlanders who were sent with the first contingent to Valcartier. This honour went to long-standing militiamen and the sons of officers and city fathers. And so, as a new recruit, Bob trained in his spare time and waited for the call that would surely come.

Like Bob, Lieutenant Colonel James Alexander Cantlie, the local commander, was also biding his time. Not satisfied to send a couple hundred of his men off to fight in a mixed contingent, he lobbied Minister of Militia Hughes for the right to form a one-thousand-man battalion. In December, the Camerons and Bob Shankland got their chance. Cantlie received the authorization he had sought and began selecting and mobilizing men. Only the best were chosen, and Bob Shankland was one of them.

On only a "moderately cold" Winnipeg day in late December, Bob officially signed up with the newly formed battalion, filling out attestation papers that listed his father, William, as next of kin. As training began in earnest and slackers "were weeded out," Bob Shankland excelled. He fitted in with these prairie Camerons, the Canadian embodiment of the First Cameronians, named for the martyred lowlands hero, Richard Cameron. And fitting in was no small achievement. According to historian John Keegan, any man can wear a uniform, but not everyone is accepted by his comrades—the "tribe." Acceptance depends on his standing "as a man among other men." Bob Shankland was accepted, rising rapidly from private to orderly room sergeant, impressing men and officers alike with his ability to learn the name of every man in the outfit, which was soon designated the Forty-Third Battalion. Bob Shankland had left one home on Pine Street, and found another with the Forty-Third. Within six months, he and his comrades would leave Canada for the battlefields of Europe.

PRODIGAL SONS

While Bob marched to war, his Pine Street neighbour Harry Clarke waited for it to end. In 1914, Harry had two sons eligible for the military—his oldest, Leo, and his third son, Charlie—and when war was declared on August 4, both boys were away. Charlie had a job in Edmonton, and Leo, who worked on a railroad surveying crew, was somewhere in the wilderness of north Saskatchewan, and was only occasionally in touch. As a child of the Empire and the son of a war hero, Harry Clarke understood an Englishman's duty when Britain was at war. But Harry was also a father, and so he postponed the inevitable conversation with his sons for as long as he could.

But the war outlasted Harry's ability to outwait it. On or around February 3, 1915, Harry trudged into the CPR station on Higgins Avenue in north Winnipeg and into the telegraph office, which adjoined the station's rotunda. He sent two telegrams: one to Leo at his last known address and the other to Charlie in Edmonton. The wires contained identical messages:

IT WOULD BE ALL RIGHT FOR YOU TO JOIN
UP. BUT COME HOME FIRST.

Sooner or later, the war would reach deeper into the country and
catch up to his itinerant sons. This was inevitable, and Harry
Clarke could not have his boys leave for war without them coming
home first to say goodbye.

Leo would only get the message after a long delay. But the
other telegram found Charlie in his modest lodgings in Edmonton.
Charles Edward Clarke had gone west to find a job, and ultimately
hired on as a night watchman in an Edmonton department store.
The work was decent and honest. Among other duties, Charlie
opened the building in the morning and closed it up again at night.
But even before his father's telegram arrived, he knew his time in
Edmonton was drawing to an end. Rumours flew that the French-
owned store would close due to the war. Losing his job was not
his only reminder of the conflict's reach. Like most cities in the
Dominion, Edmonton was gripped by war fever. One of the city's
most popular militias, the Nineteenth Alberta Dragoons, opened
the doors of its 106th Street armoury and canvassed for volunteers
who could ride and shoot, its officers unaware that the cavalryman
would soon be extinct. Nevertheless, the Dragoons mobilized 250
men and 210 horses and shipped them to Valcartier. Meanwhile,
Charlie drilled with the city's infantry, the 101st Edmonton
Fusiliers, and it is possible that his letters describing the parades
with the Fusiliers prompted his father's cable.

Within three days of receiving the wire, Charlie boarded a train
to Winnipeg. He left on a Saturday, arrived home the following
week, and by Tuesday was a member of the Thirty-Second
Battalion, made up of another prairie cavalry militia, the Twelfth
Manitoba Dragoons.

Headquartered in the nearby town of Brandon, the Dragoons' legacy included the 1885 Rebellion and the Boer War. Their regimental motto was *Ubique Honor et Equis—Everywhere Honour and by Horse.* As a successful Winnipeg businessman, Harry Clarke might have used connections to win Charlie a spot in the ranks of this respected militia. By the following Monday, Charlie was living in the Thirty-Second Battalion's barracks in the old Winnipeg Industrial Exhibition Grounds, north of the rail yards. There the troops drilled despite blizzards that had dumped some fourteen inches of snow on the city. Pumping his arms in a uniform three inches too long at the sleeves, Charlie and his comrades drilled so relentlessly that the snow on the parade ground was trampled into a thin hard sheet. Then when the quartermaster issued the men full field kits, they knew this generosity could only mean they would soon be shipping out. On Tuesday, February 16, official word came down. Charlie phoned his father and broke the news. The battalion would be shipping out by train at 8 P.M.

The Clarkes rushed to the exhibition grounds, and Charlie stole away from his unit to speak with his family. A family photo survives of this meeting, or one like it during Charlie's week in barracks. Charlie stood between his mother and father as Bet, wife of his brother Harry Jr., remained off to the side. Pride can be glimpsed in his father's expression, as well as surprise and perhaps amusement to see his boy in an oversized uniform. Despite his ill-fitting khakis, Charlie looked impressive. His body was solid but trim, honed from a childhood of hard play and physical work. Charlie stood shorter than his father, but shared Harry's long, handsome face and powerful jaw.

Somehow Charlie Clarke looked older than his nineteen years and Harry's face, despite the slight smile, betrayed a trace of grimness.

Anxiety creased the face of Charlie's mother, Rosetta, who stared defiantly into the camera. As for Charlie, he appeared not worried at all. "We were off on the great adventure!" he declared of that day. Charlie said goodbye to his parents. He said goodbye to his older brother Harry Jr., his sister-in-law, Bet, his sixteen-year-old sister, Muriel, and his little brothers, Jack and Arthur. The only member of the family he could not bid goodbye to was Leo. After leaving his family, Charlie and the battalion headed to Union Station. As the men marched along Selkirk Avenue, friends and neighbours cheered them on. When the Thirty-Second entered the station yard, another crowd greeted them and a military band struck up an old folk tune that had become an anthem for departing soldiers. The song described the beauty of the women of France, Italy, and Spain, but noted how their allure would never "bind me": "And my heart falls back to Erin's isle / To the girl I left behind me."

The soldiers were ebullient. Some hung tiny Union Jack flags from their rifle barrels. Men not from Winnipeg wore sashes proudly naming their hometowns—Brandon, Portage la Prairie, Moosin Bay, and Moose Jaw. Volunteers with the Imperial Order Daughters of the Empire (the IODE) handed out knitted socks. Finally the men boarded the waiting cars, and the crowd swarmed onto the platform and sang "Auld Lang Syne" as the train pulled away. The tears and weeping continued even after the last carriage disappeared from sight. "God, isn't it a shame," one wife moaned. A reporter for the *Winnipeg Telegram* agreed, lamenting in print: "It was terrible. 1100 of Canada's finest, their equal perhaps not to be found anywhere in the world, were going away." Like thirty thousand Canadians and millions of men around the world, Harry Clarke's third son was off to war.

But no one knew the whereabouts of Harry's first-born. Leo Clarke's last letter home reported that he was surveying for the railroad in Saskatchewan. Unbeknownst to his family, this work had ended and Leo had taken a job with a local rancher. When his father's telegram finally found him, Leo headed for home and landed in Winnipeg just hours after Charlie's troop train had departed. That his younger brother was already off to war could only have been a shock. Leo was the oldest Clarke son, and the one who had clearly inherited the family's fearlessness and appetite for adventure. From an early age, he had proven himself to be gutsy and bold, unafraid of challenges or hard work. When the family first arrived in Winnipeg in May 1903, Leo earned money for the family by selling copies of the evening *Free Press, Tribune*, and *Telegram* on the platforms of the CPR station. Seven-year-old Charlie had tagged along, fascinated by his brother's zeal.

During their first winter in Winnipeg, Leo had led his brothers Harry and Charlie on expeditions. He marched them to the frozen Red River where the boys skated, played hockey, and raced down toboggan runs on the steep banks. Afterwards, they warmed themselves inside a stove-heated shack on the ice and made fast friends among the neighbourhood youngsters who taught them songs ("pea soup and johnny cake always makes your belly ache") and games. It was no surprise when Leo became leader of the neighbourhood kids. As Charlie would later note, Leo was "handy with his fists." However, people admired him for other reasons. He was handsome, almost delicately so, with a higher forehead and narrower face than Charlie. At five feet seven and a half, Leo was a shade taller than his brother. They both had grey eyes, but just enough green infused Leo's to give his stare a piercing quality. After the family moved to Pine Street, Leo led forays into the prairie and nearby Omand's Creek with the forest of willow trees on its banks and the adjoining abandoned brick factory where they swam in a water-filled pit. In fights and races, Leo seemed always to triumph, and on Sports Day every May 24, Leo won such a quantity of ribbons he confessed that "he was ashamed to take home so many." Charlie followed his older brother through all these contests and adventures. But the most memorable and disturbing adventure they shared occurred soon after their arrival to Winnipeg. The Clarkes lived in a small house on Syndicate Street in the northeast quarter of the city, just beyond the railroad tracks and within reach of the Red River. One night in mid-October 1904, a commotion awoke the boys. The streets echoed with panicked voices and a "lurid gleam" lit the skyline.

The city was on fire.

Leo crept from the house to take a look, and Charlie as always tagged along. They followed the glow to the downtown where an inferno engulfed Main Street. The worst of the blaze consumed the Ashdown Hardware Store. Shivering in the bitter cold among the onlookers, the Clarke boys watched as the store's stocks of paint, kerosene, rifle and shotgun shells, and gunpowder detonated from the heat, launching bullets and screeching accelerant cans into the air. The night roared like battle. For the boys, this was their first glimpse of a world ablaze—of uncontrolled violence and calamity. "It was an event always remembered," Charlie would later write, "terrifying and exciting." A decade later, another blaze had erupted: a war that engulfed the world and reached as far as the Canadian West, and it was even more terrifying and exciting. Charlie had gone off alone to the fire, and Leo followed. He enlisted in the Twenty-Seventh Battalion, which was christened the City of Winnipeg Battalion and would later be reviewed by Mayor Richard Waugh. But the Twenty-Seventh Battalion would not march to war immediately. To Leo's frustration, by the time the Twenty-Seventh shipped out in mid-May 1915, Charlie had already reached the battlefield. Leo's younger brother, for once, was taking the lead.

The train that carried Charlie Clarke to war in February 1915 did not stop at the training camp at Valcartier as earlier transports had done. After switching to the Intercolonial Railway, the Winnipeggers sped to the port of Halifax on the East Coast, arriving on Saturday, February 20. The next morning, the men stretched stiff limbs and enjoyed free time in the port, a magnificent natural harbour crowded with quays, moorings, cranes, and some of the world's largest ocean liners and freighters.

Fresh from a prairie winter, the young soldiers considered Halifax's briny air, squawking gulls, and lovely weather a revelation. Many of the Manitoba boys were seeing the foaming Atlantic for the first time, and the glorious sight reminded Charlie that "it was good to be alive." Some of the men grew introspective, and spoke of home, hearth, and kin. But for Charlie, the Atlantic symbolized something else—a threshold to be crossed, a point of no return. Although he could have no idea of what was in store, he told himself: "Enjoy your life now because you don't know what is in front of you nor do you know if you will ever return.... There is no turning back, you are in it now."

A short time later, the 962 soldiers and 35 officers of the Thirty-Second Battalion marched to the quay and boarded the troopship, SS *Southland*, whose former name, *Vaderland*, was considered too Germanic to stand. After setting off from port, the men travelled in the ship's cramped and fetid hold. They slept in bunks three high, and saw only water from their portholes. The stormy Atlantic rocked the ship relentlessly, sometimes viciously, and the men looked forward to their daily climb to the upper deck to exercise and breathe fresh air. Restless lads scaled the ship's rigging like boys exploring a tree. Others lazed about, watched the sportsmen among them box, and listened to their regimental band.

Despite the illusion of a cruise, the Winnipeg men faced real danger and never forgot they were at war. The *Southland* sailed in a small convoy with another troopship, the SS *Missanabie*, which carried the Twenty-Third Battalion from Quebec. The Royal Navy destroyer, HMS *Essex*, plowed the waters ahead of them, searching for enemy subs. Both soldiers and seamen feared the German *Unterseeboot* or—as Winston Churchill dubbed it—the U-boat. The previous September, while prowling the North Sea near the Isle of May, the German sub U-21 fired a single fifty-centimetre torpedo at the British cruiser, the HMS *Pathfinder*. The *Pathfinder*'s magazine exploded, and the ship went down in minutes, the first vessel in history sunk by a submarine. A short time later, U-9 destroyed the British warships HMS *Aboukir*, HMS *Hogue*, and HMS *Cressy*, and by the time Charlie Clarke was crossing the Atlantic, U-boat aces infested the waters around Great Britain like sharks.

A lookout had spotted a sub in the vicinity of the Canadian convoy, and the crews sprang to action, issuing life preservers and beckoning British destroyers patrolling nearby. When Charlie awoke to the sound of the sea splashing against the ship's hull—and silent engines—he expected the worst. He climbed on deck. But instead of witnessing a pitched naval battle, he could just make out the spires of St. Colman's Cathedral piercing the sky in the distance. The *Southland* had retreated to Queenstown Harbour, County Cork, Ireland, where it hid briefly before sailing on for Bristol and the Port of Avonmouth.

On March 7, the *Southland* docked at Avonmouth where the men of the Thirty-Second Battalion finally stepped on English soil.

For the British-born boys, they were home. For the Canadians, England was an undiscovered land: "A new world," one soldier wrote, "a world we had read about in books." The English viewed the Canadians as a wild and foreign lot. Journalists witnessing the arrival of the first Canadian contingent the previous autumn called them "pioneers and backwoodsmen." There was a roughness to the colonial men, a disregard for authority and social rank that unnerved some of the British. As one officer lamented, "Canadians were not ordinary soldiers."

But they were happy to be there.

Charlie and the Thirty-Second boarded a train that sped east across the heart of England. They wove through pristine countryside that was familiar to even those who had never been in Britain before. "The thatched cottages, the neatly-clipped hedges, the churchyard with its headstones and tumbling wall," wrote one soldier, "all seemed to fit in with what we expected." Charlie had been born in Essex on the other side of the country. But as he passed through the quaint villages of southern England, the names on the station platforms "brought back memories of cities and towns"—Bath, Chippenham, Swindon, and Reading—that "our parents had talked about at home."

Charlie was both at home and a long way from it. The train finally came to a stop at Folkestone, Kent, right where the English Channel was the narrowest. With Calais only thirty miles away, the French coast loomed nearer than London. And with Flanders less than fifty miles from Calais, the war was at hand.

The Canadians detrained and marched to their new home, Risborough Barracks at the Shorncliffe Army Camp. The base looked ancient, its buildings a collection of metal huts that the Canadians christened "Tin Town." The Thirty-Second shared Tin Town with the Twenty-Third Battalion, the boys who had crossed the Atlantic with them, and the Thirtieth Battalion, formerly the Duke of Connaught's Own Rifles of Victoria, BC. Together, the men close-order drilled, long marched, and learned the use of bayonets and rifles. They were preparing for war. Yet, for Charlie, the experience was largely pleasant. He visited two heavenly wonders—the great wall of chalk and flint known as the White Cliffs of Dover and the chiselled mountain of stone called Canterbury Cathedral. Charlie also was reunited with some of his relations, spending Easter in Harpenden, Hertfordshire, with his Uncle Arthur, his father's younger brother. And he steeled himself against temptation. While passing through London, a "big blowsey looking woman" recognized his uniform and called out "Hullo Canada." But Charlie kept going. Later he rented a bicycle and visited Sandgate, on the coast where his mother Rosetta had spent lazy summers as a girl.

On April 21, Charlie had returned to base. A soldier a few beds down had been diagnosed with measles and Charlie's hut was quarantined. He took to his bunk, and that was when it happened: Charlie heard the "mighty rumbles" of artillery from Ypres as a battle erupted. He and his comrades peeked out from their hut and stared across the channel. They could just make out the "continual flashing" of muzzle fire from monstrous guns even though the artillery was sixty miles away.

Charlie and his friends trembled at the awesome violence they were glimpsing. "It was very exciting and fearful," he decided. He knew that something momentous was happening, but he didn't know what. He had no idea that amid these flashes, the Canadian First Division was facing its first taste of fire. Most of all, he had no inkling that friends from Winnipeg, including his Pine Street neighbour Fred Hall and Fred's brother Harry, were fighting for survival.

THE GOOD SERGEANT

Fred and Harry Hall, April 1915

Strangely, the war brought them together. The brothers Fred and Harry Hall, separated in age by nine years, had not grown up together, and were in many ways strangers when Fred arrived in Winnipeg in mid-1913. But they were going off to war together in the same militia—the 106th Regiment—after bidding their mother and sisters goodbye in the Winnipeg rail yard, and enduring the same four-day train journey to the CEF base in Quebec. In the reckoning and re-ordering that took place there, the men were divided into battalions of roughly one thousand soldiers each, moderate care being taken to keep militias together within these formations. Harry Hall and most of the 106th were formed into the 10th Battalion along with the cattlemen and cowboys of the 103rd Regiment or Calgary Rifles. But any hope—or fear—that Harry and Fred would serve together on the battlefield ended when the older Hall was transferred to the Eighth Battalion, largely made up of Winnipeg's respected militia, the 90th Winnipeg Rifles or Little Black Devils. The

Rifles were non-kilted, and had no Scottish links, but they were a legendary outfit, and a credit to the Eighth Battalion.

The brothers endured, as Harry later wrote, "drills in formation and long route marches" at Valcartier, although not once was the younger Hall given a rifle to train with. In late September, the brothers crossed the Atlantic together along with the rest of the CEF—Fred aboard the troopship RMS *Franconia* and Harry aboard the SS *Scandinavian*. Theirs was a strange homecoming: although sons of England and from a family of proud soldiers, they returned as aliens wearing the uniform of a foreign army. They wintered together at the Canadian camp on Salisbury Plain. There, Harry learned the rudiments of military life, while Fred's long experience as a soldier brought him rapid advancement, to acting sergeant in late October and later to sergeant major, making him the ranking non-commissioned officer for C Company. (Under the then-current structure, each battalion was made up of four companies, usually lettered A to D.) Fred, who had spent his adult life with the First Cameronians, was a rare commodity within the battalion—a professional. The stinging scorpion tattooed on his right arm, a souvenir from his days as a soldier of the King, was a more convincing demonstration than the chevrons on his shoulder that he was a tough battle captain.

After a winter of drilling in the Salisbury mud, the brothers shipped over to France in February 1915 with the British army's First Canadian Division. (The Canadians would not fight as an independent entity. Like the Dominion from which they came, they were an extension of Great Britain.) The Halls' initiation was gradual. In March 1915, at the Battle of Neuve Chapelle, the Canadians laid down diversionary fire for the attacking British and waited to leap from their trenches to support them when the Brits broke through. The breakthrough never came, but seasoned soldiers like Fred Hall knew that Canada had crossed a threshold. The men had been drilled and blooded and were now ready to face the enemy. As one soldier put it, "the halcyon days" were over.

In April, the Canadians marched to Flanders and the Ypres salient, a bubble in the front line that protruded into German-held territory. This area surrounding the ancient mercantile city of Ypres had represented the tragic end of the war's hopeful beginning. The two opposing armies had clashed in France and then in a series of flanking movements had worked their way north toward Belgium. At one point, as this process unfolded, the British commander-in-chief, Sir John French, had declared that the Allies "would soon be in a position to round [the enemy] up." His pronouncement was premature and the roundup never happened. But the Allies—the British, French, and what remained of the Belgian Army—were not prepared to surrender ground there. Flanders was hallowed soil for Flemish riflemen, and Britain, after all, had gone to war to defend Belgium. Already a generation lay buried there. Ypres was nothing less than, as one Brit later said, "an eternal memorial to British valour." It had strategic value too: Ypres was a major rail terminus leading to the coastal ports. For all these reasons, the Allies did not let her go. Despite ferocious German attempts to seize it, the Allies retained a twenty-four-square-kilometre swath of territory around the city, which the French Eleventh Division guarded throughout the winter. By April, the French Eleventh was weary and ready for relief, and the Canadians were ordered to take over their positions.

On April 14, Fred Hall and the men of the Eighth Battalion climbed aboard motorized—rather than the more familiar horse-drawn—buses in L'Abeele, a village on the French side of the Belgian border, and headed east to the salient. Meanwhile, Harry and the Tenth Battalion rode similar conveyances to Vlamertinghe, where they alighted and marched on to Ypres. Although they were latecomers to the war, the Canadians were not ignorant of Flanders's significance. Captain John McCrae, poet, surgeon and artilleryman, rode into the salient atop his horse, Bonfire, with hate in his heart. He had read the casualty figures of the first clash at Ypres—160,000 French, British, and Belgian casualties; and 134,000 German. For McCrae, only days away from articulating his grief and outrage in a famous poem, the dead were calling from their graves. "We would be terrible traitors to the world," he wrote, "if we stopped any time before the snake is scotched.... Germany has got to get a lot of lessons yet."

Canadians entered the city of Ypres awed and humbled by the destruction that was before them. The Cloth Hall, a six-hundred-year-old textile warehouse and marketplace, a castle of spires, turrets, niches, and ostentation, had been shelled and gutted. The city's great churches had been similarly savaged. Rubble and carrion littered the streets, and few buildings stood undamaged. Yet, civilians still lived among the debris, and the city, according to one regimental historian, was "still functioning more or less normally."

The Canadians took refuge in the rubble and waited for dusk. In the Eighth Battalion, Sergeant Major Fred Hall had more than two hundred twenty soldiers in his care as the Eighth prepared to enter the front lines. But he had other soldiers on his mind—namely, his two younger brothers, Harry and Ted. Harry, a private in the Tenth Battalion, was not far away; Fred's Eighth Battalion and Harry's Tenth were elements of the same brigade. Their brother Ted was also in uniform, but Fred worried less about him. Three years younger than Fred, Ted was an experienced soldier. He had been stationed in Malta in the first months of the war and then was shipped back to Britain in October. Ted and Harry had been able to see each other once in Winchester before Ted and the Rifles were sent to France.

Ted's deployment to the war could only have panicked their mother. But her greatest worry was the baby of the family, Harry. Fred knew this, and tried to calm her by including reassuring news of Harry in his letters home. It was indeed good that the brothers both served in the Second Brigade, where Fred could keep an eye on him. Apart from watching on and calming their mother, there was little else that Fred could do. Seasoned soldiers like Fred Hall knew that in battle, every man was on his own.

When darkness fell over the salient, Fred Hall's concerns returned to C Company and the war. Bugles sounded, and men fell in. Then the Eighth and Tenth Battalions left the city via the northern St. Jean road, which pointed directly toward the front lines and beyond it, to the town of Passchendaele. Starlight illuminated the road and the "naked, flat, and oozy" farmers' fields. The ooziness was the result of the ground thawing, releasing the foul odour of rot and death. As they edged down the road, the shadows of farmhouses loomed in the fields, but virtually all had been toppled by artillery.

When the column arrived at Wieltje, a collection of ruined farmhouses, it was met by French guides who led them along paths and trenches to the uneven, reeking ditch that was the salient's forward position. Other elements of the Canadian division were being deployed at the same time. When in place, it would occupy four thousand metres of the front. A British Division, the Twenty-Eighth, occupied the line to their right. The French Eighty-Seventh and Forty-Fifth Divisions, the latter made up of exotically attired African colonial units, held the left flank on the other side. Fred Hall's Eighth Battalion manned the right end of the Canadian sector just ahead of the high ground known as the Gravenstafel Ridge.

That first night, Fred Hall's company settled into the crude French dugouts, using their time to marshal ammunition lugged in from the rear, feeding on "iron rations" of corned beef, and facing the enemy across an implausibly narrow stretch of no man's land. The no man's land between them and the Germans was vacant. Barbed wire, an invention of North American cattlemen, was just then making its way to the battlefields of Europe.

For Fred Hall, the proximity of the enemy was the least of his worries. The trenches they had inherited from the French were foul and inadequate. Trenches varied from army to army, and those least interested in digging in were the French, perhaps because they were loath to admit that the war marring their countryside would be prolonged enough to require it. For whatever reason, the salient's trenches were "remarkable" for their disrepair, according to the Tenth Battalion war diary. The parapet or trench front varied in height along the line, with some stretches completely exposed to the enemy. Dugouts—bunkers excavated in the sides of the trenches to provide shelter under artillery shelling—were "so filthy that our men could not occupy them." The worst of it were the dead bodies that mouldered just beneath the trench floor and the human limbs that were sometimes encountered jutting out like tree roots from the trench walls.

Soldiers could do little but "keep out of sight of the enemy and not step or sit or lie down in filth." The next day, the hard work of repairing and rebuilding would begin. The front was inactive, the French having suffered only thirty casualties since Christmas. The sleepiness of the sector suggested to some that the Germans had turned their attention to other theatres, such as the Argonne. No one knew, least of all the Canadians, that the quiet along the line was a mirage, and that Germans were at that moment planning one of their most devastating and audacious offensives.

The Allies didn't know, but they should have. On March 28, a British unit had captured a German officer who, under interrogation, gave up intelligence that beggared belief: the enemy was preparing to attack the salient with poison gas. Gas was not a new weapon. On the Eastern Front, the Germans had bombarded Russian forces with shells laced with tear gas. The tear gas bomb had failed in its purpose, but German scientists had also developed a weapon system using a toxic gas, chlorine, and according to the prisoner, they were ready to deploy it. The story might have been dismissed as delusional had not the French heard a similar account from some of their prisoners. But despite the grave and alarming nature of this intelligence, it was neither appreciated nor shared.

On the morning of Thursday, April 22, Fred Hall and the Eighth Battalion stood the line. Harry Hall's Tenth Battalion had been relieved and was billeted in Ypres, which had just been shelled. The bombardment was no ordinary cannonade. Monstrous enemy guns, including the forty-two-centimetre Krupps howitzer, nicknamed *Dicke Bertha*, Big Bertha, had pounded the ravaged city and wrought yet more destruction. "Houses were seen to collapse and disappear in dust clouds," wrote one soldier. "A black pall thickened over the city, and this was streaked with tongues of fire as flames from blazing buildings spread on all sides." For some of the men, the intense barrage was suspiciously similar to the shelling that often preceded an offensive. Yet the trenches held by Fred Hall's battalion were "quiet." It was a beautiful spring day along the salient's line and so calm in places that larks could be seen and their song heard. Soldiers stretched out to sun themselves, and the atmosphere at the front remained like this, easy and uneventful, until late afternoon when the wind changed. It had been blowing in from the east for most of the day, but now the breeze shifted and began to blow from southwest. Within the headquarters of the German Fourth Army, this seemingly unremarkable change in the weather sparked excitement. The general staff had been waiting since April 15 to release 168 tons of chlorine gas into the air. The plan was to create a killing cloud that would burn a gaping hole in the Allied lines—an open gate in the front that the German infantry could rush through. But the Germans needed a steady westerly wind to deliver the gas, and for the past eight days, Thor and Woden, the Norse gods of weather and battle, had been uncooperative. Now, finally, their opportunity was at hand.

Arguably, the plan was less audacious than it was desperate. The salient had frustrated and confounded German war planners who still dreamed of a breakthrough. All manner of strategies and weapons had been considered. When the possibility of harnessing poison gas was mooted, many generals—ignoring the moral dubiousness of its deployment—strongly advocated its use. Like the nuclear debate a generation later, the potentially decisive nature of the weapon trumped morality. "If these poison gases were to bring about the fall of Ypres," said German general Berthold von Deimling, a commander during the First Battle of Ypres, in 1914, "we had to go on, come what may." Some generals, looking beyond the immediate objective, saw the gas as a war-winning weapon. Sober pragmatists like German chief of staff Erich von Falkenhayn, an old-school Prussian warlord, were more skeptical. Gas was untried, and with so much of his army battling the Russians in the east, Falkenhayn knew he had too few soldiers in Flanders to exploit a breakthrough even if gas proved effective. But the weapon was worth an experimental try, he believed. If it worked as hoped, the undermanned Fourth Army had enough riflemen on hand to gain some ground in the salient, where every metre was precious and paid for with blood. Falkenhayn had green-lighted its use.

The first indication of imminent catastrophe for the men in Fred Hall's line was the appearance of "peculiar" clouds that to some looked like the smoke of lyddite shells hitting enemy trenches.

Then, on the left of the line, an artillery observer for the Ninth Canadian Battery muttered to an officer: "There's something funny going on." The something was a six-kilometre-long "green cloud" that crept like a fog bank across no man's land. Realizing the vapour had to be a German attack, officers along the line gave the order: "Open immediate rapid fire!" and soldiers began blasting into the "grey-green" mist, firing so furiously that rifles overheated, muzzles elongated, and "fat was pouring out of the [guns'] woodwork." Canadians on the far left braced themselves. But at the last minute, the wind shifted again, and the deadly mist drifted into their left flank, the trenches of the *Tirailleurs* and *Zouaves*, the French colonial troops from North Africa.

The French line imploded, its soldiers overwhelmed by the chlorine vapour that attacked their eyes and lungs, creating a searing pain and the sensation of drowning. They felt as if they were underwater because the gas was a vesicant, designed to trigger the overproduction of mucus in respiratory systems, which the men choked on. As for the pain, when the chlorine mixed with water, namely the moisture in the men's eyes, nasal passages, throats, and lungs, it formed hydrochloric acid, which ate away at their tissues and flesh. And with the agony came terror, which might have been even more pronounced among the African troops, who were steeped in a martial tradition in which enemies faced each other honourably with swords or muskets. Death caused by a ghostly cloud wasn't war as they knew it. Indeed, more than one African might have agreed with the colonial soldier from British India who said of an earlier battle: "This is not war, this is the ending of the world."

The Germans followed the gas with an artillery barrage, and the French line, already choking, buckled and broke. Shouting "Asphyxie! Asphyxie!" soldiers tossed their weapons aside and stumbled to the rear. "The men came tumbling from the front line," said a private with the Bedfordshire Fusiliers. "[T]error-stricken, they were tearing at their throats and their eyes were glaring." The poisoned colonials fled to the rear in a mob. They trampled the wounded and slow-moving in their path, and to Canadian troops in reserve near the village of St. Julien, located two kilometres behind the front, the retreating troops in their blue-and-red uniforms looked like "rushing" and "half-staggering" Napoleonic riflemen fleeing out of time from some ancient battle. The Canadians tried to turn the retreating men, and at least one squad "got orders to shoot them down." Declared a private: "We just turned around and shot them as they were running away."

Those firing on the Algerians didn't shoot at them for long. There were more important targets to aim at. Riflemen with the German Fifty-Second Reserve Infantry Division emerged from behind the cloud, and what a sight they were. Like many enemy soldiers, they wore spiked Pickelhaube helmets, but because of the gas, they also wore masks that made them look like monstrous insects. They were an army of praying mantises, probing the air ahead of them with bayonet-tipped rifles. For the Canadians posted at St. Julien, it was the most surreal of sights. But no one missed the importance of what was happening. Six kilometres of the Allied front had collapsed, and the enemy was pouring through the breach.

Further down the line to the right, Fred Hall's Eighth Battalion hunkered down and waited. They had watched the gas cloud waft across no man's land and the German infantry scramble after it. Then shells pounded the Winnipeggers, killing six men and wounding thirty-three. Men gagged and their eyes watered because of the gas, which was not chlorine, but later identified as tear gas. The men braced for an infantry attack.

As an element of the Second Brigade, the Eighth Battalion was commanded by Arthur Currie. A lumbering, jowly western Canadian businessman, Currie owed his commission to his friendship with the son of Minister of Militia Sam Hughes. A failed real-estate developer, Currie was discovering a new métier in war. He understood that, following the gas attack, the Germans might next attack his sector of the line. Accordingly, he refused to send his reserves into the battle on the left, and instead ordered his rear echelon to Locality C—strategic ground in and around Gravenstafel Ridge directly behind the Second Brigade trenches— to shore up their position and make ready. The tactician in Currie told him that Gravenstafel Ridge was an enemy target. He would be proven right eventually, but not in the next few hours. In the late afternoon of April 22, the fighting on Currie's left would decide the future of the salient.

In the wake of the stampeding Algerians, the Germans drove deep into Allied territory, pushing toward the prize, Ypres. By 6 P.M., Canadians at the front were being shelled from behind. The Germans had advanced so far forward that they had captured Allied guns (sixteen 75-mm and twenty-nine 90-mm cannons), and turned them on their former owners. The Germans had also penetrated Kitcheners Wood, a small forest near Ypres, which was so far to the rear it was mainly used by army cooks. Just to the east of Kitcheners Wood stood the village of St. Julien. Only hours before, St. Julien was firmly in Allied hands, but now it was up for grabs. If the invaders pivoted right and besieged St. Julien, they might be able to sweep behind Currie's men, seize the ridge, and isolate the Canadian front. Hall and his comrades could not have had any idea how close they were to encirclement and oblivion. But everyone in the salient now knew the situation was grave. So Fred Hall hunkered down and waited with the Eighth Battalion, not realizing that the division's survival over the next hours would depend on his brother Harry and the Tenth Battalion.

Early on April 22, Harry Hall had been in an Ypres café, whose chairs and tables were set up along a debris-strewn street, enjoying a cognac and coffee with a couple of chums. After three days in billets, his battalion was due to return to the front within twenty-four hours, and the deployment had already begun. Throughout the afternoon, companies were marched from the city to spend the night in the countryside, which was free of shelling. But while Harry and his comrades sipped drinks, the enemy was on the march toward them. When company bugles sounded, Harry and the others bolted from their tables and fell in. Soon they were marching north. The plan was to stop at the junction where the Ypres and St. Jean roads met and rendezvous with companies already camped in the countryside. But when the Tenth reached the crossroads, they collided with the human flotsam of the collapse, a tsunami of "exhausted and gasping" colonial troops together with farmers pushing carts, some containing their wives and families. Children grasped the skirts of mothers whose eyes "looked the picture of pure terror." Horsemen charged in and out of the fleeing mob. The "fugitives" streamed across the fields and onto the road, and with them came the chemical stench of "hydrochloric acid," and more shelling. The Tenth marched against the tide, winding its way like a snake through a "confusion of transport wagons, ammunition carts, refugees, dead and dying horses," eventually reaching Wieltje, where they took cover in reserve trenches and waited for orders. The enemy's advanced position was no more than a kilometre away, perhaps less. When darkness came, they emerged from the ditches and gathered near a farmhouse. Harry spotted "kilted" warriors of the Canadian Sixteenth Battalion, a cobbling together of men from four Canadian highlander regiments, including

Winnipeg's Seventy-Ninth Highlanders, the militia his brother Fred had belonged to back home. Finally, just before 11 P.M., a courier arrived bearing orders.

They were presented to Lieutenant Colonel Russell Lambert Boyle, the six-feet-two-inch Alberta cattleman who led the Tenth. A tough cowboy, Boyle had once told a chaplain: "I may be killed, but I have no fear of being wounded. I've been wounded before and my wounds heal quickly." And he had long yearned for this moment to enter the war. Just three weeks before, Boyle had been in London where he made a case for the deployment of the Canadian division. "Let me tell you there is no force more efficient as a fighting unit than those Canadians now in the trenches," he had said. "They can't be beaten." He went outside to brief the men personally.

Harry listened to Boyle outline Currie's plan. The Tenth would be attacking a detail of Germans nested in the dense trees of Kitcheners Wood, a half kilometre to the right. Their orders were to enter the brush, clear it of enemy, and rally on the other side, where a British battery that had been taken over by the Germans stood. The Tenth had been ordered to lead what one soldier called a "cold steel" bayonet charge. The Canadian Scottish of the Sixteenth Battalion would follow in support.

Harry and the Tenth crept to the assembly area where they removed their packs and overcoats, and fixed bayonets. They formed into ranks. Harry stood among the five hundred men in the first row. Starlight softened the night and rendered Kitcheners Wood visible as "a dark blur" in the near distance. Lieutenant Colonel Boyle ran his fingers through his moustache and paced the line, giving the boys their final instructions. *When advancing, keep to the right*, he whispered. *And proceed at a steady pace.* He hadn't forgotten what this attack meant for the Tenth Battalion. "We've been aching for a fight," one man declared. "Now we're going to get it." A well-known divisional chaplain, Canon Frederick Scott, also made his way among the waiting men, slapping backs and declaring this: "A great day for Canada, boys!" The boys almost believed him. They were "thrilled," but scared.

Just before midnight, Boyle drew his sword and ordered the men forward in two files. They began their advance under the light of a pale moon. There was no foe in sight and the attack took on an unreal quality. According to one officer, "The lines went steadily ahead as if they were doing a drill maneuver." To some men, the event seemed almost like a joke, an assault on a quiet forest. But the trees were not empty. The Germans were there, hidden in a trench just in front of the tree line. They stayed their fire and let the Canadians approach as close as seventy-five yards. Then "all hell broke loose." A flare arched into the sky, illuminating the Canadians, and the Germans unleashed a barrage that thundered "like the blows of a hollow hammer." Bullets raked the ranks. Those who were not shot dove to the ground and struggled to get their bearings. Identifying the enemy's position was not hard despite the "blinding vortex of dust." Rifle and machine gun barrels spat flame along a line in front of the trees. For a brief time, the Tenth was trapped, and at least one officer despaired, recalling how the "inaction of the moment was maddening." But presently the men rose up, gave off a collective roar, and charged. They leapt into the German trench, gutting enemy soldiers with their bayonets and driving survivors into the trees twenty-five yards away. A squad of men led by Major Joseph McLaren, a St. Andrews–educated Scot from Brandon, Manitoba, charged after them unaware that the trees were saturated with more enemy. The fighting in the woods was brutal, mostly blind because of the darkness, and hand to hand, although one soldier with the Sixteenth later admitted that he "lost confidence in my bayonet and always fired." Screams echoed above the din. At one point, McLaren could be heard rallying his men.

Those not in the trees, including Harry Hall, remained in the shallow trench that they had seized from the Germans, and fired on a nearby enemy redoubt. For a short time, the westerners of the Tenth triumphed: Kitcheners Wood was cleared of Germans, and the big British guns on the far side of the forest were captured and demolished. (They couldn't be moved.) Despite this success, the Tenth and Sixteenth were too diminished in strength to hold the area for long under the shellfire that overwhelmed them, said one sergeant, the way a "tropical storm sweeps a forest." Moreover, the German redoubt in front of the woods was never taken. Lieutenant Colonel Boyle, meanwhile, had been shot in the groin. The tough cattleman who had no fear of being wounded ultimately died of one. Major McLaren, also wounded, died when a shell struck the ambulance carrying him to an aid station.

Too weak to defend the woods and too isolated to be reinforced, the Tenth and Sixteenth abandoned their conquest and withdrew. When the dust cleared and April 23 dawned, Harry Hall was a rarity—a living, breathing unwounded soldier of the Tenth Battalion. At their next roll call, only 188 men and 5 officers fell in. The Tenth and Sixteenth had stopped the German advance. They had been aided by the enemy's inexplicable slowness in capitalizing on the collapse of the Forty-Fifth Division's front—a reticence that British historian Basil Liddell Hart would attribute to the enemy's "fear of their own gas."

Despite this accomplishment, Harry's travails weren't over. The battle for possession of the salient raged on. Early the next morning, Harry and the others saw a yellowish cloud approaching from about four thousand metres away. The dragon was spitting fire again. The enemy had launched another gas attack and another offensive. This time, Harry's brother Fred and the Eighth Battalion were the target. The Germans released the gas, unleashed ferocious shelling, and stormed the Eighth Battalion line. Although they had been issued crude respirators (water-soaked "cotton bando-liers" fitted over the face), the Winnipeg men choked, burned, and clawed at their own eyes. Many collapsed, but enough hung on to hold the line. They fought desperately, almost maniacally. Men who were too ill to stand upright lay on the trench floor, loaded rifles, and handed them up to their comrades on the fire step, who shot into the attacking Germans. The Ross rifle was prone to jam when fired repeatedly and the men often had to pause to kick the bolt loose before firing again.

Harry Hall and his weary comrades were soon drawn into this fight. They relocated behind the Eighth Battalion's line ahead of Gravenstafel Ridge. For Harry, the coming days were a blur of shelling, casualties, and no sleep, which "made it impossible to grasp what was going on." But the Eighth Battalion line held and the salient endured. On May 5, Harry and his comrades were sent to billets at the French village of Merris. Harry heard that the Eighth Battalion was resting nearby at Bailleul. He had been fighting close to Fred while posted near Gravenstafel Ridge, but had no contact with him. He hadn't seen his older brother for almost a month. At the first opportunity, he wandered into Bailleul and sought out the Eighth Battalion. He spotted one of Fred's friends, another sergeant, and the expression on his face told Harry everything he needed to know.

POISON

Fred Hall, April 1915

The sergeant took Harry Hall aside, that day in Bailleul, and told him the story of his brother Fred. Of course, Harry knew the background. He had just lived through it all: the April 22 gas attack, the stampede of panicked French colonial soldiers ahead of the green cloud and advancing German infantry, and the desperate last stand at Kitcheners Wood. After stopping the Germans, Harry and the Tenth Battalion had been dispatched to the front near Gravenstafel Ridge, and although Harry never encountered his brother there, it was in this sector that Fred and his comrades had made their stand.

During the bulk of the fighting after April 22, Fred Hall was not at the front. He and the Eighth Battalion's C Company (also referred to as No. 3 Company) waited while the gas attack and subsequent fighting consumed the left side of the salient. But Currie, anticipating a German attack on Gravenstafel Ridge, kept Fred's company in reserve and posted the Seventh Battalion immediately in front of the hill, in the strategic zone called Locality C.

Currie's expectation was realized in the early hours of April 24 as the wind blew into his face. German *stinkpioniers* opened faucets on barrels of chlorine, and pointed the attached hoses in the direction of Gravenstafel.

At about 4 A.M., Eighth Battalion commander Lieutenant Colonel Louis Lipsett, from his headquarters on the ridge, spotted the murderous "bluish haze" drifting toward the line and knew that he was under attack. The poison fog enveloped the Winnipeg trenches shortly after. As the Canadians gasped and choked, German infantry with the Second Reserve Ersatz Brigade rose up from their trenches and stormed across no man's land. And despite what Lipsett called the "paralyzing effect" of the chlorine, the Winnipeggers in the trenches lashed back, calling in an artillery barrage that caught the Germans in open ground, and firing their Ross rifles until, as always, they jammed. The Canadian line wavered and trembled under the enemy battering like a metal post thwacked with a sledgehammer. But the line held.

The Toronto Scots of the Fifteenth Battalion, dug in on the Winnipeg left, were not as lucky. Gas and German marauders tore into the line, "advancing unchecked" over these trenches just as they had overcome the Algerians two days before. Lipsett learned of the breach by telephone, and he understood the danger. His position, Gravenstafel Ridge and Locality C, was in danger of being encircled by the enemy. He needed reserves to rush left and stop up the hole, and the only reserve he had left was Fred Hall's C Company.

So he had two platoons of C scramble half a kilometre to occupy the Fifteenth Battalion's now-empty trenches. Then he ordered two additional platoons to fix another problem that developed after the breach was made. The trenches on the left end of the Winnipeg line ("subsection 2c" on the trench maps) had come under intense pressure. The defenders had shored up the flank and so far had kept the Germans from isolating the battalion. But they were being attacked from all directions. German units that had broken through on the left had come up behind them and were firing furiously from a support trench and, according to one report, a mangled, tree-filled copse. In response, a squad of Eighth Battalion men climbed over the back of the trench (the parados) and charged. Among them was a husky private from Kenora, Ontario, who had everything to live for. Just before twenty-one-year-old Arthur Clarkson had sailed for France with the First Division, he had married a Scottish girl in Aberdeen. Now Private Clarkson and a handful of Eighth Battalion riflemen stormed the German positions behind the Winnipeg line, and the newly entrenched enemy lashed back with withering fire that cut them down almost to a man.

The flank was under such pressure, Lipsett "renewed [it] twice" with reinforcements on April 24. But by nightfall, he knew he had not bolstered it enough. So he ordered his final reserves, two solitary but rested platoons of C Company, to cross over to left flank and join its defence. C Company was commanded by twenty-seven-year-old Winnipeg lawyer Lieutenant Gerald O'Grady, who passed on the orders to the force's ranking NCO. Sergeant Major Fred Hall immediately began marshalling his men. Like all experienced sergeants, Fred had them check rifles, ammunition stores, and rations of water and canned bully beef. Fred was seasoned enough to know that during a prolonged siege, their lives might depend on having sufficient food and water at hand. Once assembled and equipped, the men set out in the early hours of April 25. Fred and his troops no doubt hoped to be hidden by the darkness. But according to an account in the Winnipeg *Free Press*, they crept forward under the glare of a "waning moon" and enemy flares. The force had about one kilometre to traverse.

As they approached the trenches, the men split into two groups. One platoon set off up a "gully" that wound toward the line; the other stayed out in the open, following a low ridge to the objective. Fred Hall was with the men who advanced over high ground.

With the 2C trenches in sight, clearly illuminated by the flash of mortars and heavy shells, Fred and the others may have been uncertain about the location of the Germans. They were hiding in a nearby copse, and as Hall's men mounted the brow of a hill, the enemy riflemen opened fire.

"They [the Canadians] were mown down," declared the *Free Press*. Yet, some of the platoon, including Fred, managed to dodge bullets and mortar shells and reach the nominal safety of the 2C trench line. They left their fallen comrades on the ground, but not all of them were dead. Amid the roar and thunder of fire, Hall and the others heard the wounded calling for help. Fred acted immediately. He crawled over the parados, scrambled up the hill, and returned with a wounded man. Then he ventured out again, and carried back the only other survivor he could find.

The reserve platoon that had travelled along the gully eventually arrived. But at some point during the melee, a bullet or hunk of shrapnel struck and wounded the platoon's senior officer, Lieutenant O'Grady, putting him out of commission. Fred Hall was now in command of his platoon as the enemy rained fire on their position. The German strategy was to soften the trench up, and then attack and clear it with their troops. By daylight, the Germans' chances for success appeared alarmingly high. The flank was in grave danger of being overrun. The Germans continued to rake it with fire and "one after another of the officers were killed or wounded," and the trench floor was covered with bodies, either maimed or dead. The surviving Canadians were as short of ammunition as men, and as the sun rose on this new day, illuminating a battlefield pockmarked by shelling and littered with the torn bodies of fallen soldiers, Fred Hall stared into oblivion. His battalion was besieged, and it was obvious that the remnants of his company might not survive the day. At that moment, the only resource he had left was the one military quality he had been imbued with since boyhood—honour. Fred, like his father, was an honourable man.

Frederick Matticott Hall had certainly been revered after his premature death in 1905. The Second South Lancashire Regiment had buried the elder Hall with full military honours, and an unprecedented throng of locals—"one of the largest gatherings of the townspeople that has ever assembled," reported a local newspaper—had attended. The funeral procession had wound like a sombre parade through St. Helens. Starting at Westfield Street and then filing down Dentons Green and Windleshaw Road, the mourners and pallbearers marched to the dirge from Handel's *Saul*, a funeral march noted for its sorrowful trombone, the instrument Frederick the son had learned from his father, and perfected throughout his life. Sergeant Major Frederick William Hall had come by his sense of honour honestly. It had convinced him to choose the army over a career in law when he was a young man. It had compelled him to leave the army and England to care for his mother. It had propelled him to enlist when news reached him that the Empire was at war.

And only a commitment to honour explains what Fred did next. Sometime on that morning along the 2C trench, cries echoed from beyond the parados. When the men scanned the space behind the lines, they saw a wounded Eighth Battalion soldier sprawled on the ground, "waving his arms feebly." The man was Arthur Clarkson, one of the brave souls who had charged the Germans when they appeared behind the trench the day before. Young Arthur had been languishing, wounded, on the broken ground ever since. Perhaps he had been unconscious. Perhaps his cries weren't heard until there was a lull in the firing. But his cries now were plaintive. He was a British-born boy who had been raised by a Canadian uncle in Kenora. He had worked at the Rat Portage Lumber Company, and three months ago to the day he had married Sarah Newcombe, the daughter of a Scottish fisherman. Arthur wanted to live. His cries for help, as mortars and shells fell around him, testified to it, and his comrades responded.

According to one account, two soldiers—a private and a sergeant—scrambled onto the open ground, and crawled only a few feet before one or both were wounded, and forced back. Another account claims that only one soldier ventured out for Arthur, and was immediately killed by either shrapnel or rifle fire coming from the Germans concealed in the trees.

What is certain is that Fred Hall saw Clarkson, witnessed the brave failed attempts to reach him, and resolved to bring the man in himself. He scrambled over the parados, somehow evaded the bullets and shellfire, and crossed the fifteen yards of no man's land to where Arthur Clarkson lay.

At this point, accounts again vary. Some state that Fred Hall tried dragging Clarkson back before pulling him to his feet so that they could move more swiftly. Others state that Fred immediately lifted Clarkson and held him upright. All accounts agree that Fred Hall had taken only a single step toward the trench when his head snapped violently backward. He had been hit directly in the forehead by either shrapnel or a bullet, and when he crumpled to the ground, the Eighth Battalion men watching on from trench 2C knew that Sergeant Major Fred Hall was dead. Arthur Clarkson, the man Fred had given his life to save, lived on a while longer. His cries were heard throughout the day until a shell landed almost directly on him, ending his suffering and his life, and all but obliterating his body and Hall's. After the Canadian division rallied and the Germans were beaten back, neither the remains of Fred Hall nor Arthur Clarkson were found. The battlefield had swallowed them whole. But they weren't forgotten. Word of Fred Hall's bravery spread from the survivors of 2C trench to the survivors of the Eighth Battalion. Lieutenant Colonel Lipsett heard about it and wrote in his official report how "Sergeant Major Hall was killed whilst trying to put a wounded man under cover." The selflessness and martyrdom struck a chord with soldiers and officers. An anonymous account of Fred's deed, presumably scribbled by an Eighth Battalion witness, begins with a quote from John 15:13— "No greater love has this than a man lay down his life for a friend." British military tradition requires soldiers to pay special homage to acts of devotion between comrades and Fred Hall accordingly was nominated posthumously for a Victoria Cross, the Empire's highest decoration for valour. The medal was officially awarded a few months later.

On August 24, 1915, Mary Hall was presented with her son's VC in Winnipeg. The significance of the date was not lost to Mary. She was accepting her dead son's award exactly one year, as she told a journalist, after her "Freddie went away with the troops from the CPR depot." What happened to Fred was an example of the swiftness of fate in that terrible time. Over the preceding year, a war had erupted, and in the course of it her son had lived extraordinarily, died tragically, and would soon become legendary.

Fate would catch up with Harry Hall as well. After surviving Kitcheners Wood—in itself a marvel of defiance against overwhelming odds—he remained with the depleted Tenth Battalion, which wasn't scrapped, as some feared it would be. Instead, the unit was reinforced, reconstituted, and brought up to a semblance of its former strength.

Harry and the Tenth were marched onto a new battlefield a month later near the French village of Festubert. This time the Canadians were on the offensive, although Harry and his comrades, among them two Scotsman from Winnipeg, Duncan Cross and Hector McIvor, knew their assault to be ill-conceived, if not suicidal. The battalion was ordered to attack and occupy a sector of a German trench that could not be found on any map or seen with the naked eye. The operation proceeded despite the vehement protests of Brigadier General Currie, and on May 20, Harry Hall was in the vanguard of the assault. The jumping-off point lay at the end of a narrow communication trench that ran straight as a spear into no man's land. The plan was to pour out of a hole in the trench and then attack over open ground. Even young Harry doubted the scheme. "We knew we would never make it," he admitted, and his pal Duncan agreed. They would be running through a door in the trench directly into enemy fire. "This is crazy," Duncan said. "If the forward men get mowed down, I'm ducking into a shell hole."

"I'll be there before you," Harry said, and the attack unfolded just as the men predicted. They stormed down the communication ditch, poured out of the exit, and ran into a hail of bullets. Harry, Duncan, and Hector stumbled into no man's land together and when the soldiers directly ahead of them collapsed, cut down by fire, they dodged into a shell hole, and then slipped back into the communication trench when the firing eased up. It was a smart decision. Scores of their comrades died, and no one in the battalion advanced farther than one hundred metres. Harry's lieutenant, a recent replacement as "green as grass," limped back to the trench, bleeding and weeping. "I've lost my platoon," he cried. "What shall I do?" Harry inspected the wound on the officer's head, and said, "You can go to Blighty"—slang for Britain and home. "Getting a Blighty" meant that a man had a survivable wound that guaranteed a stay in a British hospital, and might even mean a discharge from the army. Only the lucky received Blighties. At Festubert, Harry was lucky too: he was lucky to be alive, but for the moment he was going nowhere.

A luckier day found him in June 1915, at the battle near Givenchy, another obscure French village that would soon become infamously associated with death on a massive scale. At Givenchy, Harry was wounded in the arm. Although the wound itself was only moderately serious, the gangrene that set in afterwards threatened the limb and his life. He was shipped to a hospital in Great Britain, and it was while he was there that Harry learned that his brother had been awarded the Victoria Cross. The story of Fred's death came as a shock to him, of course, and the news that the Eighth Battalion had been unable to retrieve his brother's body was distressing. But he later expressed no surprise that Fred had earned the VC. Fred Hall had taken life seriously, perhaps even too seriously. This quality made it easy for Harry to understand why Fred would have charged into a hailstorm of metal to aid a stranger.

The final brave act of Fred's life was acted out only a short distance away from where Harry and the survivors of the Tenth had been posted on April 25. His brother had died so near. Yet Harry never knew.

But this was not the only sad and ironic detail to emerge from Harry's war. Both at Festubert and Givenchy, Harry had shared the battlefield with another Winnipegger whose fate would be inextricably tied to his family, his brother, and his brother's home on Pine Street.

A DEAD MAN'S MEAL

Charlie Clarke, May 1915

For Charlie Clarke, the Second Battle of Ypres was mere thunder that echoed across the English Channel. But because Ypres took such a dreadful toll on the First Canadian Division, the engagement had an immediate effect on Charlie's future. On Sunday, May 2, even before Harry Hall had marched from the salient, Charlie Clarke boarded the SS *Victoria* and "pitched and rolled" to Boulogne, the northern port that had become a key transit point in the war. Fresh troops and supplies arrived in Boulogne, and the maimed and injured departed there for Great Britain. A Canadian nurse arriving in May 1915 described its main road as "one continuous stream of ambulance wagons with the wounded," and Boulogne as being "to all practical purposes, an English town, [as] there are so many British soldiers about its streets."

There were Canadians there too. When the Thirty-Second Battalion arrived, it bivouacked on a hill outside the city, and Charlie drew guard duty. The camp's lights had been extinguished so as not to attract enemy shelling or observers, and Charlie stood his post in "pitch dark." "What I didn't imagine that night!" he recalled, and was glad for dawn. He was also glad to leave camp, with its open latrines and the gaps under the fences through which French children peered as the men evacuated their bowels. The Thirty-Second climbed into boxcars—the French conveyances claimed a capacity of *40 Hommes et 8 Chevaux*—and rumbled through the night. When the train groaned to a stop, the doors opened to reveal the sunlit streets of Steenvoorde, a village hard on the border of Belgium, and the war. The men stretched and left the train, formed into columns in a nearby open field, and marched to the village of Bailleul, where Harry Hall had slipped away from his battalion to find his brother Fred.

If Charlie Clarke encountered Harry Hall or knew that other Winnipeggers were billeting in Bailleul, he made no mention of it in the journal he was keeping at the urging of his father, Harry. Harry Clarke had given him the blank volume so that he could write down his war experiences. For generations, the Clarkes had been a family of soldiers, adventurers, and scholars, and Harry Clarke was passing this legacy on to his son. Already, the history Charlie had written made for a fascinating tale. He had a good eye for detail. Soon after detraining at Bailleul, for example, he witnessed a wondrous and frightening sight. A German airplane buzzed overhead. At this stage of the war, few flying machines were armed, and combat between them was rare. Airplanes were mainly used for reconnaissance, and with so many soldiers in and around the village, the German pilot had good reason to be curious. Charlie watched puffs of smoke blossom in the sky from anti-aircraft fire. The explosions never came close to the aircraft, whose pilot flew on unconcernedly. But Charlie was impressed. This incident marked, as he wrote, "the first shots fired" of his war.

As fate would have it, any future fire he was to experience

would not be with the Thirty-Second Battalion. Despite the protest of Lieutenant Colonel James Cowan, the Winnipeg jurist and South African war hero who had led the Dragoons, the Thirty-Second Battalion would not enter the war as a unified fighting force. Like the Twenty-Third and Thirtieth Battalions, the Dragoons would be earmarked for reserve—its men sent off to serve in existing outfits that had been depleted in the fighting. The Canadians suffered staggering losses at Ypres: the Eighth and Tenth Battalions were reduced to fewer than two hundred men each, and existing units had to be brought to strengthen them. Dragoons went to Fred Hall's Eighth and Harry Hall's Tenth battalions. About one hundred seventy men joined the Fifth Battalion, the Western Cavalry now ridden by horseless BC and prairie men. Charlie Clarke found a home with the Second Battalion, a collection of old militias from eastern Ontario, including the Forty-First Brockville Rifles, the Forty-Second Lanark and Renfrew Regiment, the Fourteenth Prince of Wales Own Regiment, and the Fortieth Northumberland Regiment. The Second was commanded by David Watson, an Anglophone newspaperman from Quebec, who with his weary eyes, creased visage, and bristly moustache looked more schoolmaster than battle captain. In fact, Watson had been a major in Quebec's Eighth Regiment, but remained just enough of an amateur soldier to satisfy Sam Hughes. Hughes gave Watson the Second Battalion, which had been in reserve in Vlamertinghe on that fateful day of April 22 when the Germans unloosed poison into the gusting wind at Ypres. The Second marched into battle just as the salient appeared to be on the verge of collapse. It was ordered to support the Tenth Battalion in its attack on Kitcheners Wood, where Harry Hall had fought. Confusion reigned from the beginning. For much of the battle, the reinforcements from the Second Battalion had no clear idea what was happening. "Fighting was in progress somewhere in the wood," declared the Second Battalion historian, "which, to the advancing men, was simply a blur against a very black sky." The confused skirmishing on the terrain around these woods, which consisted of broken ground, narrow, winding roads, and "ditches, soggy and choked with weeds," culminated in tragedy. To uproot the enemy from the left side of the line, the Second had been ordered to attack a position so unassailable that none of the scouts who had been sent out to reconnoiter returned alive. No. 1 Company charged in with bayonets fixed to their rifles and was decimated in less than two minutes. Its line "sagged, crumpled, and finally was swept away." The battalion's other companies suffered a similar fate. Three days of fighting saw the virtual annihilation of the battalion. When they left what one officer called "that place of evil" on April 29, the Second had lost 544 soldiers, and most of its officers.

Charlie Clarke was made welcome in the battalion. He reported to No. 3 Company, commanded by Captain Francis E. Birdsall, a twenty-five-year-old farmer from a town in northern Ontario that bore his family's name. No. 3 had seen hard fighting in the salient, losing most of its members in a field christened the "Mustard Patch." The survivors—the "Old Timers," as Charlie called them— shared terrible stories. Charlie could not help but look up to these men. But their tales of mayhem, poison, and death at Ypres didn't frighten him. "We were young and healthy," he would later write, "and although the rumble of guns could be heard toward Ypres, we were keen, and on a great adventure."

The adventure began drearily. The new men were put through training geared to the kind of combat that lay ahead. An important lesson included the rudiments of fighting in the war's chief terrain: below ground, in the trenches. Charlie learned that trenches were dug zigzag fashion so that an enemy incursion would not give them a clear line of fire. He was taught how to build a parapet at the trench's front, a parados at the rear, and traverses, which linked zigs to zags. He and the other new arrivals received further instruction on how to fire the problematic Ross rifle, and they were baptized into the outfit when paraded to a nearby brewery and bathed in malting vats filled with soapy water.

On May 14, Charlie and the Second Battalion marched from Bailleu, toting "full packs, overcoat, blankets, and rifles." They travelled along roads crowded with soldiers and horse-drawn limbers. They moved at night to escape the enemy's notice, clogging the back roads and byways until dawn. But night could not mask all signs of the war, which for Charlie became more tangible with every step. Shelling grew louder and the star shells that illuminated the front flared overhead in the distance. The Second Battalion was marching to war, but its route was a meandering one. They marched into a village, spent the day in a farmyard, and then set off again at night, only to trudge—apparently aimlessly—in the rain, which chilled the men to the marrow. "I took my rum issue that morning for the first time," Charlie confided to his diary.

The men harboured a "heart breaking" suspicion their officers were lost. "We wondered if anybody knew where we were supposed to go," he wrote. But there was a method to these mad wanderings. An offensive raged not far away, and because the Second Battalion stood in reserve, it moved to be in striking distance of the nearest crisis. The crisis was the Battle of Festubert, a British attack linked to a larger French campaign to the south. Festubert village sat in the Artois region, not far from Belgium, and in 1915 the French and British saw a breakthrough there as a new beginning. Located on the far side of the Artois front was a rail line that crossed the Rhine into Germany. Another strategic rail link ran to Ypres, and it was believed that a collapse at either of these points—Ypres or the

Artois—would force the Germans to withdraw, and flush the war from the trenches into the open ground where "decisive victory" waited. But Allied troops along this line faced daunting enemy defences. The Germans had dug deep and formidable bunkers in the Artois's chalky ground, and they commanded the high ground.

The Allies attacked anyway, launching a massive offensive on May 9 that history would remember as the Second Battle of Artois. The British First Army, commanded by up-and-coming staff officer Douglas Haig, struck the Germans at Aubers Ridge, a lovely eminence that Haig had coveted ever since he first spied it on reconnaissance in February. The attack failed miserably for a plethora of reasons, including inadequate artillery fire by the British who were plagued by shell shortages. (During the first two years of the war, Germany produced three times as many shells as the British.) But Haig, displaying a stubbornness and disregard for casualties for which he would later become notorious, pressed the attack on May 15 further to the south near Festubert. The Germans gave ground. The enemy's withdrawal was strategic, however. Haig failed to recognize this and ordered another attack three days later. This time, he ordered the Canadians into the fray. The Fourteenth Battalion included three fine Montreal regiments that had suffered badly defending Gravenstafel Ridge on April 24. Their mettle may have impressed General Alderson, the Canadian division's commander. He chose them to fight alongside the kilted Sixteenth Battalion, which had distinguished itself at Kitcheners Wood.

The two battalions were meant to attack in the early evening of May 18 in tandem with the British. But the Canadians were late off the mark. Due to miscommunication, Allied artillery was still firing at zero hour, so the infantry waited while the British Guards Brigade defied the shelling and stormed across no man's land, their flank exposed because the Canadians were still in their trenches. When the Canadians finally took the field, the Guards had been chewed to pieces and the Germans were ready for the next wave. The Canadians pressed on, and despite the murderous enemy fire, a few men managed to reach the German advance trench about four hundred yards away. Here the diehard Canadians made a stand, though they were trapped by mud, fire, and confusion. The Germans had already pulled back to their main line, enabling their artillery to bombard the abandoned position at will. The attackers suddenly became targets. A message sent to the rear reported on the status of the attack. "The Canadians are all blown to hell," it read. The Devil reigned a while longer. The Canadians attacked again two days later on May 20. The Fifteenth Battalion, the Canadian Scottish who suffered the "worst one-day loss" of the war at Ypres, fought alongside the weary Sixteenth. Despite fire no less hellish than before, the battalions brawled their way to an open area known as the Orchard, a position that was as far forward as any Allied soldier would get at Festubert.

But they tried a third time, bringing in Harry Hall's Tenth Battalion to storm down an abandoned German communication trench, charge into no man's land, and seize a ghostly object that no one could see or identify on a map. Despite these failures, Haig was obdurate, determined to throw men against the German defences until the effort was successful, unwilling to concede that it was a waste of life.

It was against this grim background that Charlie Clarke and the Second Battalion were called to the line on May 22. That night, the men crept toward reserve trenches near Indian Village, the unofficial name given to a collection of houses northeast of Festubert. The march to the line was eerie. They trod in the dark. A guide shepherded them at the head of the column, and Very lights—flares—streaking the sky in the distance gave them their bearings and confirmed that they were, indeed, marching to the front. As they wove single-file through a cemetery, a boy in the battalion named Jimmy tried to cut the tension by singing. "Whiter than the whitewash on the wall," he crooned, and urged the others to join in. Charlie told him to shut up, but Jimmy kept singing as the column wound by a farmhouse and a crucifix loomed at the side of the road.

> *Oh wash me in the water that you wash your dirty*
> *daughter in,*
> *So I can be whiter than the whitewash on the wall!*

Their trail led through a gutted, roofless house crowded with wounded and traumatized men. The wounded moaned and the unhinged "shook and drooled." Charlie was almost relieved to arrive at their trench, which before the attacks of the past days had constituted the front line, but which now was situated a half-mile behind the action. Charlie took sentry duty that night, but except for artillery fire and flares, the hours passed uneventfully. When morning broke, quiet had settled over the field. The sun shone and larks flew. Just ahead of their position, stretcher-bearers worked in the open, collecting dead men for burial. Charlie's section leader, a twenty-year-old banker from Quebec, Lieutenant Okill Learmonth, eyed the dead as well. He wondered aloud if any of the Montrealers killed in the previous battles and lying in the field were friends from home. He wanted to go look, and asked Charlie to come along.

Charlie had never seen a dead man before, and he was uncertain whether he wanted to. But since Learmonth was an officer and an "Old Timer," Charlie decided that "it would be fine" to join him. So he scrambled over the parapet and immediately tripped over the corpse of a soldier. There was a file of them forming a grisly line in front of the trench. To Charlie's shock, these poor souls had barely made it over the top before they were shot down. "There they were," he later recalled, "the flower of the British army hit as they went over the top."

Charlie, Learmonth, Jimmy the singer, and a corporal stepped gingerly over the first rank of corpses and crossed into the cold battlefield. They headed toward a barbed-wire fence on which dead British soldiers of the Guards Brigade dangled like rotting laundry. Yet more corpses lay contorted beside them. Charlie gazed on these dead men and felt confused. "I don't know what I expected," he wrote, "but I just felt sort of detached. This was war, and men would be killed. I who had never seen a dead body before was here amongst a dozen or more and didn't feel any special feelings." But something did catch Charlie's eye. A mess tin with a cover of fine cloth swung from the packsack of a dead man whose face had been draped in a Union Jack. Charlie found himself admiring the kit—"it was so much cleaner than my own." He picked it up, turned it in his hands, and never considered where he was standing as he gazed on it covetously. He and the others were loitering on open ground in broad daylight in full view of the enemy. He never considered that he was in danger until he heard a "swoosh and bang." Suddenly brought to his senses, Charlie turned, looked up, and spotted the "puffs of smoke" from the German artillery that was shelling them. "Run," someone shouted, and the men bolted for their trench.

"I didn't hesitate," Charlie later admitted. "I ran, and a good runner I was too. I was leading the race back toward our own trench." Charlie leaped over the parapet, hit the trench floor, dodged left, and kept on running. He followed the zigzagging ditch and sped past soldiers, bays, and dugouts, until someone he vaguely recognized pulled him aside and told him that he had reached the end of the battalion line. Charlie sat down on a crate. He ignored the food he was offered. He sat there and brooded "in a daze" for as long as three hours until Jimmy and the corporal arrived. When they found Charlie, one of them exclaimed: "Look, he still has that mess tin." This friendly voice and the realization that the dead man's kit was still in his hands shook Charlie from his stupor. He rose to his feet, acknowledged his friends, and followed them back down the line to the No. 3 Company position. Charlie Clarke was midway through his first day in the trenches. He had survived shelling and mingled with the dead. He was at war, and the violence he would be forced to witness would only grow worse.

BOMBERS

Charlie Clarke, June 1915

In the aftermath of the calamitous Battle of Festubert, in which the Canadians lost more than two thousand men and the British eight times this number, soldiers licked their wounds, and officers reeled.

"[The] son of a bitch who wrote this order never saw a trench," Second Brigade Commander Currie shouted after receiving one order. And the son of a bitch who gave the commands, First Army Commander Haig, "raged" at the Canadians for their lack of success. In private, Haig was more generous. The Canadians were "splendid men," he admitted in his diary. It was their generals who were "sketchy."

If the war gods had frowned on Haig at Festubert, they had smiled on Charlie Clarke. He had seen dead men for the first time and endured shelling, but he had survived. And the shelling had been an education of sorts in the random killing power of modern artillery. On his third night on the line, Charlie had been awakened by the "rushing sound" of an enemy missile. The dugout he slept in quaked violently, and the concussion sucked the "breath" from his lungs. When Charlie and his comrades scrambled outside, they found a hole next to their dugout smoking like a chimney and inside it an unexploded shell. Charlie was still a green soldier, but he knew he had come close to being "blown to smithereens." As he stared down at the dud and contemplated what might have been, he thanked his luck, like any good soldier would. "A miss is as good as a mile," he decided. Any man in the Second Battalion might have said the same. At Festubert, they had been kept in support and so had missed immersion in a bloodbath. The outfit's official chronicler called Festubert a "quiet tour" that resulted in just two deaths and thirty-one wounds before the battalion withdrew to billets near the village of Essars, just outside of Bethune in northern France. But as they bathed, paraded, and swilled wine and cognac, many in the battalion sensed that the arrow that missed them at Festubert would find them eventually. "The feeling generally was that the abortive operations at Festubert were not the end of the present programme," wrote a future officer in the battalion, "that something would be tried somewhere else."

"[Festubert] had served to initiate us into trench warfare," Charlie wrote later. But it was an initiation he could only have been delighted to put behind him. Charlie and the men of No. 3 Company returned to the commune of Essars and billeted with the same families that had hosted them before Festubert, taking up residence as usual in barns, sheds, cribs, and sties. The locals greeted the soldiers like old friends. Charlie and a few others from his section sheltered with their previous host, Monsieur "Ah Oui," so called by the boys because "Ah, oui" was the man's response to every question. His withered, toothless face was a welcome sight and, of course, Charlie savoured the plates of chips and eggs the local farm women cooked up for them. In Essars, the boys swam in the canal and took over the tables in the nearest *estaminet*. Charlie didn't drink. But he would go along with his comrades and help the drunken ones back to their bedrolls. In his off-duty hours, he could catch up on the news. Behind the lines, and at the mouths of some trenches, even during an artillery barrage, French newsboys could be found selling copies of the London *Daily Mail*, only one day late. He could also catch up with his letter writing. He noted gratefully that parcels and letters arrived as regularly as artillery fire. "It is extraordinary how the post manages to reach one out here," a British officer observed. "The other day we were moving about all day, over trenches and back again, and when we had been sitting still about an hour, the post came in." A letter posted in Great Britain might reach a soldier in two days. Post from Canada travelled equally fast, and for Charlie it represented a lifeline. He later declared "what a great part [these letters] played in our lives," and recorded in his journal every letter received and answered. Letters came from his mother and siblings, and his family in Essex—his father's brother Uncle Arthur and his many aunts. Then sometime after June 8, Charlie received a special letter. The missive was from his brother, Leo, who had news.

Leo told Charlie that the outfit he signed with, the Twenty-Seventh City of Winnipeg Battalion, was finally mobilizing. After a long, painful wait, Leo expected to be shipped overseas anytime. In fact, Leo's letter had arrived late. He and the Twenty-Seventh had left Winnipeg on May 13, and four days later had boarded the RMS *Carpathia* for the transatlantic voyage. Four years before, this ship had rescued survivors of the *Titanic*. Now it ferried troops toward another disaster. By the time Charlie received his brother's letter, Leo was already in Great Britain and closer to the war than he ever realized.

Charlie, meanwhile, decided that he wasn't close enough to the war. While he was in billets in Essars, he made a momentous decision. He volunteered to serve in a platoon whose members would be trained in the use of specialized weapons and tactics. The duty would be dangerous, but the men were promised front-line action and a chance to escape some of the more dreary duties of the infantryman. The outfit was known simply as the Bombers, and Charlie was immediately accepted.

When Charlie reported to the bombing officer in mid-June, he found himself surrounded by kindred spirits. They were like him—tough, restless men, eager to get out of the trenches and into the fight. Although Bombers were a relatively new addition to the British army, they had already established a reputation as daredevils. What few then understood was that the need for bombers revealed the changing nature of warfare in the early twentieth century. Bombs were hardly a new weapon: fuse-ignited, hand-thrown bombs had served a purpose in earlier wars. They had been phased out after the advent of high-functioning cannons and muskets. By the outbreak of the Great War, artillery had evolved into monstrously proportioned rifled guns that spewed shells with the power of an "express train travelling at the rate of 65 to 70 miles an hour," as one soldier put it. But these locomotive-sized shells were proving to be inefficient in the necessary work of killing men in slit ditches. By early 1915, after the conflict bogged down in the trenches, strategists realized that hand-thrown grenades could do this job. A fuse-lighted, hand-gripped bomb, just like the one their grandfathers had wielded in the early nineteenth century, could clear a swath of enemy trench if lobbed over the parapet. But bombs were volatile and hazardous to handle, almost as likely to kill the thrower as his target. Specially trained men were needed. Fearless men. So battalions in the British army, including the CEF, created special platoons like the one Charlie Clarke joined, and schooled volunteers in the finer points of this "black art."

A bombing officer led each unit. It was a perilous command, which at one juncture of the war offered its incumbents a life expectancy of just sixteen days. The British army had come up with a factory-made grenade: the Mills No. 5 was about the size and shape of an overripe peach. Activated by pulling a pin, it detonated after a five-second delay, time enough for it to reach an enemy. Overall, the Mills was a reliable weapon, but there were not enough of them. Or, really, any in mid-1915. The Mills No. 5 had been introduced that March and wouldn't be produced in quantity until well into 1916. The British arsenal also contained the No. 1 and No. 2 hand grenades, but these were unwieldy, wooden-handled contraptions that flew in the air pulling cloth streamers, which were meant to ensure that the grenades land nose first. But these weapons were problematic. Both models had a "sensitive head," which made them prone to explode if dropped or bumped—not an unusual occurrence either in transit or in the trenches. Furthermore, they too were in short supply.

So Charlie and the Bombers were compelled to fabricate their own handmade explosives. This was easier to do than some had originally thought it would be. A "dooser of a bomb," in Charlie's opinion, was a length of pipe stuffed with powder and charged with a blasting cap. Some designs were even simpler. A block of wet gunpowder when fixed with primer and detonator and attached to a "slab of wood" could empty an enemy trench as effectively as any factory-made ordnance. The Bombers also constructed "jam tin" bombs: discarded fruit jelly cans jammed with gun cotton primers, detonators, shrapnel concocted of nuts, bolts, and nails, and fused with match heads for easy lighting. The Brits called these devices

Tommy Tickler's Artillery in honour of the jam that originally filled the cans.

The boys trained exhaustively. They built bombs, and they threw them. They perfected straight-arm catapult throws, which enabled them to lob grenades into trench blocks. They honed their skills until they could blast a target consistently, without a miss. Most importantly, they trained in tandem with infantry, which reflected the primitive state of military strategy in the early stage of the war when it came to trench assaults. In 1915, at the dawn of the era of heavy artillery and air power, the British army's technique for emptying trenches depended on a combination of hand-thrown explosives and bayonet-wielding riflemen. The "bayonet men," as Charlie called them, led the charge followed by two Bombers and three bomb carriers. The Bombers tossed their grenades over the heads of the infantrymen into enemy trenches and bays. After the grenades detonated, the boys with the bayonets leaped into the ditch and impaled the survivors. It was bloody work, but it was effective enough and at that stage of the war few had better ideas for defeating enemies who hid like moles in the ground.

Almost immediately after joining the Bombers and after an initial crash course in creating incendiary mayhem, Charlie was given a chance to go to war as a grenadier. On June 10, 1915, the bugles sounded and the men fell in. The battalion was moving out and marching to the front. This time, their destination was not Festubert; they were heading to a similarly ruined French village to the south named Givenchy.

Charlie set off to this new battlefield a new man and soldier, supremely confident as only a young man could be and oblivious to the dangers that lay ahead.

ROSE OF GIVENCHY

Charlie Clarke, June 1915

G ivenchy-lès-la-Bassée was an ancient and quaint French village that knew combat eight centuries before the Second Battalion marched down its narrow streets. In the eleventh century, the village was known as Juventiacum, a cluster of peasant houses on the bank of a canal that the count of Flanders, Baudouin V, had ordered excavated in 1054. The canal linked the sea near Dunkirk with the Scarpe River, and wound by the towns of Saint-Omer and Givenchy through the vast fields of Flanders. The channel was known as the Fossé des Crêtes le Comte and was meant originally to serve as a defensive moat. It had protected Baudouin's lands well enough, but by 1915, the canal was just one water-filled ditch in a landscape scarred by thousands of miles of trenches. The Allied front line snaked four hundred miles from the North Sea to the Swiss border. When one figured in second-line entrenchments, reserve ditches, communication lines, and dead ends, the Allied trenches on the Western Front were some twelve thousand miles long.

But the only safe place for a man or woman near the front was below ground, in the effluent and muck of a trench floor. Anyone or anything above ground was a potential target. Givenchy was a case in point. The commune's square-towered church, which was almost as old as the canal, had been toppled by shellfire, and most other buildings had been reduced to rubble. Charlie, the Second Battalion, and the bulk of the First Infantry Brigade marched into the wrecked village on the evening of June 10.

Many of them—perhaps even Charlie—felt uneasy. Givenchy, just three kilometres south of Festubert, may have been too close to the scene of their last battle—a "pure bloody mess," in the estimation of one general—for the men to feel anything but anxious as they passed through it. But Givenchy, despite its ruination, offered one comfort.

As Charlie glanced over collapsed walls, he noticed roses blooming in the detritus and debris of every garden. The blossoms were as red as Flanders's poppies, and they were a surprising sight. How was it possible for such simple beauty to grow unattended amid so much destruction? And how strange it was that the soil of these battlefields produced blood-red flowers as innumerable as the lives lost on the ground. Flanders also nurtured blue cornflowers, but there had been too much bloodshed for the soldiers to notice anything but the colour of gore. Roses held a special significance for British and Canadian soldiers. While on the march, a favourite song of the men, according to soldier-poet Wilfred Owen, went "The roses round the door / Makes me love mother more." Another anthem was the ditty "Roses of Picardy." The men left Givenchy at dusk and arrived at the front in the dark, as intended. The battalion's No. 2 Company took up positions around a long, narrow, and irregularly shaped salient that protruded so far into no man's land the enemy stood only fifty paces away at the tip.

The salient had been dubbed "Duck's Bill," a phrase that evoked its odd dimensions. No. 2 Company manned the bill's fire trench, a network of miserably maintained ditches that drew the scorn of company commander Captain George T. Richardson. A famed Ontario athlete and businessman, and "one of the keenest and most competent officers" in the Second Battalion, Richardson was too fastidious to tolerate shabby defences. Repairs would be undertaken soon enough. For the moment, he ordered every second soldier on the line to stand sentry for alternating two-hour shifts. He would take no chances in this miserable, crowded place.

Charlie and No. 3 Company hunkered down on the far right of the battalion line. As he settled into the trench, Charlie looked to the right and in the murk could just make out the silhouette of willows standing guard on the grassy bank of Baudouin V's great moat. The early summer weather was lovely, and the Second Battalion's first night on the line passed without incident. This calm leaked into the next day, which the battalion's war diary described as "very quiet." The enemy was nowhere in sight. But they were at hand. When Charlie, carrying heavy jars, trudged down the trench to fetch water, he found a pump in a shed on the front line. A soldier in the shed warned Charlie to be careful when gripping the pump's lever. A shell had blasted a hole in the wall directly in front of the pump, and a German sniper had his sights perpetually focussed on the handle. He fired whenever he saw a fist and someone's hand had nearly been shot off. This was sobering information. The enemy was so close he could target a man's fingers. Charlie pumped the lever carefully using "short strokes" that did not rise as high as the sniper hole. He filled the jars and left the shed with both hands and every digit. When he returned to his end of the line, he heard gossip to the effect that an offensive would be launched soon. An order arrived from battalion HQ to reinforce these rumours. And then the men were ordered to trade in their Canadian-issue Ross rifles for British Lee-Enfields. The Rosses had their advantages. Some men considered them a fine sniper rifle, but their habit of jamming during repeated fire made them a liability in the field. Many Canadian soldiers, including Fred Hall's brother Harry, had taken matters into their own hands, leaving their Ross rifles outside dressing stations and making off with the Lee-Enfields that wounded Brits had laid down. But Charlie had yet to be in a battle where his rifle failed him, and it worried him to be switching weapons on the eve of a fight.

But the British wanted Canadian firepower to be at maximum strength. Their plan for Givenchy demanded nothing less than massive and relentless fire. The operation was launched three days after Charlie arrived on the line. It began with a massive artillery barrage. The shelling was intended to soften and confound the enemy ahead of one of the most radical schemes of 1915, which the Second Battalion and First Brigade would play a central role in executing. The plan was desperate, but the repeated failure to break through the German line in the Artois and at Ypres had been maddening, and the British general staff sought new tactics, no matter how unconventional. At Givenchy, British commanders decided to attempt a breakthrough by going underground.

Soldiers who had been miners in bleak, soot-covered coal towns in England's north were brought in to drill three tunnels under the battlefield at Duck's Bill and to plant explosives under the German trenches. It had been painstaking work. The miners, lauded as "masters with their tools," had chiefly relied on one— the bayonet—which they used to pry loose "big cheeses" of clay from tunnel walls. They also used a stethoscope to eavesdrop on the Germans in their bunkers, who they feared might attack at any time. For all their preparation and care, the strategy itself was brutal and direct. At zero hour, the explosives under the German line would be detonated, creating a chasm in the enemy front large enough for a Canadian company to charge through and exploit. The shelling that began on June 12 was the first phase in this plan. The barrage grew in ferocity the following day, and by June 15 the Allies were ready to light the fuse.

At Duck's Bill, the First Battalion, an outfit made up primarily of western Ontario men, relieved Richardson's No. 2 Company, sneaking up to the front via a communication trench called Hatfield Road. The First had fought at the Yser Canal in April, and like every other outfit there had suffered devastating losses. But they had been bucked up with replacements, and on the afternoon of the fifteenth stood the line fresh and at full strength. They could only hope that the underground blast would part the earth as the Red Sea was parted in the Bible story, giving them a clear path to the German lines. But Canadian commanders weren't relying on the mines alone to support the offensive. First Brigade Commander Malcolm Smith Mercer was an unmarried Toronto lawyer with a broom-brush moustache and a habit of leading his men from the front that would eventually kill him. At Givenchy, he showed foresight by ordering two eighteen-pound artillery pieces to the front line to be turned on any German machine-gun nests that survived the underground explosion.

The First Battalion would also receive covering fire from Charlie's No. 3 Company and a couple of No. 2 Company platoons, all newly armed with reliable Lee-Enfields. Charlie's Bomber platoon also was slated to join the fight. When the First Battalion breached the line, the Bombers had orders to follow the infantry in and use grenades to scorch and clear as much trench as possible. At 5:57 P.M., the entire brigade stood ready at their posts and waited while the miners triggered the detonation.

A minute later, the mines exploded. The result wasn't just a blast. An ungodly geyser broke through the earth, ripping the air and buckling the ground as if it were water. It was planned to secure a tactical advantage, but in the end, its effects were more on the scale of a natural disaster. The explosion killed enemy soldiers, although exactly how many would never be known. But the blast also swept over the Canadian line, crushing and burying scores of First Battalion men. The survivors were pummelled by shock waves and battered by the rain of debris that fell on top of them. According to Captain Richardson, observing from the flank, blowback from the explosion broke the backs, legs, and arms of at least fifty Canadians.

Although reeling and battered, the attackers scrambled over the parapet and launched themselves at the enemy. Initially, according to Richardson, German survivors lay deaf and disoriented in their trenches and the First Battalion "appeared to suffer only slight losses" as it stormed the enemy trench. Throughout the chaos of the attack, Richardson, observing from the flank, measured the attackers' progress by keeping his eyes trained on the "blue flag," which was attached to a pole carried by a vanguard soldier. Through the haze of smoke and dust, Richardson watched the flag reach the German line. Men poured into the enemy trench and ran in both directions. Then the First Battalion Bombers trotted in from the rear, tossing in grenades and performing the brutal work of trench clearing. It seemed the attack was proceeding roughly to plan. Barely ten minutes after the blast, the bobbing blue flag had moved more than two hundred feet to the right inside the German trench. The Canadians had seized as much as seventy yards of the front.

Then the flag stopped advancing. Its carrier had hit a wall, and Richardson knew that the First Battalion marauders had butted up against reinforcements or a trench block. Bombers on both sides entered the fray, the Canadian grenadiers tossing Mills bombs and their improvised tins of bolts and black powder, while the German Bombers heaved gas grenades meant to blind and burn. Ultimately, Richardson watched the attack die. "The flag was then seen to be slowly withdrawn, step by step," he wrote in his battle report, "and by 8 P.M., the enemy were in full occupation of their trench again."

From his position on the right flank, Charlie Clarke also watched, and was perplexed, as the attack faltered. The Second Battalion had done their best to support the offensive. The men in Charlie's trench had fired so relentlessly that even their Lee-Enfields overheated. But despite their supporting fire, the First Battalion boys began to limp back to the Canadian line. Retreating soldiers—some wounded, all battered—appeared all along the line, leaping over the parapet into the trench while the Germans washed the front with searchlights and machine gun fire. It was a pitiful sight to behold. Despite the metal in the air, Charlie's bombing officer climbed into no man's land, and began helping the retreating wounded.

The defeated men slumped against the trench walls, exhausted and frustrated. The operation had been another fiasco. Richardson's report minced no words. "This attack seemed," he wrote, "and seems from every angle one viewed it, as futile and hopeless." The body count bore out his assessment. The First Battalion suffered 464 dead and wounded. The Second Battalion lost eighty-three men.

The attack had been ill-conceived and poorly executed. Not only had the initial blast been a debacle, inflicting as much devastation on the Canadians as it had the enemy, the attack itself had been inadequately supported. The right side of the Duck's Bill had been well enough reinforced. But on the left side as few as six "sound men" stood at the fire trench. By contrast, said Richardson, the enemy trench "was lined with Germans, freely exposing themselves while firing, or while throwing bombs at the attackers in the grass below." Even the eighteen-pound guns brought to the front failed in their purpose. Masterfully directed German fire destroyed both cannons minutes into the offensive.

Throughout the attack, Charlie and the Bombers had been standing to, waiting for the order to enter the fight. But the offensive failed so completely that the order never came. Instead, the surviving First Battalion men stayed in the fire trench, theoretically ready to repulse a possible German counterattack. But these men were exhausted, and instead of standing vigil they looked for a vacant spot in the crowded trench and went to sleep. After standing sentry for a while, Charlie too slumped onto the firing step at the foot of the trench. There was no shelter. The closest dugout was already crammed with five Bombers, who filled the space like cigars in a box. Then the calm that had descended over the line abruptly ended. Shelling erupted, and within minutes it developed into a barrage like nothing Charlie had yet experienced.

Allied guns fired to ward off a German attack, and the enemy fired back to punish and harass the beaten-back attackers. Artillery fire was a routine of trench life that few soldiers grew accustomed to. Men's nerves were stretched and frayed with each explosion. Advances in siege warfare had not only created cannons of nearly incomprehensible power, they also spawned a new strain of mental illness that would plague a generation of men. Shell shock was the diagnosis army doctors gave front-line soldiers who trembled and twitched involuntarily, wept uncontrollably, remained sleepless, and hallucinated. A later generation of psychologists would call this condition post-traumatic stress disorder and attribute it to all forms of combat. But doctors in the Great War blamed battle fatigue on shelling and no one who had lived through a barrage argued with the diagnosis. The feeling of sheer helplessness that was the product of being shelled drove even stalwart men mad. When a barrage began, a soldier could do little else than keep low, retreat inside himself, and hold on. Which is what Charlie Clarke did. "I sat up," he later recalled, "and leaned forward with my elbows on my knees, my chin resting on my hands and my jacket open at the throat."

He remained in this upright fetal position until a shell fell near him and virtually on top of the dugout where the five Bombers were huddled. "Smoke and fumes filled the air," Charlie would later write, "and falling dirt rained down." A heartbeat later, the wounded began to shriek. A soldier who had been sleeping just to Charlie's left in a funk hole (a bunk carved into the trench wall) cried out in pain from the shrapnel that had gouged him and was now emptying him of blood. Charlie, miraculously unhurt, scrambled to his feet and followed the trench to the dugout, which was so ravaged and broken Charlie felt certain it had received a direct hit. In fact, it hadn't. The shell had missed the dugout, but landed close enough to kill two of the five men inside. Charlie tore his way into the mound of earth, sandbags, and timber, and helped out the survivors. Later, he marvelled at the fickleness of war—how five men could be squeezed so tightly in a bunker that there was barely room for them to breathe, and yet three would emerge alive after the bunker was destroyed. Charlie later asked himself: "How do you account for this?" To underscore the irony, one of the survivors was drenched in the shell's yellow lyddite guts. Even Charlie had lyddite on the back of his coat, along with bits of other men's bones and flesh.

Dawn brought a new day, but it would be no less terrible than the last. Charlie was once again dispatched to fetch water from the pumphouse. With a two-gallon jar in each fist, he headed down the zigzag trench to the left of the line. He had not made many turns when he stopped, appalled at what lay before him, which was nothing living. Literally. The one-hundred-yard block of friendly trench that Charlie had just entered was guarded by a detail of corpses. "Just dead men," Charlie later recalled, "laying head to toe." They had been killed during the night's barrage. Instead of picking random victims from a variety of sectors, the war gods had chosen to kill every man in this trench, without exception. Charlie gingerly made his way down the line, taking pains not to tread on corpses. He kept clear of the ditch walls, which seemed to be on the verge of collapse. When he arrived at the pumphouse, Charlie realized he risked more than a hand wound when he reached for the handle. One of the two eighteen-pounders brought to the front line had been hidden in the pump shed, which German fire destroyed along with the cannon. Remarkably, the pump itself was still working. Charlie crawled to it, filled his jars, and retreated back to the doubtful safety of the trench. He walked past the army of corpses and returned to his post. It was then that Charlie contemplated the narrow space separating the living from the dead in this Great War.

Upon his return, Charlie's corporal gaped at him as if he were a ghost and announced that he had just reported Charlie killed in action. Charlie had been gone a long time, but this was not the reason his superior had given up Charlie for dead. While he was away, stretcher-bearers had come down the trench lugging a dead man on a litter. The corporal had lifted the blanket, inspected the dead man's face, and had been persuaded that the face belonged to Charlie. But Charlie survived that day and ultimately the battle.

When they left the front for billets, the Second Battalion wound its way back through Givenchy. The village remained ruined and desolate, but the roses still bloomed: perhaps they were even bloodier and more beautiful than before. They poked through the rubble and blossomed like open wounds. That the flowers could flourish in the aftermath of the fruitless battle that had just concluded was the ultimate irony. Dead men guarding a length of trench had become so commonplace that no officer had bothered to have the men removed for burial. But natural beauty surviving and enduring in such a terrible quarter was truly remarkable, and caught the eye of every soldier marching past. Charlie saw them, slipped from the column, plucked a blossom from the ground, and took a long moment to contemplate this "red rose so lovely there amongst the ruins."

THE HUGE PICNIC

Charlie Clarke, June–September 1915

After Givenchy, the Second Battalion marched northeast into a place where a mild rot tainted the air. The city dwellers, soldiers from London, Manchester, or Toronto, cringed at the stench. Only the country boys, such as Charlie, understood.

Flemish farm buildings—a pigpen, stable, chicken coop, cattle barn, and pigeon loft—surrounded a flagstone courtyard. The manure from all the livestock went into an open pit at the centre of the courtyard, which drained into a nearby cesspool. Flanders rain flowed into the pit and adjoining pool, turning the collected dung into "fine liquid manure," which the farmers loaded into tanks and spread across their fields. When they were spraying, the reek carried for a "mile or so." Hence, the stench that tinged the air after a rain or humid day: it was fertilizer. The rot was not completely benign. Men wounded in these fields often contracted terrible infections when the decay—"nitrates, potash, and bacteria"—seeped into their lacerations. And when the smell merged with the other competing stenches of the war such as blood, human effluent, unclean bodies, festering wounds, and mouldering dead, it became unbearable. Nevertheless, for Charlie and many of the farm boys he served with, sniffing the potent odour of manure was one of the few occasions where the reek of decay in the air was innocent of sinister meaning.

And innocent is how Charlie and others would remember the front-line village of Ploegsteert, which the men called Plugstreet or Wood Camp. Charlie and his comrades limped there on June 27, by way of a snaking communication trench they christened Mud Lane. On the way, he had expected the worst. But when he arrived, he found Plugstreet to be very different from the crudely maintained fronts at both Festubert and Givenchy. Plugstreet's trenches were sound with "proper bays, good parados, and parapets, and communication trenches." But what Charlie and his comrades found even more astonishing was the unspoiled condition of the battlefield. The belt of countryside along this stretch of the trenches still possessed some of its pre-war beauty. Trees were verdant and grass grew in wide patches in no man's land.

But beauty in anything could be beguiling, and no one trusted it. In the British army, routine dictated that soldiers began each day as if they were engaged in a fight to the death. Infantrymen rose before dawn and at twilight stood to at the fire trench, awaiting the enemy offensive that always came at first light, if it came at all. But even though the Second Battalion perpetuated this tradition at Plugstreet, the men quickly realized that no German attack would be coming at first light. Soldiers on both sides of the line seemed to go through only the motions of war. Machine gunners fired ritually. Snipers sniped occasionally and without much aggression. And artillery pounded away like a heartbeat. But for all intents and purposes, Plugstreet remained quiet, as the Second Battalion war diary would record again and again throughout the summer of 1915.

The Second Battalion settled into a line that slunk, meandered, and hiked from St. Yves to the bottom of the Messines Ridge, through Plugstreet features such as La Douve Farm and La Petite Douve Farm that later became famous. Plugstreet Wood, a patch of forest unmolested by shellfire, ranged out on their right flank and included "pleasant trench shelters rustic in its cultivated beauty," according to Second Battalion historian William W. Murray. But as much as the soldiers appreciated Plugstreet's bucolic and relaxed ambience, everyone seemed to agree that the quiet was too good to be true, and that a bloody brawl lay around the corner.

To prepare, the men were told to "get busy," as one Canadian remembered, with shovels, sandbags, and orders to shore up the line. Charlie did his share of digging. But as a Bomber, he was spared much of the daytime drudgery of infantry life. In his new role, Charlie's territory was no man's land, and his element, the night. Already in 1915, bombing platoons were becoming the Great War version of Roger's Rangers, the 1812 irregulars who fought using native tactics of stealth and surprise. At their peak of audacity, the Bombers would resemble Second World War marine commandos or special forces operatives. Like elite soldiers of any era, the Bombers attracted unusual men. Some were like Charlie— young, patriotic, and eager for battle. But the platoon also attracted its share of adrenaline addicts, misfits, wild men, and malcontents who were too individualistic and flawed to thrive in the regular army. Unsurprisingly, some of the most idiosyncratic Bombers were Scotsmen.

There was Private Bill Craw, a thirty-year-old clerk from Renfrewshire, Scotland, who left his home, journeyed across the sea to Brandon, Manitoba, and took up farming with a fellow Scotsman. In the 1911 census, Craw is listed as a "Domestic" or manservant, which might have described his role as farmhand, or might have been his attempt at wit. If a joke, Bill Craw was that type of man. On bombing patrols, he wore a ragged balaclava cap similar to the headgear adopted by commandos of the future, and struck a soldierly balance between meticulousness and good humour. Charlie found him to be full of surprises. One surprise was his penchant for poetry. In the early twentieth century, verse enjoyed broad popularity and a wave of poets, including British versifiers Wilfred Owen and Rupert Brooke, and the Canadian John McCrae, would scribble and die in the trenches. Bill Craw was the Bombers' poet and everything inspired him, even the banality of trench life. His poem "My Dugout" is an example.

A tin of old bully, some potatoes and bread,
Is the grub I've to eat, or I'll starve till I'm dead;
Some photos of fair maids, pinned on the wall,
That oft to my mind, found joys do recall;
A bunch of old letters, all tattered and torn,
That keeps my old heart from getting forlorn;
Some woodbines and matches, scattered around,
Is all I possess in my home in the ground.

Another Scot was the Bombers' jokester. Known as the Hielandman (Gaelic for *Highlander*), he was the source of an endless stream of creative curses, stories, puns, and gripes. Charlie marvelled at how he could irritate others, even when unconscious, his nocturnal snores, snorts, and restlessness making it impossible to sleep when sharing a dugout with him. But the Hielandman was forgiven all on patrol because he was daring and able to "move in no man's land with anyone." Charlie's best friend was another Manitoba boy. Twenty-two-year-old William Abraham "Bill" Roe hailed from a farm near Portage la Prairie. The second oldest of five children, Bill was like Charlie—a prairie son whose youthful zeal drove him to the army and the Bombers. The platoon had no shortage of zeal. Bomber Fred Tyo, a farmer from Marintown, Ontario, so excelled at battalion sports events that he was dubbed Pole Vaulter. The Bombers boasted a handful of Ottawa Valley lumberjacks and "wild woodsmen" who were agile, "nimble of foot from riding the logs," and tough as old-growth timber.

A bombing officer commanded the platoon, but an inspired NCO held the men together as a unit. Sergeant Edward Moody was from a town in Hampshire in southern England, one of seven children raised in a solid working-class neighbourhood. Moody's father spent his career as a brewer's labourer, and by the time Edward was fifteen years old, he was a stable boy. Ten years later, he was still living in the family's Banning Street house, but he yearned for more. In July 1913, he sailed from Southampton to Quebec City. He hoped to become a farmer, but a little over a year later, he sailed back to Europe aboard a troopship. By the summer of 1915, he was a "beloved" member of the Bombers.

Doug "Big Dolly" Ledgerwood was a hulking and naive Manitoba farm boy about to lose his innocence forever. Little Bill from Fife was another devilish Scotsman. And there were other men whom Charlie become acquainted with during what one officer called the Plugstreet lull, a time of relatively low stress that enabled the men to bond and build esprit de corps. This process of team building was necessary because by June 1915, the battalion was almost exclusively made up of newcomers brought in to replace the dead and wounded of recent battles. As one officer ruefully noted: "The original Second Battalion had been virtually destroyed at Ypres. A few score had lingered on, and some went beyond Festubert and Givenchy; but in the main the complexion of the Battalion had altered." Those who had survived on the battlefield were disappearing by other means. Before the summer's end, Battalion Commander David Watson would be promoted out. "Davie," as the men called him, was a sometime martinet, often lacking flexibility. But he was considered an able fair dealer who empathized with his soldiers and was genuinely disturbed by losses. Command of the Second went to Major A. E. Swift, a Boer War veteran and one of the few professional officers commanding a battalion in the Canadian division.

The replacements and survivors banded together at Plugstreet, and in the absence of serious fighting set to work improving the front. They occupied a stretch of trench in the D-4 sector, but knew the line according to its landmarks. For example, the line skirted Dead Cow Farm, where the carcass rotted in the farm's pond. There was also the Devil's Elbow, the bend in the line from which Charlie and the other Bombers crawled each night to patrol no man's land. Venturing between the lines after dark, owning and commanding no man's land, became key to being a Bomber. In other parts of the front, grenadiers went out at night to attack sleepy German positions or to guard the work parties that ventured out to string razor wire and shovel out entrenchments. But at Plugstreet, the Bombers' main job after dark was to man a listening post, which had been dug precariously close to the German line, its location made necessary by a slight rise in no man's land that blocked the view of the enemy trenches from the Allied side. Conditions on Charlie's first night at this post were a scout's nightmare: a cloudless sky and a bright shining moon offered no shadows in which to hide. One Plugstreet sentry called stars "our great friends of the midnight watch," but most soldiers hiding in no man's land preferred darkness. Especially on that first night. Just ahead of his hole, Charlie heard the echo of hammer blows and he knew he was only yards away from a German work party. And if enemy workers were at hand, then an enemy patrol was nearby "on the look out for such as us." He and his fellow sentry remained still and ultimately went undetected. But the near miss was a revelation that every Bomber experienced sooner rather than later—that no man's land was a mean, crowded, perilous place where a soldier was always in danger.

The danger was not always the enemy. One night that summer, a sentry along the fire trench shot at the listening post while Charlie manned it. The sentry was skittish and confused, but when the friendly fire continued after Charlie's one-hour shift had ended, his hot-tempered replacement shot back. The man was later court-martialled and imprisoned for his fury. Charlie never pitied the condemned soldier. "If he never got back to the front line again," Charlie mused, "he got out of a lot of misery...." Charlie suspected that the kid was court-martialled because he had a German surname and ancestry. If true, he may have been one of the few *Deutschländers* at Plugstreet anxious to fight. After so much killing at Ypres, Festubert, and Givenchy, both sides seemed inclined to live and let live.

As June turned to July, casualties remained light, fighting rare, and soldiering was reduced to ritual. At the beginning and end of every day, the two sides exchanged fire at stand-to. But the volleys were perfunctory and half-hearted, as this poem posted on the wall of a Plugstreet dugout testified.

Early every morning
As the stars begin to tire,
Without the slightest warning,
Our maxim opens fire;
A German gunner answers back,
And one by one the rifles crack,

All down the line you can hear the rattle,
And then begins our morning battle;
And as the dawn creeps in the sky
A couple of shells go whistling by.
The bullets are flying in every direction
Just as the larks begin to carol,
And all because the machine-gun section
Wanted to warm their hands on the barrel.

Artillery fire also became routine, and amounted, according to one British officer, to "a short afternoon of hate at 3:30 punctually every day."

The Bombers occasionally brought havoc to the enemy, heaving grenades in the German trench that sprawled so invitingly, in some stretches, only one hundred yards away. But even the Bombers were restrained, reluctant to upset the status quo. So both sides compensated for their lack of aggression by obsessing over their trenches—digging, building, and repairing until they had transformed the line into what one soldier called a "grim and formidable" barrier. The Germans also slaved away at their fortifications, and "every night the picks and shovels of 300 or 400 men could be heard merrily at work," recounted a British captain with the Royal Berkshire Regiment.

Charlie Clarke would also be nostalgic about Plugstreet. "The summer of 1915 was a lovely summer and at times our life took on the atmosphere of a huge picnic." Charlie used the time to perfect his Bombers' trade. With each eight-day tour of the front, whether in the woods or at Devil's Elbow or Dead Cow Farm, he and the others—Sergeant Moody, Bill Roe, Bill Craw, and the lumberjacks with their great physical strength and Québécois accents—grew more adept at moving stealthily between the lines. When in billets, they practised throwing Mills bombs and the strangely configured Hales grenade with its brass fixtures and long "wind vane" of a tail. While these factory-made devices became more plentiful, the men spent less time building their own; in time, handmade bombs would become a thing of the past.

Charlie was tempted to give up the Bombers' duties only once. The offer came from his old platoon sergeant, a fellow famously known as a hunter and hoarder of food, who took care to provide for himself and "a few followers." Recalled Charlie: "They had a packing case set up for a table, some empty ammunition cases for seats; keeping the choice pieces of meat they would have real feasts." During one tour along the line in the woods at Plugstreet, this sergeant asked Charlie to serve as his personal cook. He had identified Charlie as a resourceful scrounger and talented cook, and he hoped to harness his talents for the benefit of himself and his entourage. Charlie agreed to give it a try. He scouted local orchards in search of fresh fruit to stew. He roasted beef in a Dutch oven he fabricated from scraps of metal. One way and another, he rustled up tasty meals for the sergeant and his hungry circle. The job not only fed Charlie, it also protected him. As the sergeant's man-servant, he was excused from night patrols and work parties. He "lived the life of Riley." But after the tour in the woods was over, Charlie quit working for the sergeant. "I wasn't really cut out to be a cook," he said.

It didn't matter. The picnic would soon be over. The Plugstreet summer with its low casualties, relentless excavations, and idyllic weather was drawing to a close. The first harbinger of change was the arrival of dignitaries. In late July, while the Second Battalion was billeted in the Piggeries, a pre-war hog farm whose "bricked and covered sties" now held as many as two hundred soldiers, Canadian Division Commander Alderson, Prime Minister Robert

Borden, and a scion of royalty, Prince Arthur of Connaught, inspected the troops. Not one of the boys was glad to see their leaders. High-profile visits always preceded an offensive, or worse, a transfer to some awful place.

Prime Minister Borden, wearing his trademark grey serge suit, marched through this Canadian battlefield with purpose and newly acquired gravitas. Canada's increased role in the war had elevated his status. Under Borden's leadership, Canada had raised a second division of volunteers for the British war effort, and in return the prime minister had been invited to attend a meeting of the imperial war cabinet, which was a rare gesture to a politician from one of the dominions. But as much as anything, this token of respect revealed that the Plugstreet summer of 1915 was coming to an end. The Canadian division had hard battles ahead.

September brought rain that soon filled listening posts and trenches with muddy sludge. On September 20, the Second Battalion was relieved on the line by the Torontonians of the Third Battalion, and by 9 P.M. that evening, Charlie and his comrades were on the march to billets at Bulford Camp near Neuve-Église, a base one British soldier called "admirable" with "huts well-built and commodious," and a meadow that the men used as a cricket pitch. While at Bulford, the men were marched to the nearby village of Nieppe, and given their first "bathing parade" of the summer.

The vats of hot water gave Charlie and his fellow Bombers the welcome opportunity to wash away a season of lice, grime, and stink from their skin. And even as they wallowed in the suds, the men were already constructing revisionist memories that would define Plugstreet as "idyllic," "rustic," and the summer of their lives. In Plugstreet, the Bombers had been able to train, patrol, and bond under non-crisis conditions. But in fact, the tour was far from the holiday that some men later recalled. A rot hung in the air and permeated the length of the ninety-mile British line. The reek wasn't the manure-tainted fields of Flanders, but human decay. During June, July, and August 1915, the British army lost 64,388 men—killed, wounded, or lost to disease and accidents. The Canadian division hemorrhaged 2,068 men during this same "quiet" period. According to historian Paul Fussell, a calm day on the British line could consume as many as seven thousand men, dead and wounded.

Try as they might, the men of the Second Battalion couldn't scrub off this stench. The body count would continue to mount at an accelerating rate. For Charlie Clarke, the war was not only about to grow more violent and desperate, it would soon become more personal.

BROTHERS-IN-ARMS

Charlie and Leo Clarke, September–November 1915

Charlie Clarke's life and war would change in the autumn of 1915, and the force responsible for this change was the army on the march to Bulford Camp in late September.

The Bulford camp was a prime target for long-range artillery or a breakout force of Germans. A sprawling tent city on the Flanders plain equidistant from Ploegsteert and Bailleul where soldiers assembled, trained, and rested, Bulford was also the Second Battalion's new headquarters. On September 23, the battalion was midway through a three-day billet at the camp when Charlie heard a rumble in the distance—the sound of drums and bugles—and knew an army was approaching. But he and his friends did not arm themselves with rifles and fall in. This approaching army was not the enemy. It was the Second Canadian Division, the reinforcements from home that Prime Minister Borden had promised and delivered to Great Britain. Now this new division was making its way to the battlefields of France and Belgium to rendezvous with the Canadian forces that had been fighting since March. The battalion's arrival was an event, to be sure. It doubled Canada's military presence on the continent to two divisions of roughly thirty-eight thousand men in total. More significantly, within the British Expeditionary Force, the Dominion was now a two-division corps—the Canadian Corps.

Charlie had already heard that the Second Division had arrived in France and was expected in the war zone. As soon as he heard the drums, he sprinted off down the road. He was beside himself with excitement for good reason: he knew his older brother, twenty-two-year-old Leo, was among the new troops.

Charlie and a few other soldiers met the approaching columns and stood on the side of the road as the marchers filed past. The Second Division boys may have been fresh, but they were road weary, having marched all the way from Bailleul and before that Fletre and Meteren. But with Bulford Camp in sight, the band leading the march was now playing a lively ditty, which couldn't help but put added spring in the soldiers' steps. Charlie carefully eyed the passing troops for any sign of his brother's battalion, the Twenty-Seventh City of Winnipeg. Finally, he recognized a man he had worked with at the Eaton's store back home. "Hello Bill!" Charlie shouted to his old friend, and not long after Bill passed, Leo Clarke marched up.

Charlie recognized his older brother immediately. Army life hadn't changed him much in the fourteen months since the brothers had last met in Edmonton. Leo was as trim and strong as ever. He remained a shade taller than Charlie and his face was a shade thinner. His grey-green eyes were piercing and bright. Charlie ran into the column and fell in beside his brother as they marched. They chatted excitedly, mainly about small things, and Charlie marvelled at how good it felt to speak with "someone from home."

Charlie marched with his brother into camp and was pleased when he learned that Leo's battalion was being billeted not far from the Second Battalion. In the next few days, the brothers visited one another when not parading, bathing, or standing for inspection. But the Clarke reunion was short-lived. As Charlie later said: "Soon enough we had to go our separate ways." The Second Battalion was sent back to the Plugstreet area. Leo's battalion was marched to Locre, a village located just southwest of Ypres, where they were being readied for their first descent into the trenches. Both brothers wondered when they would see each other again.

There was no telling. The war was finally heating up. Two days after Leo arrived at Bulford camp, British and French forces launched an offensive at the French village of Loos, which British First Army Commander Sir Douglas Haig later called the "greatest battle in the world's history." He may not have been exaggerating. Allied forces had attacked with poison gas and a host of eight hundred thousand men. But the offensive failed, and the most that the Second Battalion historian William W. Murray could say of the debacle was that its soldiers fought "with that heroic vigor that is the special endowment of the British rank and file."

Fifty thousand men would be killed and wounded at Loos. There also would be a notable casualty off the battlefield. The Loos failure caused the British monarch and his ministers to re-evaluate the war's leadership and sack BEF commander-in-chief Sir John French. He was replaced by Douglas Haig, who enjoyed the confidence of the Empire's war cabinet despite his middle-class birth and questionable intellectual skills. Haig did have a solid military resume in his favour. He had fought in the Sudan and Boer War, served in the war office, and enjoyed a term as chief of staff in India. He entered the Great War as the aide-de-camp to King George V, and rarely passed up an opportunity to criticize French in front of the monarch and other commanders. Haig's discreet lobbying had the result he intended and in late 1915, the British Expeditionary Force had a new battle commander. Haig vowed to bring about a decisive victory and may have even believed his own promise.

But all this lay in the future: Haig would not assume command of the BEF until early December. That fall, Charlie still languished in the "muddy and wet"—no longer idyllic—trenches of Plugstreet. In the opinion of most, "torrential rains, blustery winds, sleet and cold" transformed this front into a place of general wretchedness. But Charlie's brother Leo was too new to the war to care much about the weather. By October, he and the Twenty-Seventh Battalion were posted on the Ypres salient, manning an uneventful stretch of the line near "Tea Farm," which was near the West Flanders village of Kemmel where the men regularly billeted. Leo and his outfit were bogged down in the same sluggish routine that Charlie's Second Battalion had endured for two seasons. It was inertia interrupted occasionally by heartache, as evidenced by the Twenty-Seventh Battalion's war diary for October 16: "Dull morning," the passage began, referring to the weather as well as the war, and then finished with a description of the death of twenty-seven-year-old Private Cyril Brimble, who succumbed in a dressing station after being gut shot by a sniper. Born in Somerset, England, Brimble had embarked on a new life in Winnipeg, only to find an early grave in an obscure Flemish churchyard.

The men in Charlie's Second Battalion who prayed for any deliverance short of death from Plugstreet's boredom and wretched weather eventually got their wish. On October 9, the Second was transferred north to the D1-4 sector, just ahead of the Flemish village of Wulverghem. Charlie was not displeased by the move—it placed him closer to Leo. Both divisions of the Canadian Corps now occupied more than five miles of trenches from "Wulverghem to Kemmel and St. Eloi." Kemmel, where Leo and the Twenty-Seventh regularly took its rest, was a reasonable four-kilometre hike from Wulverghem where the Second Battalion was defending the line. But this was the only good news. The Wulverghem front itself was too broad for the Canadians to be able to defend effectively en masse. So thin were they along the line, one Canadian battalion history lamented: "Had the Germans attempted to drive in force at this time, the position would have been alarming." The only consolation was that the German line was "as thinly held as our own," as one officer with the Tenth Battalion noted.

But this was a small consolation given the other challenges that made Wulverghem such an odious place. Along the D1-4 trenches, the Second Battalion stared across the line at the vacated village of Messines, a ghost town now taken over by German soldiers. Messines sat on high German-occupied ground that was so nearly unassailable the village's church steeple still stood defiantly in plain sight. Messines looming there almost overhead made the men "feel naked," Charlie later mused. An officer with the Sixteenth Battalion complained that Messines "looked right into your eyeballs."

And the Germans in the trenches were even closer. In the Second Battalion sector, the enemy trenches sliced the field only sixty yards away, the distance of about half a football field. The limited extent of no man's land made the work of the Bombers problematic and even more perilous than usual. "This was something new to us," Charlie admitted, "and would make 'listening post,' patrols, or covering parties tricky."

Sometimes it seemed that the Bombers' commanders were making their lives as difficult as the Germans' were. The platoon had a new bombing officer: Lieutenant Horace Pym, a thirty-seven-year-old British soldier of the old school. Pym was the type of man Rudyard Kipling had in mind when he wrote his ditties. A child of the Empire, Pym had been born at sea when his family was sailing to New Zealand. Like many Brits of his generation, his career touched every corner of the globe that British maps had coloured imperial pink. He had served in a cadet militia in Australia, trained in artillery in England, and fought as a cavalryman in the Boer War with the mounted regiment Lord Strathcona's Horse. At five feet nine, Pym was a tallish man for the time, and he wore the war paint of a hardbitten soldier of the King—a tattoo of a "clasped hand, dagger, and heart" on his left forearm, and an "anchor, wreath, and star" on his right.

From the first day, Lieutenant Pym made it clear the Bombers would no longer be spending nights babysitting work parties and languishing in listening posts. Under his direction, his grenadiers would take the war to the enemy. They would be audacious, aggressive, and utterly focussed on killing Germans. Charlie appreciated the man's spirit. Pym would, Charlie realized, "lead us on a merry dance." In fact, it was a death dance. Some nights, Pym would emerge from headquarters reeking of the rum he had consumed to bolster his courage. The lieutenant was smart enough to know the inordinately short life expectancy of bombing officers. On one occasion, he led a foray into no man's land with a mandate simply to crawl through shell holes and mud up to the German fencing, and then remove a length of barbed wire with wire cutters to bring back. Some British (and perhaps Canadian) commanders were ordering their chief scouts and bombers to collect these souvenirs as proof that their nocturnal rangers were patrolling with sufficient aggression. Charlie, however, saw the act as "show off"—a needless risk of life and limb. Possibly egged on by Battalion Commander Swift, Mr. Pym made a habit of these suicidal souvenir hunts.

Pym also ordered grenade attacks on enemy trenches with a regularity that bordered on bloodthirsty, in Charlie's estimation.

Clearly, the live-and-let-live ethos of Plugstreet would not be abided any longer by the BEF's high command. Even between offensives, the war would be taken to the enemy. The Bombers were not the only special soldiers under pressure to generate a body count. Sniping was also encouraged at Wulverghem. On both sides of no man's land. Both Canadian and German marksmen hid in lairs and searched for targets—a head raised above the parapet, a reckless soul moving over open ground, or a soldier exposed in a listening post. Charlie wasn't on the line very long before a sniper targeted him. In time, dodging bullets became a routine, albeit terrifying, occupation. "When you were laying out in no man's land," he said, "the crack of a bullet hitting a post or the parapet behind would just about split your head." Because these shooters were themselves exposed, they preyed on each other, and according to one scouting officer, "lived in a murderous world of their own, developing feuds with unseen enemy snipers."

But snipers were not the greatest threat at Wulverghem. The Germans had perfected a new hazard—the rifle grenade. This was a simple bomb that could be launched from a gun barrel. But the new technology gave German grenadiers the ability to rain down hate on Allied trenches even during the day. So these were the factors that made Wulverghem a mean "murderous world": reckless marauding, intense sniping, and long-range grenade attacks against an aggressive enemy hunkered down only sixty paces away. Remarkably, when the battalion's first tour of Wulverghem came to an end, the Bombers had not lost a man. They left the trenches with a full complement and billeted in the tiny village of Dranoutre, just behind the line. Charlie had seen more French and Flemish villages than he could remember, but he sensed Dranoutre was special. The people were notice-ably kind and the farm wives cooked exceptionally tasty chips and eggs, served up with a smile for a modest price. Dranoutre also boasted an *estaminet* or two where the men could find courage in glasses of wine, brandy, or *Jenever*, a Belgian gin flavoured with juniper berries. Most of the Bombers when not parading or training chose to drink. The platoon, after all, included "real lumberjacks" and "Scotch coal miners," tough men prone to do "crazy things" and they regularly consumed wine and cognac as if it were essential fuel. As before, Charlie sometimes accompanied his comrades to local cafés out of solidarity, but he limited himself to non-alcoholic grenadine and helped the more drunken boys home at the end of the night. Charlie was a rare Bomber who enjoyed eating more than imbibing.

Whenever possible, Charlie stayed away from the *estaminets*, and instead knocked on farmhouse doors in quest of a home-cooked meal. It was on one such hunger-driven foray that he arrived on the doorstep of the Flagolet family. The head of the household, Joe, was a gracious host and his wife, Louise, was more than happy to fry up a plate of chips and eggs for him. The first visit proved so comforting and the meal so delicious that Charlie returned day after day. He found comfort in the earthy and unadorned life of these plain, honest folk that surely reminded him of prairie people. Similarities between Canadian farmers and those he encountered behind the lines on the Western Front consoled him. The differences fascinated him. He was intrigued by the construction of the boxlike Flemish farmhouse with its central fireplaces, little more than a "pit in the floor with the huge chimney that you could look up through and see the stars." He marvelled at how Belgian farmers harnessed their dogs to pull carts or run on a treadmill to churn butter. He delighted in how men combed their hair with the brushes they used also to polish their boots, pants, and jacket. But the Flagolets of Dranoutre fascinated him even more.

He loved watching Madame Flagolet sit and weave lace during his visits, "her nimble fingers switching the needles from side to side as she worked on intricate patterns." She was barely a decade older than Charlie, but senior enough to mother the young soldier, and perhaps harmlessly flirt as well. Charlie quickly became close to the Fragolet's two children, who practised their school-taught English on him and sat enraptured as he spun tales for them of Winnipeg and western Canada. Before long, *chez* Flagolet became Charlie's "home away from home."

But Charlie's true home away from home was in the company of his brother, and as soon as he could, Charlie hiked to Locre, hoping to find the Twenty-Seventh Battalion in billets. To his relief, he found Leo alive. But his brother was restless and frustrated, complaining that the Twenty-Seventh Battalion was as new and green as he was. Leo seemed determined to make up for lost time. He informed Charlie that he had requested transfer to the Second Battalion. Charlie could see that his brother was itching to join him.

Who knew why? Three years older, Leo may have felt responsible for his younger sibling. But if he believed he could look out for Charlie, Leo was mistaken. As a Bomber, Charlie was beyond the reach of anyone to protect. When the Second returned to the trenches, Lieutenant Pym's "merry dance" of mayhem continued, with assistance from Bombing Sergeant Moody. Both the officer and the NCO pressed the men to expand their skills. It was during this period that the platoon experimented with a new weapon: the British army had developed a rifle-launched bomb to match the German ordnance. The British issue was similar to a Hales grenade, but it was attached to an eight-inch rod that could be jammed into a rifle muzzle, and be dispatched by firing a blank round. These grenades gave off a terrific kick when launched, Charlie noted, and represented the culmination of much experimentation with delivery systems.

The army presented the Bombers with a number of devices to sample in the field. The West spring gun was a catapult meant to throw bombs across no man's land. The Leach Trench Catapult was a Y-framed slingshot, larger but otherwise identical in design to the slingshot prairie boys used to drill rocks at gophers. But the rifle grenade proved the best and most reliable of the new front-line weapons. Charlie and the others practised until they could "place a bomb pretty close to a target at any distance up to a limit of three hundred yards." Now the Bombers had the capacity to rain their own hate on the enemy from the relative safety of their trenches.

Their earthworks remained an imperfect refuge. The German Bombers had become expert with their rifle grenades. They were skilled at triangulating the location of an attack and responding in kind. So the Bombers developed a system to overwhelm and confuse them: they attacked in packs. Two men acted as observers while the others moved up and down the line firing from every trench bay. For the Germans, it was as if they were being strafed from every direction. Rifle grenades changed the Bombers' war, but their best weapon remained their audacity. One night, Bill Craw, the balaclava-wearing trench poet, ventured out on patrol. Pym had ordered him to lead a patrol to the German wire, perhaps with a mind to fetch back a snippet of rusty barbs. But when Craw's group got there, enemy sentries in the nearby trench spotted them and opened fire. Craw's Bombers scattered and one by one crept back home. But Craw stayed behind, tossed a bomb into the German trench, and then hunkered down in a shell hole as the Germans swept the field with fire. Bill the poet held his ground, lying "doggo inside the wire for upwards of two hours," according to one report, before slipping back to the Canadian line.

There was a price to be paid for keeping up this tempo of attack, and the price was dear. On November 5, one of the platoon's beloved originals, Sergeant Moody, was killed in the line of duty. He had mothered the wild woodsmen, ne'er-do-wells, and eccentrics of the platoon since the beginning, and the Bombers buried their leader near headquarters in ground that would be known a century later as R. E. Farm Cemetery.

That autumn was notable for goodbyes. On October 11, the battalion lost another popular leader, Captain Bob Mercer, whose death from random shelling was, according to the battalion's history, a "blow." Two weeks before that, another revered leader, Sergeant John Layland, had been killed.

On November 11, another type of death was registered. But this one was not unwelcome. Charlie's brother Leo, who had volunteered to be a sniper, registered his first kill, making a terse entry in his diary: "Shot my first German at 3 P.M."

November 11, 1915, was also memorable for Charlie. Indeed, it was life changing, although Charlie had no inkling of its importance when he awoke. On the line near Wulverghem, he went through his usual morning ritual. He had been assigned to go to headquarters to fetch the platoon's rum ration. As a rule, the drinkers among the Bombers were guaranteed an extra swig because several like Charlie never imbibed. Later, the men had enjoyed the informal truce that always fell over the line at breakfast. Even at contentious sectors like Wulverghem, sniping, bombing, and general warring was put aside while men on both sides cooked and ate their morning meal. After they had eaten, the Bombers, many of whom had been up all night, retreated to a dugout for a nap. Late on this morning, however, long after the breakfast truce had ended and snipers had returned to their lairs, Charlie stood in the trench and glanced behind him over the parados, where he spotted a khaki-uniformed Canadian soldier running over open ground toward his position. With snipers at the ready on all sides, the act was sheer madness. Others around Charlie noticed the approaching soldier, and stepped up, mumbling how the man had to be "a crazy mutt" to expose himself in this way, and awaited the shot that would bring him to earth. Who could this reckless soldier be?

When the runner approached near enough for his face to be visible, Charlie realized he knew him. It was Leo. To Charlie's amazement, the crazy mutt was his brother Leo Clarke.

The same day that Leo had registered his first sniper kill, he had also made another note in his diary. The passage read: "Joined the Second Battalion to be with Charlie." Leo's transfer had been approved, and Charlie could see that he "hadn't wasted any time." He had reported to battalion headquarters, and then had immediately set out in search of his brother, even running over open ground so as not to waste a minute more than he had to. Ten months after his father had sent each of his sons an identical telegram, the Clarke boys were together and at war.

A NEW YEAR OF SLAUGHTER

Charlie and Leo Clarke, December 1915–January 1916

On New Year's Eve, the brothers Leo and Charlie Clarke stood in the dark in the cement-hard, ice-covered trenches of Wulverghem and counted the minutes until the end of 1915, their first year of war. How strange it was to remember how the year had begun! Twelve months earlier, Charlie had been living in Edmonton, eking out a living as a department store guard. Leo had been wintering on a ranch in northern Saskatchewan. For the Clarke boys, war had been a rumour. Now almost ten months after Charlie's enlistment in Winnipeg, the war had become horrifically tangible, a reality that had been unimaginable when they joined up. Who could have foreseen the hundreds of miles of trenches, the gas attacks, the gangrene, no man's land, the devastating effects of machine gun fire, locomotive-sized shells, forests reduced to charred kindling, great rusty walls of barbed wire, corpses stacked like timber, or the filth, the body lice, the shell shock, and on and on. None of it was predictable; all of it had become the facts of life for millions of Western Front soldiers.

Both Charlie and Leo had seen and done incredible things. On the last day of 1915, they might have posed the same question a soldier with the Sixth Northumberland Hussars asked on that day: "Will this ever end?" For most, the answer was almost uniformly bleak. "There was a hopeless sort of outlook," the Hussar recalled of that moment, "a belief that we were there for keeps. That it would never change."

At 11 P.M., the stroke of midnight, Berlin time, Leo, Charlie, and the other bombers huddled in a Wulverghem bay heard signs of hope. Barely sixty yards away in the German trenches, laughter, singing, and happy shouts wafted across no man's land. The enemy was celebrating the New Year—not the war, a battlefield victory, or their nation. They were dancing on the grave of the odious year that had just ended. And they were heralding the promise of the future, another year, 1916.

Nineteen fifteen had been awful—it was the year of inertia, entrenchment, and the Second Battle of Ypres (Second Ypres). But 1915 had also been inordinately eventful for Charlie Clarke, particularly the last month. In many ways, his world—as well as his war—had changed, and much of the change began the morning of November 11, when he spotted his brother traipsing over open ground toward him.

Now Leo was a member of the Tenth Platoon and had settled into life at the front. But the elder Clarke found the infantryman's life—an endless cycle of "sentry duty and going out for rations," as Charlie described it—as unappealing as his younger brother had done.

Leo wanted to fight. But he had been in the army long enough to understand how, for most riflemen, the rhythm of the war tilted toward inertia. The infantry fought only during offensives. It was scouts, snipers, and bombers who took the war to the enemy on a daily and nightly basis. Of these three outfits, the Bombing Platoon enjoyed—or perhaps suffered—the most freewheeling and dynamic duty. Leo wanted to be a Bomber, and based on Charlie's recommendation and good standing, he was quickly accepted.

Bombing duty, of course, was extremely dangerous but it also offered perks. At Wulverghem, the prime bonus was the right to sleep in the dugout that Charlie and Bill Roe had constructed. Almost immediately after being shifted to the D1-4 trenches, Charlie had lamented the primitive state of the fronts' shelters and bunkers. So he and Bill had scrounged shelter frames from the battalion engineers and constructed their own dugout along the line. Heated by a stove fashioned from the bricks of a derelict farmhouse and fuelled by coal the Hielandman had stolen from the company sergeant major, the dugout's comforts were the envy of the battalion and a sanctuary that Leo had entree to. He was now an elite soldier.

In no man's land at night, Leo exhibited the same zeal and fearlessness that Charlie had shown, and before long he was mixing it up with the enemy. On November 20, Leo recorded in his journal: "Lots of bombs and hand grenades for both sides." The Clarke boys celebrated each other's birthday. On December 1, Leo turned twenty-three years in billets at Wood Camp, and as a gift he received a fresh bath. The brothers warmed themselves in vats of water as the thunder of an "artillery duel" wafted in from the nearby front. On December 8, Charlie turned twenty years old in the trenches. His gift was the prospect of chips and eggs in his new home in Dranoutre. The Second was due to leave for billets that evening, and Charlie looked forward to dinner with the Flagolets.

Perhaps Charlie's best birthday gift came from the enemy. While he dawdled and packed in the Bomber dugout, a deafening rush of wind echoed and a violent shudder—as if the earth beneath

119

them had been pulled like a carpet—drove them to the ground. Around them, dust and flying debris filled the bunker, and the soldiers knew that a shell had found them. But no one was hurt from the direct hit that should have atomized them. When they filed outside, they found a shell lodged in the bunker wall. They had been hit by a dud and spared certain death. It was the best birthday gift of all, but their good fortune hadn't been complete. On landing, the shell's nose had pierced the dugout, and sent shards of timber flying through the air. Splinters struck Leo, gashing him in three places. The laceration on the right side of his body was deep and had the ugly aspect of a gunshot wound. No one thought Leo was in danger of dying, but he was dispatched to the Second Canadian Field Ambulance near Dranoutre, and then transferred by ambulance to the Second Casualty Clearing Station at Boulogne on the French coast. Casualty clearing stations (CCS) were the nearest equivalent to a front-line hospital in the Great War, and the Second CCS was considered so close to the action that it was already moving the bulk of its supplies in the event Boulogne needed to be evacuated. Had Leo's injury been more serious, he would have been sent to a hospital in Britain, where thousands of wounded and dying men languished. But Leo was patched up in Boulogne, discharged three days later, and rejoined Charlie and the Bombers in rain-drenched Dranoutre.

Leo's time with the Bombers had begun ominously. He had been with the Second Battalion barely a month before he was wounded. Charlie would later interpret Leo's bad luck as a grim premonition. But on the Wulverghem line in December 1915, such luck was not exceptional. Before the month was up, the Battalion would lose five members of their ranks to battlefield deaths and forty-one to wounds. The casualties had a variety of causes. The primary killers were enemy artillery and rifle grenades. But snipers, stray shrapnel, disease, friendly shells, accidental discharge of their own rifles, and an occasional suicide felled many others. Plain foolishness and bad luck also could be fatal. The body count and the senseless violence that generated it was confounding, disheartening, and exhausting, and any reprieve was seized upon as a welcome if momentary escape. All the men looked forward to Christmas.

Happily, the Second Battalion spent Christmas 1915 in billets. They were relieved in the trenches on December 24 and were in Dranoutre by evening. The next day, the men gathered for what one officer called a "monster Christmas Dinner." It was held in the Bailleul music hall, where brigade and divisional officers broke bread with their men on tables "all laid with white cloths and silverware." It was an epic regimental dinner. But Charlie and his close friends wolfed down their food, snuck away, and stole back to Dranoutre. Carrying delicacies such as coffee and cuts of beef, they appeared at the door of the Flagolet farmhouse. Joe greeted them and ushered them to his table, and Louise fed them "jam fitters" and cooked their steaks, and the Canadians, unable to spend Christmas in their own homes, were able to share it in the sanctity of someone else's. It was a memorable Christmas, a merging of different languages, religions, and traditions, and when the day was over, a man might have been tempted to look on the enemy and the war differently.

The feeling would not have lasted for long. Early on December 30, after the Second Battalion returned to the trenches, the hate resumed in earnest. After a quiet morning, the enemy began to strafe the trenches with mortars and rifle-launched grenades, transforming the front into "a very hot place," according to one infantryman. During the barrage, twenty-six-year-old Private James Harty, a farmer's son from Renfrew, Ontario, was nestled in a dugout when he glanced out the entrance and spotted a man bleeding and exposed in the open trench. When "Rod" Harty, as his friends called him, bolted out to summon a stretcher-bearer, an exploding grenade cut him down. Private David Lucas, a lad from Smiths Falls, Ontario, and a survivor of Second Ypres, also died in that strafing. Charlie, Leo, and the Bombers responded with a ferocious attack of their own, which the battalion's war diary noted "eventually silenced" the enemy. Whatever emotions Leo Clarke may have felt in the aftermath of this bloody frenzy were compressed in a journal entry that left the numbers alone to convey them: "Two of my men killed," he wrote, "seven wounded."

And then it was New Year's Eve.

At 11 P.M. Charlie, Leo, and the other Bombers listened to the incongruous, unwarlike sounds as the enemy joyously celebrated the arrival of 1916 on Berlin time. And the call went out. A German shouted "Happy New Year" in English, and a Canadian would have been forgiven for interpreting the greeting as an invitation for a truce. There had been a truce the previous year. On Christmas Day 1914, British troops in trenches at Neuve Chapelle were also greeted with German goodwill. The enemy erected a sign declaring "Merry Christmas," which heartened so many Tommies that they joined the Germans in carol singing and eventually rose from their cold ditch and met their enemies in no man's land to mingle and shake hands. When a sergeant protested this fraternization, a soldier responded: "Shut up, it's Christmas time!"

Now the Germans were again reaching out across no man's land with friendly calls and the launching of star shells that streamed the "lovely and clear night" like peacetime fireworks. There would be no handshaking this time, however. By the end of 1915, fraternization with the enemy was a criminal offence. Battalion leaders were reportedly under strict orders to prevent any truce. On Christmas day, a British sentry reportedly shot a sergeant with the Sixth Black

Watch as he made his way to greet the enemy. Only one British unit disobeyed this stern edict, and the junior officer responsible was sent home in disgrace. Indeed, as 1915 bled into 1916, there could only be one response, and it came at the order of Lieutenant Pym, who arrived in the trenches from battalion headquarters with hot rummy breath and murder on his mind. Pym announced the Bombers would wish the enemy Happy New Year with a strafing. And it would be no ordinary grenade attack. Pym ordered a barrage worthy of the occasion.

So on New Year's Eve, as the Germans sang and celebrated, the Bombers let loose a strafing along the length of the battalion front. According to Leo Clarke's journal, the men launched one hundred grenades and floated an equal number of star shells to light the mayhem. Illumination was scarcely necessary to witness the result: Charlie could hear the devastation. "The shouts of joy turned to cries of pain and rage," he later recalled. "The screams could be heard all along the line where just before greetings had filled the air."

The next day, January 1, 1916, aerial observers reported a long line of stretchers carrying away dead and wounded. Although his conscience ached and he "felt bad" for the attack, Charlie reminded himself: "This was war."

As it would later turn out, the strafing was a fitting beginning to his second year on the Western Front. The coming twelve months promised to be as terrible as the last. This time would be—as he later put it—"a year of slaughter."

THE RAID

Charlie and Leo Clarke, January–February 1916

There was a game played in the Western Front in early 1916. Charlie Clarke dismissed it as a new fad, just like the show-off tactics of so many bombing officers. The fad was trench raids— nighttime incursions into German territory with the aim of harassing, killing, or capturing enemy soldiers. And the idea for the raids came from the very top, a product of frustration with the stalemate that had settled over the Western Front, and the determination of the British high command to "dominate no man's land." Practically speaking, domination could be achieved in two ways— harassment of the enemy with grenades during the day and direct attacks on their positions at night.

In terms of the latter, there was already a tradition of raiding in British military culture; it had its origins in India. Nightly "irruptions into enemy positions," noted historian John Keegan "… was a traditional feature of the Indian frontier." And it was Indian units in the BEF that brought raiding to the Great War. An Indian Corps sally against a German trench near Ypres in 1914 was probably the first British raid, although many Brits later blamed Canadians for the practice. "Canadian toughs had pulled off a fine effort, and since then such entertainments had become popular work with the Staff," complained poet soldier Siegfried Sassoon. By early 1916, lamented Charlie Clarke: "Raids were to be the thing."

Bending to pressure from battalion headquarters, one of Charlie's officers, No. 2 Company commander Captain George Richardson, volunteered to plan and lead a raid at Wulverghem. That Richardson stepped forward was no surprise. George Taylor Richardson was hero material—pure born-and-bred Canadian aristocracy. The scion of a family of wealthy grain merchants, his legend as one of the best players in the history of hockey rounded out his pedigree as a northern prince. At Queen's University, his sporting prowess was legendary. This reputation served him well among soldiers, who tended to equate sporting and military values. The idealists and the amateurs in the trenches admired the Tommies who dribbled footballs in no man's land, and the British lord who argued that a "sporting spirit" was essential to being a soldier. If any man possessed such spirit, it was George Richardson. He was a man who had played at men's games— hockey, football, commerce, and war—and had excelled at them all, with one possible exception. His business acumen was doubtful. Richardson's brother James was the brains of the family grain empire and George, to his frustration, was known mainly as a hockey player. But after April 1915, Captain Richardson's skills as a wartime leader were unquestioned. During the hell that was Second Ypres, he hadn't wavered, despite seeing his company all but annihilated. Brigadier General Currie described him as "brave, noble, and generous." He was also sufficiently down-to-earth to understand the power of his wealth. He reportedly carried "gold in the heels of his boots" in case of emergency. And privilege hadn't seduced him into believing he was immortal. When Richardson went to war, he told his family he didn't "expect to return alive." Still, he lived to see 1916—most of the men he had signed up with hadn't. Some were tempted to think that ambition drove George Richardson to volunteer to lead the trench raid in the D-3 sector, but battalion historian Murray wrote that honour was his only motivation. And as an old hockey player, he might have yearned for a good fight.

A good fight the raid would be. Forty solid men—volunteers all—were to be gathered together, trained meticulously, and unleashed in a commando operation against a strategic stretch of enemy trench. The marauders would reach their target by using "tubes of ammonal"—the Great War equivalent of the Bangalore torpedo—to blow an alley in the German wire. Once through, they would leap into the German line and wreak havoc, killing or capturing every enemy in sight, and destroying whatever weapons that couldn't be lugged back.

The clandestine operation was deemed so important that Richardson was assigned a new rank: Officer Commanding Raid. But the plan was far from a secret, at least among the Bombers. Charlie wasn't enthusiastic about it: he still considered raids to be a gimmick "to stir up the lagging minds of the troops," and he worried that battalion commanders competed over who could mastermind the most daring strike. On one hand, good sense compelled Charlie to stay away, but on the other hand, as a Bomber he "didn't want to miss anything." He was among the eight men who volunteered and awaited word, only to learn his name had been removed from the roster.

When he investigated, Charlie discovered that his brother was responsible. Leo had appealed to one of the officers, probably Lieutenant Richard de Warren Waller, a twenty-eight-year-old

farmer from Elkhorn, Manitoba, who was also leading the operation. Leo pleaded that the raid was too dangerous for brothers to
take part in. What if they were both killed? But if only one brother
were to be accepted, the privilege should fall on the eldest. The
officer agreed. Charlie was scratched, and Leo became a raider.
Charlie wasn't disappointed. He told himself that he was relieved
to be clear of an operation aimed at "looking for trouble."

And there was little chance for the brothers to debate. Once the
raiders were chosen, they were designated a "Special Duty Party"
and sequestered at "Anti-Aircraft Farm," where they were briefed
and trained. This training area was located well behind the lines,
allowing the raiders to rehearse unobserved. Captain Richardson
wanted there to be nothing left to chance. Engineers created an
exact duplicate of the trench to be attacked, and the men rehearsed
every aspect of the operation—from demolition of enemy wire
with ammonal tubes to setting up a communication post in the
German trench.

By February 8, the raiders were as primed and ready as their
rifles and torpedoes. Charlie was ready too. He and the other
Bombers had been given assignments designed to support the
incursion. Charlie and a partner were to man one of two flanking
parties to be positioned in no man's land on either side of the
raid's operational zone. Their instructions were to make sure no
German patrols bumbling in the dark stumbled accidentally on
Richardson's men. Charlie was assigned left flank with a partner
who was new to the platoon. Implausibly, the man had been the
battalion commander's subaltern, but had grown restless as a soldier
servant. He had "heard so much of the Bomber's exciting lives," he
told Charlie, he couldn't resist volunteering.

The flankers were ordered to be at their posts for the duration
between 1 and 5 A.M. Charlie and the new man crawled into no

man's land shortly after dark. It is not clear why he set out early. He may have feared for Leo and resolved to be extra conscientious. It is also possible the flank guards were ordered out well in advance of the raid to seal off the operations area. It's possible that weather was also a factor in the commanders' minds.

Up until the night of the operation, Flanders had been predictably rainy, turning no man's land into a bleak and muddy landscape that was perfect cover for the raiders. But at dusk on February 8, the weather suddenly turned wintry. A light snowfall powdered the ground. Then the clouds that had produced the snow vanished, revealing what the battalion history termed a "brilliant, moonlit night." The combined appearance of starlight and snow was a stroke of ill luck that endangered the entire operation. The snow created a bright backdrop that would reveal anyone in no man's land. And the bright moon was extra illumination that only made matters worse.

It was an awful night to be between the lines. Charlie and his partner crawled silently to the Canadian wire where Charlie— already an experienced patroller—began to "pick" through the barbs like a man squeezing through a hedge. He could only assume the new man was on his heels. But when he heard someone mumbling, Charlie turned and couldn't believe his eyes. The former batman had powered on a flashlight. The act was suicidal. If German sentries only fifty paces away saw the torch, they would rain in machine gun fire and mortar shells. Charlie extinguished the man's light with a curse, and asked how in the world he could be so stupid.

"I couldn't see where I was going," he replied. After a beat it became clear the light hadn't been seen. They crossed through the wire without further incident, and arrived at their assigned position, armed with a small arsenal of Mills bombs. In advance of the operation, the Bombers had prepared more than three hundred Mills bombs, each one inspected and armed with a detonator. Charlie always carried nothing but grenades in no man's land. A rifle was too cumbersome and while a handgun was a fine weapon for night patrol, pistols were issued only to officers. The Bombers on the other flank were armed as he was. They lay down on the cold ground, waited, and watched.

There was no movement around or near them—nothing to suggest that enemy patrols were skulking in the area. One in the morning, the start time for the flanking teams to be in position, came and passed. Of the explosions, gunfire, shouts, and screams that one associated with a raid, there was nothing. Eventually, far to the right, Charlie heard grenades detonate. A salvo of machine gun fire crackled briefly. Then quiet descended on the front, and Charlie wondered if the raid was over. Had the bomb blasts and machine gun reports been the operation? They remained at their post, Charlie later said, "straining our eyes into the dark of night, but nothing happened."

Just before dawn, Charlie and his partner crept back to the line. Charlie immediately headed down the trench. Following zigzags and traverses and passing by bays, dugouts, and funk holes, he made his way to sector D-3 where the operation had been launched. He needed to find out what happened and whether Leo was all right. When Charlie arrived, he found a handful of downhearted men loitering aimlessly about and was given the sad news. The raid was a "fizzle"—a failure. One man was missing, and one man dying.

This was the story Charlie was told. Just after dark the night before, when Charlie Clarke was in no man's land, Captain George Richardson moved his men into position at the D-3 trenches. They huddled in a communication trench that intersected the line and waited for the order to proceed. But the raiders were glum and worried, exuding none of the bluster men usually showed on the eve of a daring attack. The problem was the moon and the thin carpet of snow.

Some of the men—perhaps even the officers—hoped that the operation would be postponed until conditions improved. But Richardson lacked the authority to scrap the raid independently, and there was still hope that the night might darken, and the snow melt. So Richardson ordered the first step of the raid to proceed. Two teams of three men each climbed over the parapet, each party armed with a fifty-pound ammonal tube that would be slipped into the German wire and detonated at the prescribed time. In seconds, the men disappeared into the dark, and Richardson waited. But the night didn't improve, and worse, there was also an indication that the enemy was alerted.

According to reconnaissance, the opposite trench was "heavily manned" and "very much on the alert." Why? It was anyone's guess. But the raiders' only advantage—surprise—had been lost.

Richardson couldn't see going on with the attack, and set off for battalion headquarters to confer. HQ agreed, and the operation was cancelled. A relieved Richardson returned to the D-3 fire trench and informed fellow officer Waller. The torpedo teams had to be recalled, so Richardson and Waller both climbed over the parapet and into the snow-bright battlefield. They slithered forward, each officer tasked with finding and bringing back one of the demolition parties.

Waller found his team short-handed. Only two men lay at their post. The third man was missing and it was not clear whether he was lost, captured, or dead. Waller ordered the two men to the line, and then continued to scour no man's land for the missing raider. Richardson found his team complete and sent them back. And for a brief time it appeared as if the raid would end without penalties and losses, as long as Waller's missing man could be found. But when Richardson, following his team in, had made it back to within twenty yards from the Canadian trench, something happened. He or someone in his demolition party had been spotted. An enemy machine gun opened up and Richardson was hit with a spurt of fire, the worst wound being a bullet to his hip. He lay sprawled on the ground, unable to move.

A group of raiders waiting in the trench had seen Richardson fall. Two of them, James Murray, an eighteen-year-old bank clerk from Nova Scotia, and Oliver Denman, a signalling corporal from Sault Ste. Marie, climbed over the parapet, and crawled to the OC Raid, who was—they later reported—"conscious, but that's all." Richardson couldn't move; he had to be carried. Corporal Denman was a tall lad—six feet. But he was slender, and young Murray, although thicker than Oli Denman, was only five feet six inches in height. Richardson was a "well-built man," and the young soldiers struggled to pull him forward under the violent machine gun fire that was still coming from the German trench. They had no success until the raid's ranking non-commissioned officer, Sergeant Jack Maxwell of Winnipeg, snaked over to them and helped the boys pull Richardson to the line and into the trench.

Richardson lay on the ditch floor, his head in Denman's lap, a circle of men around him. Despite the work of stretcher-bearers attending to his wounds, everyone sensed their leader was dying. He whispered, and Denman leaned close and thought he heard the man murmur a question. It was a strange recitation, which he may not have identified correctly. But after Richardson died in the dressing station at R. E. Farm, someone decided that the man's final words had been from a poem by Rudyard Kipling: "There is one task for all; / One life for each to give. / Who stand if Freedom fall? / Who die if England live?"

Who dies? This time it had been the Canadian prince, George Richardson. The luck that had helped him—against the odds—survive the shrapnel, shells, bullets, and chlorine at Second Ypres evaporated on the morning of February 9, 1916, near Wulverghem, where he died in a scuttled operation that achieved nothing.

Leo Clarke survived the ill-fated raid, as did Lieutenant Waller and his missing demolition man, who turned up unharmed. Leo said little about the operation, and Charlie never knew what happened, other than the attack had been a muddle. But like everyone else in the battalion, he held Richardson in high esteem and the next morning, to avenge their martyred leader and vent their spleen, the Bombers lined up along the front with rifle grenades and rained down a storm of hate on the enemy. But even this attack seemed ineffectual. "We had no ginger to us," Charlie admitted. Everyone was in mourning.

They mourned for him in Canada too. James Richardson heard of his brother's death two days later by private cable. He was at his home in Winnipeg and confessed to a reporter that the news "deeply moved" him. Perhaps he had begun to trust in his brother's luck, and took his survival for granted. George Richardson had no such faith. He had made arrangements to distribute his fortune after his death, by establishing a thirty-thousand-dollar trust to educate orphans of Second Battalion men killed in action.

In a war in which so many lives were lost, and so many had become inured to death, Richardson's passing was shocking. It seemed to prove that the Great War was not only stealing most of a generation. It was also stealing the best of it. Richardson's men attempted to sum up the man with an epitaph more fitting than a Kipling poem. At the battle captain's internment in Bailleul cemetery, the largest funeral to date for any Canadian at the front, a squad of his soldiers laid a wreath on his grave, inscribed with a valedictory that read simply: "To One Who Played the Game."

PADRES

John Pringle and Frederick George Scott, 1914–1916

I n time, every father's son wanted to be a Bomber.

Nightly forays into no man's land had made the Bombers famous within the Second Battalion. For many infantrymen, the Bombers were heroes and daredevils. Moreover, as their weaponry grew in size and sophistication, they were privileged to wield state-of-the-art field ordnance. Indeed, the Bombers' arsenal grew more deadly with each passing month. After the rifle grenade, the most important development was the mortar. And like the rifle grenade, it was first introduced by the Germans in the form of a *minenwerfer* (mine launcher), a portable field cannon that was able to spit out two-hundred-pound shells.

Described by Charlie as a "fearsome thing," the Minnies generated grudging respect among the Bombers. So much so that British armourers soon responded with their own trench cannon—the Stokes Mortar, a length of "stove pipe" on a stand that lobbed three-inch mortar shells. The first time Charlie witnessed the Stokes in action, he declared: "Now there was something!" The

Germans were impressed too. When the Stokes was tested against the enemy in the Second Battalion sector, German bombers fired back with Minnies. Charlie watched one of the enemy shells fall, cartwheeling like a wrench in the air. The mine landed at the feet of a kid named Tommy, and reduced him to a husk small enough to "put in a sandbag," according to Charlie. Tommy had come out to watch the demonstration, and became part of it.

Tommy's evisceration didn't dissuade men from volunteering to serve with the Bombers. The possibility of sudden death was part of the allure. Infantrymen envied them their nocturnal lives and their reputation as wild men, as well as their post-breakfast naps after their morning shot of rum. Bombers had swagger and style. Rank-and-file soldiers were forever confessing their longing to join up. One admirer was Sergeant John Percival Pringle, the company quartermaster.

As quartermaster, Pringle was responsible for allocating supplies ranging from food, uniforms, and weaponry to entrenching tools. When he made the rounds of the trenches, he would "stick his head" in the Bombers' much-envied dugout with its sturdy walls and stove, and pay the wild men a visit. To Charlie, Sergeant Pringle was admirable in his own right. Six feet tall and weighing more than two hundred pounds, Pringle was tough and formidable. Charlie marvelled at his "huge hands [that] could span your head" and his ability to "almost lift you up with one hand." Pringle came by his strength honestly, having been a homesteader in northern Alberta before the war. And he was the progeny of another strong and determined man. The sergeant's father was Presbyterian minister Reverend John Pringle, who had travelled the north as a Klondike missionary, preaching to prospectors, homesteaders, general store owners, and mountain men. His son and namesake hadn't followed him into the ministry, but he did inherit his father's love of the rugged life. Young John briefly studied civil engineering at Queen's University, but ultimately chose to be a lumberman in the north. When war broke out, he was thirty-three years old and homesteading in the Spirit River area north of Grande Prairie. When he made up his mind to enlist, he had to hike most of the two hundred miles to Edmonton to do it. He arrived in Europe with the First Contingent, and by early 1916 he had risen to quartermaster sergeant. Big John Pringle, however, yearned for more.

On those days when Pringle found Charlie in the Bomber dugout, he squeezed inside, his huge form completely filling the cramped space. As he warmed himself in front of the stove, he would muse and "talk of joining the Bombers." Pringle would have been welcome. For one thing, he had God on his side—or at least, his dad did. The quartermaster's father, Reverend Pringle, was a chaplain in the Canadian Third Brigade, and a regular visitor to the Second Battalion. The elder Pringle was the sixty-two-year-old shepherd of a Scottish Presbyterian congregation in Nova Scotia when the war broke out, and surprised no one when he enlisted. He had spent too many years as a Yukon missionary, ministering to "gamblers, robbers, evil doers of every description," to miss this adventure. Anyone who had ever met Reverend Pringle understood how bold and rugged his faith was. The anonymous author of "Thanksgiving Day Service in Gailbraith's Saloon, Nov. 22, 1898" certainly did:

> *For though it was snowin' and blowin'*
> *And howlin' to beat the band,*
> *When Parson Pringle dealt the cards*
> *All the boys took a hand.*

For he wasn't one of them gospel sharks,
Or a collar and necktie swell,
That tries to scar' you into Heaven,
With visions of red-hot Hell.

But a genuine sky Pilot, he was;
Who knew, though we looked rough without.
There was good coarse gold inside the dump,
That just wanted washing out.

There was good coarse gold within soldiers too. The elder Pringle's fame as a missionary ensured that his application was accepted. He sailed on the same troopship that carried his son, and whenever possible he visited John in billets, and at least once in the trenches. And when he appeared, Padre Pringle always asked: "Where is my son, John?"

Padre Pringle was not the only man of God at the front. As soon as war was declared, ministers across the country volunteered. The fighting parson, like Charlie Clarke's grandfather Beaumaurice, was a tradition in the British military and in the Canadian one too. During the wars against the followers of Louis Riel, churchmen criticized the government for not enlisting enough ministers. By the time the Great War erupted, some of Canada's most-respected clergymen were part-time soldiers associated with one militia or another. The novelist and minister Charles Gordon of Winnipeg was a Seventy-Ninth Cameron Highlander, who enlisted despite reservations about his age (he was fifty-four) and temperament (he thought of himself as "no fighting man"). Frederick George Scott was another literary man of God. Known as the Poet of the Laurentians, Scott, an Anglican minister and chaplain of Quebec's

Eighth Regiment Royal Rifles, was on the street in Quebec City when news of the conflict reached him. He reportedly turned to a friend and muttered: "I have got to go to war." Scott too sailed with the First Contingent, with a son in tow.

Scott and Pringle belonged to an army chaplaincy of thirty-three padres who had been selected because of their zeal. Some, like Scott and Pringle, were sent with the first waves of troops overseas. Others, including such prominent parsons as Alexander Gordon, a founder of Queen's University, drummed up support for the war at home before being deployed to Europe. Charles Gordon toured western Canada, where he proclaimed "the most stirring appeals for prompt and large enlistment," according to the *Canadian Annual Review*. Gordon even penned and recited a pro-war poem for a meeting of Winnipeg's Canadian Club:

> *O Canada! A drum beats through the night and day,*
> *Unresting, eager, strident, summoning*
> *To arms. Whose drum thus throbs persistent?*
> *Whose? Old England's, Canada, Old England's drum.*

Such propagandizing wouldn't fly in the trenches. Even overzealous Minister of Militia Hughes knew this, and counselled his padres to be "friends and guides of the 'boys'" and forgo "windy" sermons. Insightful padres, like Canon Scott, understood that a chaplain inspired by example, ruefully admitting that a panicked officer might inspire sympathy, but if a parson turned and ran from danger, "six hundred men would say at once: 'We have no more use for religion.'"

When they reached France, Frederick Scott and John Pringle showed themselves to be among the best and bravest in the Canadian Chaplain Service, which by the war's end would number over five hundred members. As the First Division's ranking padre, like other padres, Scott participated in church parades, Sunday services, and presided over burials. He also went to the front whenever practicable and wandered the trenches spreading cheer and providing moral support. At night, he presided over burials. And like many other padres, the war affected him deeply. He was preaching in a brick building along the Yser Canal on April 18, 1915, when he was struck by a premonition. "I had the feeling," he later said, "that we were resting on the top of a volcano." The eruption was the Second Battle of Ypres, which Scott witnessed first-hand. He acted as both parson and patriot when he told attacking soldiers at Kitcheners Wood that "they had a chance to do a bigger thing for Canada that night than had ever been done before." But the war's violence challenged Scott's understanding of earthly and spiritual matters. "There was something uncanny," he once noted, "about the arrival of shells out of the clear sky. They seemed to be things supernatural." And his musings grew increasingly dark, as revealed by his poem "Requiescant," which he penned between the battles of Ypres and Festubert:

In lonely watches night by night,
Great visions burst upon my sight,
For down the stretches of the sky,
The hosts of dead go marching by.

Scott's determination to wander the front lines may have been because he had sons in the army, notably his second-oldest boy, twenty-six-year-old Henry. Henry Hutton Scott joined up in 1916 and became an officer in the Eighty-Seventh Battalion. Padre Scott sought him out whenever duties allowed, and admitted to experiencing "great joy" whenever Henry's battalion was bivouacked nearby. Padre John Pringle was also a good father who never missed a chance to visit his son John. More leader than marauder (he never became a Bomber), Quartermaster Sergeant John Pringle was eventually promoted to Lieutenant and given a platoon to command.

Of course, padres were not popular with everyone. Some men considered them and their apocalyptic vision a nuisance. Few had enlisted to punish the diabolical Germans, as Anglican padre Richard Macnamara insisted. Most, such as one young soldier in the Second Battalion, simply hoped that "the war'll be over by Christmas." Still, chaplains with a human touch tended to be popular. Charlie Clarke and Bill Roe once encountered Padre Scott staggering through the streets of Saint-Jans-Cappel. When Charlie hinted that perhaps the padre had imbibed too much, Scott went along with the joke. "You know boys, I have been on the wagon for forty years," he said, "and now I have water on the knees."

Padre Pringle returned to Canada on leave in the summer of 1916 to report on life in the trenches and rally the home front. In Winnipeg on June 13, he regaled the Women's Canadian Club with examples of trench humour, such as the Plugstreet wit who had erected the sign: "Any German, Austrian or Hungarian trespassing on these premises will be severely slapped on the wrist." His speeches turned serious when describing the war's awesome technology, such as the airplane, the machine that gave new earthly meaning to the spiritual title sky pilot, as he'd been called in the poem written in his honour. He told them nothing of mouldering corpses, body lice, grenade duels, shell shock, and how the war had converted swaths of Belgium into a "dreary, sodden waste," as his fellow chaplain Scott observed. Perhaps Pringle understood what his audience wanted to hear. Perhaps he couldn't bear to describe horrors he knew his son was experiencing. As the elder Pringle charmed Canada, Lieutenant John Pringle was preparing to lead his men into one of the Second Battalion's most desperate operations.

When Padre Pringle returned to France, he wandered into the Second Battalion's zone. In his postwar account, *One Man's Warfare*, Charlie Clarke does not reveal whether the padre appeared at billets or at the front. But Charlie was on hand to hear the father's usual question: "Where is my son, John?" And Charlie heard the sad inevitable answer: his "son was gone." Lieutenant John Pringle had been found draped over the barrel of a German machine gun, in an emplacement he had charged in order to save his platoon from being cut down. In a battle report, Pringle's commanding officer lauded his devotion to duty and recommended him for a decoration: the Military Medal.

Padre Pringle insisted on presiding over the burial. He laid John to rest in a crowded cemetery near the French village of Albert, adorning the plot with a simple black cross and delivering the eulogy, a friend later said, "with trembling lips and tear-dimmed eyes." It was the one service, in a lifetime of sermons, session meetings, christenings, and funerals, the churchman and father could never have imagined having to preside over. Padre Pringle remained in the army and at the front after his son's death. His devotion to the men never diminished, but his vision darkened. He grew to see the war as a dark crusade and argued that it should not end unless "it ends right, with righteousness dominant through our victory." His zealousness might have surprised some. But how could Reverend Pringle not see the Great War as a crusade? His son did not die only to have the unrighteous reign supreme in the peace that followed.

Padre Pringle was not the only chaplain to mourn the loss of a child. After enduring a rainy day near the front and experiencing "a strange feeling of gloom I could not shake off," Canon Frederick

Scott rested in billets when his host, a local curé, appeared at his bedroom door with a letter. The curé grasped Scott's hand and said: "My brother, have courage." Scott knew then: "My son is dead." Henry Scott had died six weeks after John Pringle in a nearby battlefield. But young Henry's body was not immediately recovered. After he was killed during an attack, Henry's retreating men were forced to leave his remains in a shell crater. When Padre Scott arrived at the position, he refused to allow a squad of men to try to bring his boy back. He would not have men die for a corpse—even that of his son. Yet, Scott would not abandon his boy to an anonymous grave. He went about his duties. When he heard that fighting in his son's sector had subsided, he set off to there, travelling by foot and cadging rides in an ambulance and a motorcycle sidecar. He arrived at the old front line after dark. The roads were almost empty. He was struck by the stench of tear gas that tainted the air and a procession of passing ghouls—mounted soldiers wearing gas masks that gave their heads an eerie equine aspect. As Scott later remarked: "They looked like horses upon horses." At daybreak, Scott found his way onto the battlefield where Henry had died. With the help of a young runner from brigade headquarters, he waded through fog, mud, and human remains in search of his boy's shallow grave.

The story went that a makeshift marker had been planted where his son was laid before his comrades withdrew. Scott and his helper eventually found it—"a lonely white cross that stood at a point where the ground sloped down through the mist." There was no body beneath the cross, but they probed the surrounding ground with an entrenching tool until they unearthed something white. "It was my son's left hand," Scott wrote. He knew it from Henry's signet ring. Then, as Germans sniped at them from the distance, Scott took his son's ring, reburied the body, and with the courier as the only other mourner, delivered the funeral service. Today, Henry Scott lies in the Bapaume Post Military Cemetery.

But in early 1916, this grief and these deaths lay in the future. Henry Scott had not yet enlisted. John Pringle, still alive and still the quartermaster, regularly visited Charlie Clarke in the Bombers' solid and warm dugout in the trenches near Wulverghem, and dreamed aloud of being a hero, never realizing that fate would give him just enough life to fulfill this wish. And John's father, the padre, sought him out on visits, always happily asking: "Where is my son, John?"

THE LAST LARK

Charlie and Leo Clarke, March–April 1916

On March 15, 1916, Charlie was hunkered in the trenches of Wulverghem when he heard a strange and beguiling sound utterly foreign to the battlefield.

Charlie and the Second Battalion had returned from billets the day before and had been bombarded with a cacophony of sounds—the enemy crack of sniper fire, and the thunder of incoming grenades and *minenwerfer* mortars. The Bombers responded by strafing the enemy with their own rifle grenades and a salvo from ten trench mortars. The fierce counterattack silenced the enemy, reported battalion commander Lieutenant Colonel Swift in the war diary. Then the next day, amid this aggression-induced silence, Charlie heard the song of a lark.

The lark was common to Belgium and northern France, and soldiers often heard its trill behind the lines. Sometimes they were spotted in unlikely places. Soldier poet John McCrae saw larks in the sky while presiding over a funeral at the Second Battle of Ypres, in 1915, and incorporated the sighting in a poem he composed afterwards. But in most areas along the front, the war had driven the larks away.

Yet, Charlie had heard its distinct piping and was moved by the song. It was the last beautiful sound he would hear at Wulverghem for a long time. That same day, enemy grenadiers stepped up their attack against the Second Battalion line. They mortared, bombed, and strafed so incessantly and ferociously that their actions had to be personal. The Bombers responded with a cannonade from eighty rifle grenades and fifteen trench mortars. The enemy grenadiers again fell silent and licked their wounds.

If shelling, as Chaplain Charles Gordon suggested, was a "spell of hate," then the struggle between the Second Battalion Bombers and their German counterparts was loathing of an especially virulent kind. The feud had begun two weeks before. The Second Battalion had been resting in billets outside of Dranoutre, Charlie's favourite billet, when another rare event occurred. A German warplane appeared overhead like an oversized buzzing insect, and the pilot lobbed bombs on the village. Then the enemy, employing some of its monstrous long-range cannons, shelled lovely Dranoutre. The Bombers were incensed. When mobilized to return to the front, Charlie and Bill Roe rushed ahead of the battalion with "blood in their eyes." Contrary to their usual practice, they moved forward in daylight and followed the maze of communication ditches to the bomb depot, located just behind the Second Battalion line. Ahead of them, German grenades and mortars were falling on the fire trench. They could hear no response from the outfit being relieved, so the two Bombers wasted no time in taking action. Mounting Newton Pippin grenades on their rifles, they turned their backs on the target and fired the rockets over their shoulders. They didn't bother moving to the fire trench, even though shooting might have been easier from there. They were loath to waste time. They fired from where they stood in the support trenches, and blasted away until the chastened enemy gave up and halted their barrage.

Their blood still up, the Bombers punished the enemy the next day—firing off salvos of grenades from up and down the Canadian line. The Germans lashed back, and a full-on grenade battle broke out. Bombers on both sides of the divide strafed, blitzed, and barraged each other, and Charlie's group charged up and down the line from bay to bay, firing relentlessly until the Germans again blinked and silenced their rifles and mortar tubes. Emboldened by their victory, the Bombers blasted the enemy the next day and the day after that. "We went after Fritz again in the morning, then again [in] the afternoon and again at night," Charlie later declared. They burned, peppered, and clouted the enemy with Pippins and Hales without respite, and earned the admiration of commander-in-chief Haig, who mentioned the Bombers' exploits in dispatches ("The Canadians continued to harass the Enemy....") which Charlie read in the pages of the *Daily Mail*.

The battalion retreated to billets at Dranoutre, and Charlie revelled in the company of the Flagolets before returning to the line, yet again, where the rain of steel and fire continued. The German Bombers, of course, responded in kind, and Charlie had the sense that "things were working up to something."

Leo felt the pressure too. The grenade battles the Bombers had waged were deadly. The Bombers had to position themselves in an open trench or bay to fire off ordnance, and their situation made them particularly vulnerable. On March 14, as German aircraft buzzed overhead, the enemy blasted the Second Battalion line with *minenwerfers*. Leo recorded no fewer than "three narrow escapes" in the course of the day's exchange. The next day—the same day Charlie heard the rare warble of a lark—a massive two-hundred-pound *minenwerfer* shell blew up only ten paces away from Leo, blasting him with wind and blanketing him with earth. The near miss exhilarated him. "Ha! Ha!" he wrote in his diary. "Almost covered with dirt, but not hurt."

Then the next day, the "something" Charlie had been expecting began. After a calm early morning and peaceful break-fast, the Germans unleashed an artillery bombardment of almost unprecedented ferocity against D2 and D3 trenches, cannon fire so heavy that it might have included guns of warships anchored off the Belgian coast. The Bombers did not even consider responding. In the face of this terrifying storm, their grenades and mines amounted to insect stings. And there was no way a man could survive outside of the dugouts and bunkers. The concentrated fire—a metal tempest of some 995 shells—created a two-hundred-yard killing zone focussed squarely in the Second Battalion sector that went on for five hours. The pelting amounted to a unique and sustained expression of hate where even dugouts were vulnerable to direct hits. Only luck and near misses offered protection. The Bombers fortunately enjoyed both. At one point, a cluster of shells landed a mere three yards away from their dugout, plowing a new one-hundred-yard trench in the open ground. They survived but still felt the effects. "Our dugouts had heaved and tossed all through it," Charlie remembered, "and the concussions had been terrific." According to Leo, the shells fell so near and with such violence, they were forced to flee. "We beat it from our dugouts to the signaller's dugout at [trench] D3, and had several close chances...." These chances included unexploded shells that protruded from the earth like half-buried carrion. Leo counted two hundred duds that might have killed countless men had they detonated.

When the shelling ended and the smoke cleared, the Second Battalion men emerged from their burrows into terrain so trans-formed as to be almost unrecognizable. Their reasonably ordered front was now cratered, marred, and devastated. Remarkably, their casualties were lighter than expected. And because the Germans did not follow up the barrage with an infantry attack, many in the battalion puzzled over the attack's meaning. Why had nearly a thousand shells been expended, and why were they thrown at such a narrow stretch of the line? Charlie knew. The enemy artillery fire had no objective, just a target. The Bombers. "Looking back I believe [the barrage] was to try and stop us," he later wrote. The Germans meant to punish them for their relentless attacks. Before the Second Battalion left the line, there would be more attempts at vengeance. And the Bombers and the battalion's artillery gamely answered. When their tour finally ended, Charlie struggled to compose a fitting postscript for their unofficial battle. On March 20, he wrote in his diary: "Worse trip we have had since Givenchy." The Second Battalion left the line and then received sad news. They were to leave Wulverghem and their beloved billets at Dranoutre. For the first time in months, the battalion was being shifted to a new theatre. When news spread of the posting, the battalion's "old boys"—veterans who had come over with the first contingent—groaned with dread. The battalion was returning to the Ypres salient.

It would be returning without the Clarke brothers. On March 27, Charlie's number finally came up. He was granted leave. He would be London-bound along with six other Bombers whose passes had arrived. Although Leo would not be granted leave, he also won a short reprieve—of sorts. In April 1916, he fell ill and feverish. Unable to fight and potentially contagious, Leo was consigned to hospital with the flu.

When he first fell ill, Leo likely treated the virus as a nuisance and simply hoped it would pass. This strain of influenza—later identified, somewhat unfairly, as the "Spanish" flu—was just entering the world as a force of destruction, and few understood its seriousness. Eventually, it would equal the Great War in its lethality, striking armies on both sides of the front, and metastasizing into a worldwide epidemic that would kill between fifty and one hundred million people. Analysts would compare this two-year pandemic with the Great Plague. Some even argued that the flu laid waste to so many German riflemen that it affected the course of the war. Although the epidemic is believed to have germinated in a US military base in Kansas or the British base in Etaples, France, there is evidence the scourge attacked its first victims on the Western Front as early as 1916. Leo Clarke and an untold number of his fellow soldiers may have suffered from an early and perhaps weaker strain. Whatever afflicted him, Leo was soon sent from the line to languish in the No. 3 Canadian Field Ambulance, a mobile dressing station located just behind the front at the Belgian village of Wippenhoek.

The No. 3 Ambulance was part of a sophisticated army medical network that had evolved from virtually nothing two years earlier. When war broke out, the Canadian Army Medical Corps was made up of a meagre twenty officers and five nurses. At the war's peak, the corps had grown to include a benign force of two thousand nursing sisters posted across the front in both Canadian army hospitals and field ambulances. This network also included casualty clearing stations, advance aid posts positioned precariously close to the trenches. Like ambulances, these stations acted as first-response centres where lightly wounded soldiers could be patched up and returned to their units, while more serious cases could be triaged, stabilized, and shipped to larger hospitals.

Because field ambulances squatted within shelling distance, working there could be as dangerous as being on the front line. Orderlies and ambulance drivers fetching the wounded from the front were regularly killed. During the Second Battle of Ypres in April 1915, the No. 3 Field Ambulance lost a pair of orderlies when an ambulance wagon accidentally rolled across German lines, and enemy riflemen opened fire. And shellfire regularly struck horse-drawn patient transports both on the way to and away from the front, killing both the wounded and the men and women trying to aid them.

There were many other ways to die in field stations. They were sheltered under canvas tents that offered no protection either from the shells that occasionally struck them or the cruel weather that afflicted Flanders in winter. One front-line nursing sister complained that wind and rain made it "almost impossible to keep things from getting wet." But few doctors and nurses had the luxury of worrying about rain (or even shelling) during or right after a battle, when the wounded, maimed, and dying inundated the station. The Great War's monstrous engagements created body counts that strained hospitals and, indeed, imagination. "They come in such numbers that the tent is soon filled," complained one panicked surgeon. "I can't cope with them all! Many are white and cold, and lie still and make no response...."

If the numbers of wounded men exhausted doctors, the magnitude of the wounds confounded them. Breakthroughs in industrial warfare had ushered in an array of terrible weapons that mutilated, disfigured, and dismembered on an industrial scale. And the efficiency of the military medical system meant more and more of these ghastly wounded men were living long enough to reach aid stations where often little could be done for them but to look on in horror. "Some of these new patients have dreadful, dreadful wounds," Canadian nursing sister Clare Gass confessed in her diary in June 1915. "One young boy with part of his face shot away both arms gone & great wounds in both legs. Surely Death were merciful." As many men left clearing stations for the grave as to larger hospitals for treatment. The military cemeteries that sprang up alongside these stations underscored how ruthlessly merciful death could be.

As it happened, in April 1916, the No. 3 Field Ambulance where Leo Clarke recovered from the flu was uncharacteristically quiet. The ambulance's war diary lists periodic visits by ranking officers from the British Second Army and the Canadian Corps. On April 22, a "minstrel troupe" entertained the patients. Although still bedridden, Leo Clarke grew stronger. But his progress was slow and this must have frustrated him. Leo had been with the Second Battalion for fewer than six months, and he had been relegated to an aid station twice, once wounded and now inexplicably incapacitated by a little-understood disease. As Charlie's older brother, and as the undisputed leader in all their youthful games, he must have been dismayed to find himself playing a lesser role. He had always looked out for Charlie and now he was prevented from doing that.

But if Leo yearned to watch over his younger brother, he need not have hurried his recovery. Charlie left the trenches on March 27 together with the Hielandman, who also had been granted a pass. They set out that night, riding ration limbers as far as Dranoutre, and then boarding a train to Boulogne, where they caught a boat for England. Once on British soil, Charlie immediately headed for his Uncle Arthur's home in Harpenden, a village just north of London that was known for its horse track and straw weavers. When he arrived, he made a ritualistic transition to civilian life by retreating to the dining room (a sometime guest room for billeting soldiers), peeling off his khaki uniform, and unwinding the cloth swaddling his legs. He then handed these articles to Uncle Arthur for delousing. Newspapers at the time had exaggerated the prevalence of lice in the trenches and civilians were apt to insist that their soldier-guests go through this routine. Charlie then put on a "dress suit" belonging to Arthur and was transformed into the civilian he had been two years before.

In appearance, he was now an unremarkable twenty-three-year-old boy. Although, by March 1916, able young men like Charlie had become a rarity in England: those who were not dead were in France. Arthur and his sisters—Charlie's maiden aunts Ethel and Gertrude—doted on him as the precious commodity that he was. They took him to London and showed him the sights. He may have been shocked, or simply overwhelmed, to find himself in the British capital after so many months in the trenches. In any event, extended family seems to have kept him fully and happily occupied, because he left no record of his impressions. Fortunately, other soldiers did. They were astounded at civilized London's actual proximity to the horrors of the front. For example, one astonished British soldier once described how a comrade "had breakfasted in the trenches and dined in his club in London." They trembled at how alive London seemed with its innumerable cafés, restaurants, pubs, and women. And they chafed at the surreal attitude of civilians about the war. "England looked strange to us returned soldiers," said soldier poet Robert Graves. "… The civilians talked a foreign language; and it was newspaper language. I found serious conversation with my parents all but impossible." Soldiers on leave literally laughed aloud at the antiseptic exhibition trenches that had been dug at Kensington Gardens to show the home front what trench life was like. One returning soldier visiting Kensington admitted he had "never seen anything at all like it before."

The English Clarkes steered Charlie away from things that might remind him of the war. They visited St. Paul's Cathedral, the Tower of London, and Westminster Abbey. They took in a variety show at the London Coliseum and rushed him out when belly dancers appeared on stage. "I don't think the dear boy wants to look at this vulgar thing!" declared one of his aunts. They left the Coliseum and the dancers and before Charlie knew it, his leave was over. "All good things come to an end," he lamented. He slouched back to France and the war, loaded down with happy memories, knitted socks, and food parcels.

After recovering in hospital, Leo, like Charlie, was granted leave and paid his own visit to the Clarke family in England on May 9, revelling in their attention, regaling them with stories of life at the front, and displaying—as his Uncle Arthur noted—a "simply enormous" appetite. Leo finally returned to Charlie and the battalion three weeks after falling ill. For both brothers, this respite had been a chance to enjoy the blessings of life away from the front—little things such as the song of a lark—that they would not experience again for a very long time.

SHIFTING GROUND

Charlie and Leo Clarke, April–May 1916

Charlie Clarke returned to the war from leave at its most formidable spot—the Ypres salient. On April 6, he reported for duty at Poperinghe, the old Flemish town the soldiers called Pops, and received orders to join his unit on the eastern edge of the salient, at the Hill 60 sector.

Charlie was entering the salient for the first time. He had no first-hand knowledge of Ypres and no illusions. The salient was infamous. Old-timers in the battalion spoke of its "evil reputation." Their stories were whispered in hushed and often inebriated voices, and they taught Charlie that Ypres was a dreaded place. When he arrived in the salient in April, it hadn't changed much from the previous year. The city had been further reduced, if that were possible, to piles of debris and rubble. Its grandest building, the Cloth Hall, was now utterly wrecked. Only the scaffolding that held up sections of battered wall made it possible to imagine the building that once stood in its place. The environs of Ypres were equally devastated: a cratered wasteland of mouldering corpses, decay, and ruin that was so complete not even night masked the destruction. Canadian army chaplain Frederick Scott observed how Ypres's "grim ruins on either side of the road stand out hard and somber in the dim light of the starry sky."

Charlie found the Second Battalion in one of the most contentious and confused—even by Ypres's standards—sectors of the line. Hill 60 (in army usage, hills were identified by the number denoting their height in metres above sea level) was a much-coveted prominence on the eastern slip of the salient that was presently occupied by the Germans. The battalion was posted in the Allied-controlled low ground just ahead of the hill, a squalid and rutted place festering with rats ("great big monsters") and pounded relentlessly by artillery fire that came literally from every direction because the enemy occupied positions to the east, north, and south of the hill. Charlie marvelled how shells fell in "from in front and in between ... and from left or right or from behind." It is no wonder a Sixteenth Battalion officer called this zone "the most hated position" in the salient.

"The history of Hill 60," declared the battalion's historian, William Murray, "was the history of trench warfare at its worst." The hill itself, a 46-metre prominence, afforded artillery observers a clear view of Ypres city, the plain, high ground to the north including Observatory Ridge and Mount Sorrel, and virtually everything on the salient. "Violent undertakings," declared Murray, had been waged for this view. The hill had been taken by the British and then lost again. This back-and-forth grappling had transformed the Allied-controlled trenches beneath the hill into a maze of abandoned ditches, dead ends, and communication trenches, some of which drove right into the enemy network.

In his first hours after reporting back for duty, Charlie almost became a casualty of this muddle. The Hielandman was also back, and both Bombers were ignorant of the local terrain. They had been ordered to help reorganize the battalion's stockpile of grenades, and so they set out to find the munitions depot. The depot was clearly marked on the trench map that Charlie carried, but the map proved to be useless. The men wandered along seemingly miles of ditches and became thoroughly lost. Fed up, they resolved to go to the fire trench on the front line where soldiers rarely trod unless ordered to be there. But they went anyway, hoping it would give them their bearings, making it easier to work their way back to the depot.

They crept along the front-line trench, searching for the junction that led to the rear supply area, when bullets began to fly. Charlie felt the wind of one graze his head. Another kicked up earth at his feet. The two men threw themselves down, looked ahead, and realized to their shock that they were now staring directly into no man's land. On the other side, only about one hundred fifty feet away, they could clearly make out the German front line. The ditch they were following had opened up onto the enemy front and into the sights of an underachieving sniper. Charlie and the Hielandman survived by crawling backward out of the line of fire. But such was the anarchy of Hill 60, and the sector would only get worse.

The hammer fell immediately. On the way to the trenches from their billets in the divisional reserve area outside of Poperinghe, the battalion endured shelling and tear gas. Then the Bombers hunkered down on the left side of an old bridge that crossed the Ypres-Comines rail line. This bridge lay along the front line, and the Second Battalion infantry took up positions on both sides of it. That the battalion was split in two made this sector awkward to defend, particularly since the bridge dividing it was a magnet—"a calibrating point," in the words of historian Murray—for machine gun and sniper fire.

From the moment Charlie and the rest of the battalion settled in, they fell under "unusually violent" attack from almost every weapon in the enemy's arsenal. The Germans pitched at them nasty bombs the boys called "Sausages" and "Rum Jars." These claimed fewer casualties than they might have mainly because they landed behind the line or in the rail cut behind the bridge. Battalion HQ and the high-traffic communication trenches "Jackson Street" and "Larch Wood" were pounded viciously. And the enemy paid special attention to the sector's munitions supply depot, located in a hillock the men called the Dump, which was a treasure trove of every weapon, tool, ordnance, and gadget of the British war effort, including "barbed wire, corkscrew stakes, concertina wire, lumber, petrol tins, sandbags, trench periscopes, [and] picks and shovels...." The massive barrage was more than an "ordinary strafe." Then to make matters worse, as Charlie noted, the "Gods joined in." A thunderstorm broke over them that was so charged and violent, the soldiers had difficulty telling cannon fire from lightning claps. But the Gods weren't competing with the war. They were issuing a warning: the Germans were about to attack.

The Second Battalion lodged in trenches, bays, and dugouts expected it, but their eyes were focussed up toward the slope of Hill 60. Instead, the assault came from below. Late in the day on April 26, at or around 6:30 P.M., the earth beneath the Second Battalion's soldiers' feet fell away. Literally. Some men, particularly those in dugouts and bunkers, must have feared an earthquake was swallowing them. But a Second Battalion scout who witnessed the surreal attack knew that it was no act of God or nature. "I saw a mound rising in No Man's Land," recalled Sergeant Dick Reynolds, "like a giant mole was pushing up the earth."

Just as the British had done at Givenchy, the Germans had burrowed tunnels under no man's land, stockpiled explosives, and detonated them late on that April day. The resulting explosion transformed no man's land into a geyser of mud, clay, and stone. "The mound rose to a fair height," Reynolds wrote, "then broke with a roar, and earth was shot into the air, blotting out the sun." But the premature night was short-lived. The earth crashed down in a muddy wave, flooding long stretches of the Second Battalion fire trench, burying men who had been out in the open, and trapping untold others in their dugouts and bunkers.

Ironically, the blast also tore away a swath of the German parapet, exposing the enemy as completely as a soldier whose uniform had been blown from his body. Reynolds could see enemy infantrymen scrambling like ants in their trench. And in the ash-grey sky above their heads, more shells began to fall behind the cascading earth.

The Germans followed up the underground blast with another devastating cannonade, making the air so thick with ordnance and metal, it was as if every gun in the German arsenal was in play. "I thought I'd seen artillery fire before this," Reynolds later confessed, "but it was nothing—the air was simply alive with a snapping, crackling, whistling." This torrent of fire was concentrated immediately behind and at the flanks of the Second Battalion position, and was clearly meant to isolate it and keep reinforcements at bay.

Those soldiers of the Second who hadn't been killed, buried, or concussed knew what was next—a full-on enemy infantry offensive. Charlie scrambled from his dugout and into the main fire trench. In the process, he was nearly knocked down by running men. The barrage had blown a massive crater just in front of the trench on the far right, and these men were fleeing as if from an inferno or flash flood. In many ways, the offensive was both. German troops had spilled into the quarry-sized pit in no man's land and were attacking toward the devastated Canadian line. And many of the men bolting past Charlie ran as if the Second Battalion front had already collapsed. "The Germans are in our trench," one panicked soldier shouted. "The Germans are in our trench."

Charlie found himself standing with a Bomber named Bert. Together they tried to corral the retreating men and stem the panic. But the frightened men just pushed past them, heedlessly stampeding in the direction of a communication trench at the rail cutting that led directly to the rear. Within moments, Charlie and Bert were alone. Determined to find out what was going on, they moved up the trench, Charlie clutching a Mills bomb in his fist, alert for Germans. It wasn't easy to see anything: dust and smoke hung in the air like fog. The trench wall had crumpled in places, filling the ditch with heaps of earth, which they had to clamber over.

They soon covered a distance marked by about ten bays and waded through the soft soil into the No. 4 Company trenches. These, they discovered, were thoroughly wrecked. Just ahead of the line and not quite visible in the haze lay a lunar-sized crater 130 feet long, 85 feet wide, and 30 feet deep. So enormous was this pit that it reached almost across no man's land, its "lip" lying a mere 20 feet away from the Canadian trench. If and when the Germans occupied the crater, it would constitute the new German front line.

But miraculously, the Germans did not yet possess the trench. Not every soldier along this line had died or fled. A group of hardy No. 4 Company survivors were not only manning what was left of the fire trench, but they also were defending the crater. Moments after the blast, a handful of men had recovered their senses, taken stock of the situation, and charged into the crater to head off the attack they knew was coming. Fortunately for them, they reached the far end—the German end—of the chasm, and managed to set up a makeshift parapet before any enemy appeared. By the time Charlie and Bert had clambered into the No. 4 Company sector, this advance squad was locked in an intense firefight with the Germans. Their quick thinking had momentarily saved the Canadian line from being overrun. But No. 4 Company—neither the men in the crater nor those in the fire trench—could not keep the Germans at bay for long. They were too few. Charlie didn't know the exact state of the battle in the crater. But he instantly realized the danger they were in.

"We had better get those men back in here," Charlie told Bert. They scurried back along the line as far as the bridge and then dodged down the communication trench. Before long, they collided with a group of Second Battalion men who were in the process of tearing sandbags and timber from the walls of the trench. They had already given up on the front and were building a "block" or barricade against a German assault. A grim-faced officer oversaw the work and urged the panicked soldiers on with the pistol he held in one fist and the grenade he clutched in the other. All the men expected the enemy to arrive at any moment. They were so wired and tense that one soldier tossed a grenade at Charlie and Bert when they made their appearance. Fortunately, the bomb detonated behind them.

It was obvious that the situation was combustible. The officer, like his grenade, was about to go off. "He scared me more than anything," Charlie later reported. But Charlie and Bert managed to calm the men down and convince them that the battle was not yet lost. The Germans had not yet breached the front-line trench— but they would unless these men came back to defend it. He even argued that the front line was the safest place in the Hill 60 sector because it was receiving no direct shelling. Many of the men calmed down, understood what he was saying, and followed Charlie back down the communication ditch to the front.

They arrived just in time. About twenty-five German Bombers, the vanguard of the enemy attack force, were now attacking the No. 4 Company stalwarts defending the pit, lobbing grenade after grenade at them. Behind them, other Bombers were poised to run through the crater, burst into the Canadian line, and wreak more destruction. Some of the enemy lugged cylinders containing an "explosive similar to 40% dynamite," which they planned to deploy to demolish trench blocks and any other obstacles. Other Germans toted spades to either construct a new parapet along the Second Battalion trench or club the Canadians to death in hand-to-hand combat. But the enemy was making no headway. They seemed rattled and slow, and Charlie would later guess that the mine explosion had buried, killed, and maimed as many Germans as Canadians. This may have been true, but Allied artillery spotters also contributed to the defence. They had immediately detected SOS signals from the front, assessed what one officer called an unfolding "catastrophe," and called in a barrage. The Canadian gunners did not hesitate, and an "avalanche of metal shrieked down on the German front," according to the battalion's official history, "churning it into a welter of exploding earth."

But this avalanche didn't stop every German. Some enemy attackers braved the cannon fire and hopped from shell hole to shell hole across no man's land. Others broke into the crater and fought their way up to a Canadian listening post that was linked to the Allied line by a short tunnel or sap. A few brave Germans followed the sap into the fire trench. But by this time, Canadian defenders had returned to their posts. They spotted the German Bombers, and chased them back into no man's land. A few Canadians chased the Germans down the sap and won back possession of the listening post after a few minutes of fighting. Another quick-thinking officer kept the Germans at bay by building a trench block right in front of the sap in the No. 1 Company sector.

The listening posts were not the only vulnerable points. The Germans soon began to march across the breadth of no man's land. To fight them off, every living Second Battalion rifleman stepped up to the parapet and unleashed a series of "rapid fire" volleys into no man's land. They shot at the enemy. They shot at shadows. They shot into the shape-shifting clouds of dust, grime, and ash drifting over the field. Meanwhile, a few of the men who had rushed into the crater were still alive and fighting. They were outnumbered and under intense attack, but they were holding their own.

While these Canadians battled the enemy, scores of their comrades, buried by the initial blast, struggled to unearth themselves. A great many had been crushed or suffocated immediately and would remain interred below Hill 60 forever. But many of the men who had been trapped in dugouts and bunkers were still alive. Immediately after the blast, when Sergeant William Hoey of No. 1 Company scrambled down his stretch of the line to tally damages and round up survivors, he noticed that a dugout containing five of his men had been buried under a mountain of dirt. If Hoey remembered rightly, Frank Donley, a rifleman named Cumming, and three other men had taken cover in this bunker.

Hoey was an old soldier, a forty-two-year-old Irishman from County Wicklow. Standing only five feet six, he was a fussy rooster of a man whom some of his soldiers called "Dad." Now he gambled that Donley and the others were still alive in the dugout. As grenades and bullets flew around him, Hoey began digging with his bare hands. While he clawed at the soil, he shouted out to men who began to appear around him and organized a defence. A private soon pitched in and helped him dig. Later, a captain appeared and began pulling up fistfuls of earth alongside him. The men scraped, tore, and dug for an hour before burrowing down into the dugout and finding the structure intact and all five privates inside alive.

The freed men thanked God and their sergeant for their lives. "God bless this brave man," they later wrote in a report detailing the incident.

God blessed more men than Sergeant Hoey that day. The German offensive was beaten back, and the crater and the Canadian line were successfully defended. But the battalion paid dearly for their heroics. Ten men were listed as missing and assumed buried in the blast. Forty-four men were confirmed dead, including Lieutenant Robert Bertram, a twenty-nine-year-old son of a Northumberland country vicar, who had just been appointed bombing officer for Charlie's platoon. (Bertram had replaced blood-thirsty Lieutenant Pym, who had been transferred out to oversee mortar operations for the battalion.) By dying within days of his promotion, Bertram had confirmed just how dangerous the job of a bombing officer was. More than sixty men in the battalion were wounded, including Charlie's bombing sergeant and four members of the bombing platoon.

But the Bombers' body count didn't stop there. Within days, both Bert and the Hielandman would be gone. Bert finally decided that being a Bomber was incompatible with his dream of surviving the Great War. He transferred to headquarters and took up the infinitely safer job of orderly room clerk. The Hielandman survived the blast and the ensuing battle on April 26, but was sitting in a dugout three days later when a rifle grenade landed at the entrance. Out of the four men squeezed inside, only the Hielandman was wounded. A knife-like metal shard struck him in the shoulder. He went away to hospital "quite happy," Charlie noted, certain that he had finally been gifted a Blighty and deliverance from the war, at least temporarily.

The battalion soldiers finally achieved their deliverance on May 2, when the Toronto Regiment arrived to relieve them. This time, while they were in billets, the depleted Bomber platoon gained at least one good man. Leo Clarke returned, having recovered from his bout of influenza. The outfit he came back to was shaken: many of his friends had died, been wounded, or moved on during his absence. And another thing had changed: Charlie's standing had grown. He had saved the day at Hill 60, and there was a rumour he was being recommended for the Distinguished Conduct Medal. Leo had missed all this.

Leo may have regretted his absence from the battle, but Charlie didn't. Hill 60 had been "heavy going" and he was relieved that his brother had not shared the peril. Leo arrived just as the Second Battalion took up a position along an obscure stretch of trench near the Ypres-Comines canal called the "Bean and the Pollock." The tour was, as Charlie said, "uneventful." Perhaps too much so. "An unusual quiet had settled over the sector," reported the battalion's historian William Murray, "a suspicious quiet." And any grouser who predicted that trouble was afoot would be proved right. In early June, a fierce battle would erupt north of Hill 60, and once again the salient would be threatened.

This time, the Second Battalion would not be called upon immediately. Instead, the initial offensive would consume the Third Canadian Division. But the violence would rage closer to home than Charlie and Leo could guess at the time. The battle would be the testing ground for a man from their home and neighbourhood whose fate was tied to their own.

SANCTUARY WOOD

Robert Shankland, June 1916

Early in the morning on June 4, 1916, the Canadian Scots of the Forty-Third Battalion took up position in a beleaguered stretch of ruptured trench on the eastern slip of the Ypres salient. This battalion included hundreds of men from the Seventy-Ninth Cameron Highlanders, among them Ayr-born Robert Shankland from Pine Street in Winnipeg.

The Forty-Third Battalion had been ordered to take up position ahead of a Flemish forest known as Maple Copse. But when the Forty-Third arrived in the middle of the night, the trees of this copse were only a memory. The ancient forest, which included Sanctuary Wood and Armagh Wood, had been pummelled by hours of mercilessly concentrated artillery fire and reduced to "charred, jagged stumps." Although darkness had fallen when Bob Shankland arrived, the bleakness of the landscape was made visible under the glow of "orange, red, and green" Very lights that the Germans launched into the sky. One officer with the Forty-Third called the forest "a scene of indescribable desolation," and pondered how it was possible that only a day before, this patch had been a "beautiful wood consisting of large trees up to two or three feet in diameter, and with thick leafage and abundant underbrush."

Bob and his battalion had come to relieve the Princess Pats, whose ranks had been drastically reduced in ferocious fighting. What the Pats left behind was a picket line of corpses nested in the tangle of splintered trees and, beyond them, the engineers of this destruction—the German army, which was hastily shoring up its new position and preparing to lash out at the newly arrived Canadian regiment. This was the enemy that Shankland and the Canadian Scots would face during their first tour of the front. Behind the German line, the devastation was even worse. Just visible under the glare of arcing Very lights were more scorched and splintered stands of trees, stretching east up the slope of the most-coveted high ground in the salient. At its crest, Sanctuary Wood linked up with Tor Top, which the army now identified as Hill 62. The vestiges of Amargh Wood jutted up against the slopes of adjoining Mount Sorrel, which a day before had been Allied-controlled territory overlooking the German lines.

Now Mount Sorrel was in German hands and the battle over it—described simply by one defender as "hell"—had erupted the previous morning. But when dawn broke on the morning of June 2, in the trenches of the former front line on the far side of Mount Sorrel, there was nothing to suggest to its defenders, the Fourth Canadian Mounted Regiment, that the day would be anything except routine. One officer said it was "calm, beautiful, and noticeably quiet." There was some activity, a perfunctory shelling of Sanctuary Wood to the north, and the occasional enemy mortar, which one officer considered "as harmless as a bottle of milk if you stand flat against the front face of the trench."

In fact, the Fourth CMR's chief worry that morning had its source not in the actions of German officers, but of Canadian leaders. An inspection had been scheduled, which got off precisely at 8 A.M. when division commander Major General Malcolm Mercer and the Eighth Brigade commander General Victor Williams arrived from headquarters. They had ranged this far forward to get a first-hand look at this stretch of the front, which had recently been identified as problematic. Mercer was so worried about the defences there that he had asked the Canadian Corps' new commander-in-chief, Lieutenant General Julian Byng, to join him. The dour son of a nearly broke earl, Byng—"Bungo" to friends— was a banjo enthusiast and sometime thespian who had joined the Tenth Royal Hussars when he was twenty almost on a lark. But he rose through the ranks of the British military to replace Lieutenant General Edwin Alderson as commander of the Canadian Corps. Alderson was competent enough and devoted to his men, but he had clashed with Ottawa's militia minister, Sam Hughes, and was sacked by British commander-in-chief Haig to prevent a political rift between Great Britain and Canada. By June, Byng was still adjusting to his new command, and declined Mercer's invitation to inspect the trenches.

Byng might have considered the trip to the front too reckless, with its errant Minnies and rifle-launched grenades. Perhaps Mercer had misgivings as well. But Mercer was too conscientious to put off the job. He hailed from Pennsylvania British loyalists who had decamped to Ontario after the American Revolution. Born on a farm, he had studied law at Osgoode Hall and spent his off hours drilling with the Second Queen's Own Rifles. With musket-barrel straight posture and a commanding moustache, he stood out as one of most promising citizen soldiers in the Dominion when war broke out. He hadn't disappointed on the field. He had kept his head at Second Ypres, and was one of the few soldiers in the corps with the mettle to stand up to Sam Hughes. (He had defied Hughes by coming out against the flawed Ross rifle.) So, on June 2, it was not surprising that he and General Williams made their way to the shade of Mount Sorrel to reconnoitre first-hand, and strategize ways to toughen the front in the face of worrying enemy movements.

The mist blanketing the German trenches that morning only added to the sense that something was wrong. Intelligence revealed that the Germans had amassed artillery and troops in the area. Furthermore, they had been seen and heard reinforcing their trenches and digging saps into no man's land in an apparent bid, according to one insightful private, to "form a new line." Even riflemen understood what was going on. But if Mercer and Williams truly wondered what the Germans were up to, they got their answer from the enemy that morning. Shortly after their arrival, the enemy loosed a barrage over the area, which quickly proved to be no normal exchange of "hate." One soldier called it "the biggest we had ever been in."

The barrage not only shook and battered the earth: it seemed to liquefy it, turning it into jelly, according to one sergeant. Projectiles were so dense in the sky, the area seemed to be enveloped in "a cloud of steel." Geysers of earth shot up and compressions buckled the air. The Germans were throwing their arsenal—"every conceivable type of gun, howitzer, and trench-mortar"—at the four-mile Canadian front that wound and wove over the ridges and copses of Mount Sorrel. Every segment of the Third Division line was getting it, but the hardest hit seemed to be at the base of Mount Sorrel, where Generals Mercer and Williams were trying to stay alive. Somehow, they survived the initial volley and, reeling but unhurt, scrambled for cover. But there were no bunkers in the area deep or strong enough to offer protection against such a vicious barrage. Even steel-girded "elephant dugouts" were collapsing under this fire. By midmorning, recalled one officer, "our front line was practically destroyed and a large portion of our men were wiped out." Yet, the generals survived. Williams was wounded, clipped by shrapnel from a mortar, according to one report, and then carried to the most secure lair in the Fourth CMR sector—a bunker dug into the face of Mount Sorrel called the "Tunnel." As for Division commander Mercer, he and his aide, twenty-nine-year-old Captain Lyman Gooderham, remained unhurt at 1 P.M. when the shelling inexplicably ceased, and a silence so eerie and complete overcame the front that one soldier wondered if he had died and "gone to heaven."

But the silence was only the enemy taking a breath before the next phase of their planned attack: the detonation of a series of mines along the Canadian line that shook the ground "like a ship on a rough sea," Lieutenant J. H. Douglas later recalled. "It was not a jerky motion, but a gentle, slow movement, and the ground we were lying on rose, what seemed to me, about ten or fifteen feet." Mercer and his aide, Gooderham, made a run for it, getting as far as Armagh Wood when the shelling resumed and Mercer's leg was broken under him from either a bullet or shrapnel. Gooderham dragged Mercer to cover, but again there was none. Mercer was later killed when a German shell detonated beside him. After the shelling and mine explosions, six battalions of tough and cocky Wurttemberg riflemen swept out of the German saps and trenches, assaulted the ruptured Canadian line, and killed and captured everyone in sight, including Gooderham and General Williams, ailing and bleeding on a stretcher in the Tunnel.

With artillery now bombarding the Canadian rear to impede the movement of reserves and reinforcements, the Wurttembergers seized the ravaged high ground of Mount Sorrel, Observatory Ridge, and its adjacent hills. Some German patrols even marched as far as the town of Zillebeke, but were beaten back, "paying the penalty in full," one private declared, "for their rashness." The main body of Wurttembergers stopped their advance along a line in Armagh Wood and Sanctuary Wood. In some places, they dug in; in other areas, they settled into Canadian reserve and communication trenches. By the end of the day, they had fulfilled an Allied nightmare—they had breached the salient and were now in command of high ground overlooking Ypres city and the armies ensconced around it.

When news of the German breakthrough reached Corps headquarters, and the enormity of its ramifications sank in, a dismayed General Byng ordered that the lost ground be taken back. The next day fresh troops marched on the new front under a furious hail of fire and gas from the enemy. One of the six battalions that braved the shelling and tear gas to mount the counterattack against the Germans was Bob Shankland's Forty-Third Battalion.

But Shankland's outfit would not be in the vanguard of this operation. They were placed in support, ordered to secure the burned and pounded thicket known as Maple Copse and the corpse-filled trenches there. This ditch and its adjoining bays were too broken and mauled to offer anything in the way of shelter. So the men of the Forty-Third took cover among the fallen stands—what their chaplain Charles Gordon called "a matted welter of trees." No sooner had the Canadians arrived than the Germans lashed out "with heavy rifle and M[achine] Gun fire and commenced an attack," wrote the Forty-Third Battalion diarist. Shankland and the Forty-Third fought back and, at the cost of four dead and fifty-eight wounded, took control of the wood and their position, shouting the highland call, "We'll hae nane but

Hielan Bonnets here." This was Bob Shankland's first taste of real war. He was a lowlander, but the border region where he was raised historically was a contentious swath of Scotland, and he had grown up with tales of the Covenanter Richard Cameron and the Cameron regiments, and their promise that a "Cameron never can yield."

Neither he nor his brethren yielded during that first skirmish at Maple Copse. But in the historic six-battalion Canadian counterattack that was launched in the sector soon after, the Forty-Third was detailed to a support position. They were to deliver supplies and help with the casualties. When the fighting got underway, this proved no easy assignment. The counterattack was poorly conceived and a plethora of men were wounded. Nowhere was fighting more intense than on their flank in Sanctuary Wood, where the unsynchronized attacks took place over a ninety-minute period. In some stretches of this field, tear gas hugged the ground like mist, and "withering enemy fire" cut men down as they tripped and plodded through the dead forest.

The Canadian assault ultimately sputtered, and a cold drenching rain made the situation worse. Headquarters decided to postpone further attacks for four days, until June 8, and to use this time to dig in. The pause didn't stop men from dying. Work parties in the forest approaching Observatory Ridge were particularly vulnerable as the enemy was able "to shell it from three sides—half right, front, and half left," according to a Sixteenth Battalion officer. All through the subsequent nights, as the enemy pounded Observatory Ridge Road, men fell dead and wounded, and the call, "Stretcher bearer!" rang out hour after hour. Many of the stretcher-bearers who responded were Winnipeg Camerons, who worked non-stop. They delivered wounded to the rear and water to the men at the front, lugging it in petrol cans. At one crucial juncture, a detail was needed for a high-risk mission to fetch a squad of wounded from inside Sanctuary Wood.

Sergeant Major Robert Shankland volunteered for the detail. His superiors could not have been surprised. Twenty-eight-year-old Shankland had already been identified as an exceptional soldier, a solid leader, and a lad to watch. He had risen from private to the rank of company sergeant major because of his smarts, earnestness, and attention to detail. Like all true leaders, he paid attention to his men. He learned the name of every soldier in the battalion and proved his intelligence and efficiency by excelling as orderly room sergeant. Now he was showing initiative and courage, volunteering to lead a squad of stretcher-bearers into the twisted mire of Sanctuary Wood, in order to bring out wounded men.

The counterattack of June 4 was an angry backlash at the enemy that one private with the Thirty-First Battalion complained "should never have been delivered." Nearly four thousand men from the Third Division were killed or injured in those ruined woods. Yet many survived thanks to the efforts of men such as Robert Shankland. With German shells raining down and hot metal lacing the air, Shankland guided his men into this mass of twisted wood and emerged alive with survivors. According to a later citation, Shankland and his squad had even saved soldiers who had been partially buried. The mission was considered an act of bravery and "marked devotion" that Bob Shankland's superiors could not dismiss as simple call of duty. Even by the rigorous standards of the Camerons, Shankland's leadership had been extraordinary. He was nominated for a commendation and, in due course, received his medal: a silver medallion hanging from blue-and-red ribbon. One side of the medallion bore a relief of King George V. The other side featured these words: "For Distinguished Conduct in the Field."

On June 13, the Canadian First Division finally won back Mount Sorrel, Hill 60, and the Sanctuary Wood ridge. The assault was launched at night, at the instigation of the division's commander, Major General Arthur Currie. He knew that night attacks were rarely ordered in the British army. But he also knew that his men would be fighting against long odds, and he wanted to give them the best possible chance to reach the German line. His gamble worked. The Canadians overran the German positions, which had been pounded, pummelled, and shattered by shelling from a battery consisting of 218 cannons, including some of the most lethal guns on the front. Canada vented its fury and avenged the death of Malcolm Mercer and the nine thousand others who had been killed or wounded in the melee the men later called the "June Show."

Some survivors of that battle, such as Mercer's aide, Captain Lyam Gooderham, celebrated the victory as a German prisoner of war. Others limped away from the salient vindicated, and even proud. The Canadian contingent had faced its greatest crisis since Second Ypres, and it had persevered as a Corps and as a country. No one left Mount Sorrel the same. Least of all, Bob Shankland. But far from exhausting or unnerving him, the battle for Mount Sorrel seemed to make wee Bob stand taller, as he and the Canadian Corps marched to its next great campaign—an Allied offensive that was about to be launched in France's Somme River valley.

A SADLY DEPLETED BUNCH

Charlie and Leo Clarke, June–August 1916

As Bob Shankland was experiencing war for the first time at Mount Sorrel, Charlie and Leo Clarke were not far away, recovering from their "grueling tour" at Hill 60. They had been in reserve billets near Ypres city, ensconced in what were known as the "Railway Dugouts," caves tunnelled into the slope of the embankment supporting the rail line. But despite being in billets, the Second Battalion languished near enough the front to see enemy observation balloons floating eerily over their line. They could not escape the sensation, often justified, that they were being watched.

The Ypres salient was so small that nothing that happened there happened in isolation. When the Germans on the eastern flank attacked Mount Sorrel, Charlie and his comrades were shaken by the thunder of enemy guns and stood ready to be deployed. They weren't sent to the front that first day, but they edged closer to the fighting that night, moving under the cover of darkness to the Dickebusch Huts, a reserve position strategically located southwest of Ypres. They had received their pay packets that day, and many of them passed the time playing cards. Harry Lukka, a Greek-born Bomber the men called the Greek, ran a game of crown and anchor. As the salient trembled and shook, the Greek grew rich, winning a kitty of what looked to Charlie like several thousand francs. Harry was having a run of luck, and what could be more important to a soldier than that? The next day, while the Canadian Corps mounted its angry, premature counterattack on Mount Sorrel, the Second Battalion continued its march to the front, moving through the communication trenches that ran along the Ypres–St. Eloi Road. Just as a man could make his way from the North Sea to the Swiss border and never leave a trench, a soldier could cross the salient below ground as if he were a mole.

They had barely started when a shell exploded in their midst, spraying shrapnel into the leg of the bomber everyone knew as Little Bill from Fife. Charlie was ordered to shepherd Little Bill to an aid station. They limped back toward battalion headquarters, Bill gleefully happy at his luck: his wound was sufficiently serious to justify his removal from the line, but not serious enough to lead to death, disability, or disfigurement. Then a shell blew up beside them on the edge of the trench. It was a miss, but frighteningly close and Bill cried out. What could be more terrifying for a soldier than believing his luck had changed, or that a sadistic fate planned to kill him all along? Little Bill from Fife hobbled off as fast as his injured leg could carry him. He was clearly determined to exit the salient alive. Charlie let him go. "He had a good Blighty," Charlie thought, "and didn't want anything more."

Little Bill's luck had held, but Harry Lukka's didn't. When Charlie caught up with the battalion and the Bombers along the line at a jumble of smashed trees called Square Wood, he spotted a pair of legs sticking up from the trench. The legs belonged to the Greek and marked the far end of the Second Battalion sector where the Bombers manned an outpost. Lukka had been on duty there when an errant shell burst close to his head and decapitated him. The Bombers stretched what was left of Harry on the parados until "he could be looked after." In the meantime, he reminded the men how quickly a soldier's fortunes changed in war. But the Greek's ill luck didn't rub off on the next man, Charlie. He had been ordered to take up the Greek's position at the far end of the line. He was in this outpost, carving a funk hole in the trench wall, when the Germans began to rain down eighteen-pounders. Charlie would later guess an observer had spied him digging, and brought down fire directly over his spot in the trench.

From a distance, the shelling looked like a direct hit. And after the barrage ended, brother Leo and a squad of Bombers rushed over with spades. They expected to find Charlie either dead or mortally wounded, buried under five feet of earth. Instead, they found him pressed into his funk hole in the wall of the only stretch of the trench that hadn't collapsed. He was gnawing on the end of a candle (as was his habit during mind-numbing barrages), and curled up like a cat. Charlie had narrowly escaped the Greek's fate, although bad luck had nothing to do with his narrow brush with death. The outpost was particularly vulnerable. The Germans loomed directly ahead, one hundred yards or so away on the far side of a meadow that was divided in the middle by a rare cluster of standing trees. Further down the line, there was more space (four hundred yards in some places) between the Second Battalion and the enemy. But there was no denying that the enemy loomed near.

Fortunately, reinforcements stood nearby as well. The Forty-Third Battalion, Bob Shankland's Winnipeg Scottish, was positioned on the Second Battalion's flank, occupying trenches about sixty yards to the left on the far side of a marsh. Charlie was taken aside by the bombing officer and given an assignment. He was to set out that night, find the Forty-Third's trenches, and inform its commanders of the Second Battalion's exact position. (More and more, the platoon's leadership was going to Charlie whenever they needed "someone to take over a special job.") When darkness fell, Charlie and a bomber named Ed Harris slipped into no man's land with a covering party of Bombers in tow, a patrol that included brother Leo. Their first destination was a spot where Charlie had earlier in the day spied what appeared to be a wounded Canadian trapped between the lines. The Bombers silently crept across broken ground "torn up with shell holes" and eventually found the man "on the edge of Sanctuary Wood." He was indeed Canadian and still alive. But he was badly injured, having languished in no man's land for three days, lying between two corpses who had been comrades he had watched die. The Bombers had brought along a stretcher party, which carefully loaded the injured man and bore him away. Charlie meanwhile had checked the other two bodies and detected no signs of life, but he did find a pistol on one, which he took and holstered. Then Charlie and Ed Harris left Leo and the other Bombers "in the dark of night" and headed left toward the Forty-Third Battalion lines. Besides his newly found pistol, Charlie carried a pair of Mills bombs. Harris, for reasons Charlie couldn't fathom, lugged along a rifle, which most Bombers found too cumbersome for night patrols.

They picked their way across a field pockmarked with water-filled craters. They stopped and took cover in a shadowed recess whenever a German Very light flared overhead. After crawling across a ruptured nightscape of muddy hollows—moving from one deep shell hole to another—Charlie leapt into a ditch and found himself face to face with a startled soldier. Charlie felt sharpened steel pressed against his stomach, and realized the man was about to gut him with a bayonet. For a moment, Charlie wondered where he was. Had he "landed in with the Germans"? So dark was the night, Charlie could make out no details of the man ahead of him. But he focussed downward. "My eyes followed the bayonet to the rifle to the man," he noted, and realized the weapon was a British Lee-Enfield. "We had found the Forty-Third."

The rifle-wielding sentry kept his bayonet pressed against Charlie's midsection as he identified himself and relayed the message. Not quite convinced, the sentry called over another soldier and then sent for an officer. Although his gun was still raised, the sentry now "talked quite friendly" and revealed why he was so tense. "You came at a hell of a time," he said. "We are just going to attack."

When the officer arrived, he confirmed the warning. The Forty-Third was only minutes away from launching an operation to clear the Germans from a stretch of communication trench directly ahead. The plan was to bust down a trench block, and drive the Germans back. "Hurry up," the officer urged. "Get back to your own trench."

Charlie knew what the attack would bring: a German artillery barrage against the entire Canadian line. Charlie immediately thought of Leo and the other Bombers still in no man's land who would be caught up in the shelling. Charlie and Ed Harris slipped back into the night. Now, however, they made no attempt to move stealthily. They ran full tilt, doing their best to avoid holes and hollows they would have normally ducked into for cover. They made their way to the right and found Leo and the other Bombers about where they had left them. No sooner did Charlie blurt out a warning about the Forty-Third's offensive than he realized it was too late. "Up went the German S.O.S. signals. The sky was full of flares and flashes of guns," Charlie later recounted, "and here we were right in the middle of it."

Machine gun fire cut the air over their heads and shells fell all around them. The battle was on, and safety—the Second Battalion fire trench—was two hundred yards behind them. So the five Bombers leapt into the closest shell hole as the German barrage, laid down by the same guns that had devastated the defenders of Mount Sorrel, grew feverishly intense. Deafening, ground-buckling explosions cratered the earth around them, seeding the air with hot metal. A soldier caught in the open under an artillery barrage had little recourse except to crawl into a hole or hollow and wait it out. Yet no man in this situation could feel safe. Every shell that missed was still a strike on a man's eardrums and sanity, and there was always the temptation to run. And sometimes, braving the fire and withdrawing was the more prudent move. Soon after the barrage began, Leo and another man signalled that they were making a run for the Canadian line two hundred yards away. Charlie watched them climb out of their hole and disappear into the darkness, the smoke, and shell flashes. Charlie stayed put. The hollow they hid in was so shallow that they were battered with "clumps of mud" that sprayed over top of them from the lethally close explosions. They pressed down against the floor of the crater, and worked to "make ourselves as small as possible."

Four hours later, the barrage eased and Charlie and his two comrades decided to make a dash for their line. It was 4 A.M. If they waited any longer, dawn would arrive, and they would be trapped in no man's land. As they ran toward the Second Battalion trench, Charlie spotted gear on the ground and scooped it. Only after the three battered, reeling, and filthy Bombers arrived at the Canadian ditch did Charlie realize the discarded equipment belonged to his brother Leo.

What had happened? Was Leo all right?

Charlie found his brother alive. But Leo and the man he had escaped with hours earlier were mauled and badly shaken. They had survived the closest of calls. While they were racing back to the trenches, a shell had burst above their heads, producing a heat flash that knocked them to the ground and scorched Leo's uniform. It was at that point that Leo had discarded some of his heavy equipment in order to run faster. Later that day, Leo reported to a dressing station, and Charlie quietly marvelled at the irony of it. He and the other men had spent the night in a shallow hole in the middle of a firestorm. Yet, not a single flash or shard of shrapnel had found them. Leo, on the other hand, was making his third trip to hospital. "I was beginning to think," Charlie later admitted, "that I was born lucky."

As fate would have it, Charlie was on the line a week later during the Canadian counterattack that led to the recapture of Mount Sorrel. The Second Battalion manned the same trenches along the marsh, but did not take part in the initial nighttime assault. Prior to the offensive, the attacking battalions remained well behind the lines to escape the "savagely concentrated" enemy barrage in that sector. It had been left to the Bombers to man and hold the fire trench. They had taken up positions along the line, suffered through the shelling, and shivered during a heavy slashing rainstorm. Charlie was hunkered down in the trench with Doug Ledgerwood, a tough and resourceful Manitoba farm boy the Bombers called Big Dolly. When the order was given to attack, the Thirteenth Montreal Scottish Battalion rose up from a reserve trench and charged from behind the lines.

But the rain had turned the ground to mud, and when the Montreal Scots tried to leapfrog the fire trench, many slipped and fell into the ditch. And the trench wall proved too slick, for the soldiers were unable to claw their way out. Charlie and Big Dolly took in this "pitiful" scene—brave men "slipping and slithering in the mud" as they struggled to go over the top. Thinking quickly, Charlie and Dolly fell to hands and knees, and created "stepping stones" with their bodies. In this way, they "gave a hoist up" and out of the trench to as many as twenty soldiers. Charlie later wondered how much he had really helped them. "We helped them climb up and over," he later mused, "to go into the maelstrom of shot and shell and most likely to their death." Despite the cost, this attack achieved its objective. Mount Sorrel and the high ground linked to it were re-conquered, and the enemy was driven back to its June 1 positions. But Charlie's concern for the soldiers of the Black Watch he had boosted into the line of fire were justified when the wounded limped back later, their bare legs awash in blood and their kilts in tatters after having been snagged in the razor wire in no man's land.

By this stage of the war, all the Canadians deserved pity. Even before this offensive, Charlie had declared his platoon "a sorry sadly depleted bunch of Bombers." The salient was to blame: it had claimed thousands of casualties. And for those men at Ypres who were spared death or maiming, the awful place seemed to seep through the skin and attack a soldier from the inside. When Leo Clarke returned to the line from the dressing station, the Second Battalion had been moved back to Hill 60, where they were placed in reserve. During a particularly punishing artillery bombardment, the Bombers had taken cover in a dugout twenty feet below ground. The bunker was cramped and claustrophobic. The walls and ceiling shed dirt with every detonation on the surface above, which made the men nervous. The tension probably explained why Leo decided to tease Charlie about some girlfriend, and why Charlie snapped and leapt on his brother. The tussle was short-lived, and afterwards Charlie decided: "It just goes to show what being down that tunnel did to us." Charlie would remember that moment as the only time at the salient when he lost his composure.

Charlie wasn't the only one to snap. Even the most stolid of the Bombers started to unravel. The poet Bill Craw, so controlled under fire and so fastidious as a soldier, had stopped shaving and obsessing about his appearance. After he let buttons fall from his uniform, and frayed in other ways that seemed out of character, he was sent to hospital with shell shock.

Fred Tyo, the lumberjack and sportsman who had been so adept at pole-vaulting during battalion sporting contests, had also cracked, and was pulled from the line. To Charlie's regret, the men replacing these veterans were not their equals. As casualties mounted up, company sergeants were loath to let good fighting men join the Bombers. Instead, they sent to the platoon men whom Charlie dismissed as "loose livers." While in billets, these ne'er-do-wells drank to excess, squabbled among themselves, and raved obliviously. Later, they wandered into the night and collapsed. "We would find them in a ditch," Charlie recalled, "or under a hedge."

The way men lived on the line was starkly foreign to any human being. But it was clear that some men adapted better than others, and that many would never adapt. One replacement was a "timid little man" who only came alive in billets. Inspired by a bit of beer, he would sing in a low voice Charlie considered quite beautiful. And when he did sing, the little man often broke into a popular pre-war song, a sad song, about a child's yearning for an absent father: "And a little child shall lead them, / Lead them gently on their way."

That the little man loved this particular song was fitting. Most soldiers were children in a way, or at least they could be described accurately as boy soldiers. Charlie was still a teenager when he enlisted, and some boys lied about their age and joined up at fifteen or sixteen years. But even among the boys, some were better able to bury fear, buck up, and soldier on. The little man with the beautiful voice wasn't one of them. He simply didn't belong, and one morning he proved it. The little man and Charlie had been ordered on "a long hike" behind the lines to fetch food rations for the Bombers. On the way back from the supply wagons, the little man simply disappeared. One moment, he was following Charlie in the dark as they crossed an open field. The next minute he was gone with half the food ration. It was as if he was finally consumed by the war or his own fears. Charlie would hear years later that the little man had been felled in his tracks by a stray bullet, but proved too timid even to cry out.

Moreover, the Bombers' efficiency was flagging. The battalion attempted to improve discipline by bringing in a sergeant major from the outside, instead of promoting someone from the platoon. But the Bombers were an elite and exclusive troop and this newcomer was resented. Their resentment didn't last long. The replacement was killed on his second day on the line, before some of the men even knew his name. Having learned their lesson, the battalion elevated one of the Bombers, Corporal William King, to serve as their new sergeant. King was twenty-eight years old; he had not a day of pre-war army experience. (He had been a carpenter in civilian life.) Ironically, King's promotion somehow instilled him with military ardour. Under King's command, Charlie and the other grenadiers were roused early from their billets and drilled all day, with physical training in the morning and bombing practice in the afternoon.

They were assigned a new punctilious officer. Lieutenant Frank Strachan, a Kingston, Ontario, hardware-store clerk and pre-war militiaman, had been the company sergeant major before being given a field commission and dispatched to the Bombers. The decision to bring in an exacting outsider may have been another effort to browbeat discipline into the squad. But Strachan's spit and polish only cultivated resentment again. For most of the Bombers, he was too exacting, finicky, and armylike. Charlie considered him to be "an old woman." But Strachan was savvy enough to recognize potential, and he promoted Charlie to lance corporal. And the Bombers soon resumed their private war at the battalion's vanguard.

After serving in reserve in the Hill 60 sector, the Second was eventually ordered to man the front. For everyone but replacements, the battalion had returned to the scene of one of their most nightmarish battles. The crater excavated during the German mine strike still marred the middle of no man's land like a dry lake bed, and this chasm became the Bombers' primary battlefield. The Bombers defended an advance outpost in the crater and kept the enemy at bay through a strategy of incessant harassment. It became a tense and lonely campaign. "We were so isolated out in the crater," Charlie later recalled, "aware all of the time that the Germans were just a few feet away."

The hemorrhage of good men continued. On July 30, William King, the Bomber's newly minted sergeant major was killed, exactly ten days after his promotion. According to Lieutenant William Murray, recently appointed battalion scouting officer, the enemy had bombarded King's outpost in a mine crater with grenades and mortars. By the time Murray and two of his scouts reached the outpost, King was already mortally wounded.

King's fast death put an emphatic punctuation mark on the end of the battalion's tour of the salient. In early August they received orders to march west. For Charlie, the Second's summer in Ypres had been worse "than even the old timers had expected." During this season at Hill 60 and Sanctuary Wood, the Bombers alone had lost four sergeants and two officers. The unit's battered state is

Left: Lionel "Leo" Clarke was one of over 620,000 Canadians to go to war between 1914 and 1918. Despite his battlefield heroism, upon his death in the trenches, his brother remarked how "boyish" he looked.

Right: Fred Hall earned a VC for a daring attempt to save a fellow soldier at the Second Battle of Ypres. A complex man, Fred Hall was a consummate musician and a former law apprentice who long before the war confessed to his mother: "I have always had the feeling that I would die on the battlefield."

Left: Robert Shankland, a modest cashier before the war, steadily climbed the ranks. He was a lieutenant at the battle of Passchendaele in 1917, when his initiative helped win the day for the Canadian Corps, and earn him the VC. He later said of his exploits: "I played poker with the Hun. That's a game of bluff."

Above: Charlie Clarke (second from left) stands between his father, Harry, and his mother Rosetta, just before being shipped out for war in early 1915. Rosetta's stern glare mirrored the stoic anger of hundreds of thousands of Canadian women who watched sons and husbands march off to war. Charlie's sister-in-law Bet stands on the far right.

Right: A young Fred Hall wears the uniform of the Scottish Rifles, the British regiment he served in for 12 years until leaving to care for his mother and siblings in western Canada.

Top: March from the Somme. (From left) William Roe, Charlie Clarke, and Fred Harrison slipped from billets to have this photo taken at the French town of Bruay to commemorate having survived the battle of the Somme, their boots and khakis still caked with the grime of this historic slaughter.

Right: A group photo of sergeants from Second Battalion. Willam Roe, an original with the Bombers and one of Charlie Clarke's best friends, sits on the bottom row, second from the left.

Below: "The suicide squad." Survivors of the Second Battalion Bombers photographed in June 1916 after a devastating tour of the Ypres salient. Charlie Clarke identified the men as follows, in some instances specifying only last names: (Back row, from left) Lt. Frank Strachan, Red Davis, Fred "Pole Vaulter" Tyo, Larry Dods, Charlie Clarke, Smith, Ed Harris, McCarthy, William Craw. (Middle row) Jack Dyler, Keeham, Arpad "Babe" Urquhart, Doug "Dolly" Ledgerwood, W.J. "Bill" Rendle. (Front row) Red Barrett, Harold "Chinky" Keeling, Dave Reynolds, Ross Findlay, Pat Armstrong, Dave Gordon, Leo Clarke.

Top: The Clarke home at 785 Pine Street (later Valour Road), circa 1916, where Leo was raised. Said brother Charlie of the neighbourhood: "Pine Street had no road, nor sidewalks, nor sewer or water or light. Just swamp and open fields."

Above: A grim-faced and grieving Harry Clarke receives his son Leo's VC from Canada's Governor General in February 1917. He also received a letter from King George V, and would treasure both the decoration and letter for the remainder of his life.

Right: An unidentified Second Battalion Bomber shouldering a rifle grenade, probably a Newton Pippin, in the trenches. The Bombers often discharged the weapon in this way: firing the grenade over their shoulder with the rifle butt braced against a sandbag. Although unidentified, this Bomber could be Charlie Clarke, and according to the Clarke family, this photo may have been taken at Wulverghem, where the Canadians first employed rifle grenades.

Below: A troop of what appears to be German prisoners. According to the Clarke family, this photo may have been taken towards the end of 1915. At the end of that year, wrote Charlie Clarke in *One Man's Warfare*, "just when the 'Jerries' (Germans) were starting to call out 'Happy New Year,' we let loose, on our whole Battalion front.... The screams could be heard all along the line where just before greetings had filled the air." (p. 32.)

Top: An identified but pleased Bomber with a British trench mortar, the Allied answer to the devastating German *minenwerfer.* Charlie wrote of this weapon: "It looked forever like a piece of stove pipe with two short legs and a base plate that it rested on…. Just the thing for a real good strafe."

Middle: Charlie and Leo's Second Battalion comrades. Whether the men depicted here included friends such as the Hielandman, the trench poet Bill Craw, the "Pole Vaulter," and "Big Dolly" is unknown. But if this photo was taken in early 1916, as information from the Clarke family suggests, most of the soldiers in this photo did not survive the war.

Bottom: The muzzle flash of a British cannon, probably firing at night. Millions of shells were expended in the Great War. Unexploded shells are still being recovered from French and Belgian farm fields a century later.

Top: Valour Road, March 1946. After the war, Charlie Clarke eventually married, settled into a house on this street, and raised a family. Here his wife, Amy, stands with his sons Leo Jr. (left) and Richard. Subsequent generations of Clarkes would perpetuate the Valour Road legacy.

Above: Robert Shankland still in uniform years after the war. The only Valour Road VC hero to return home, Shankland served in the Second World War and remained closely associated with the military for the remainder of his life.

Three generations of the Clarke family stand in the plaza at Valour Road and Sargent Avenue during the unveiling of plaques in 2012 commemorating Clarke, Shankland, and Hall. (Top row from left) Don Presant, Jennifer Clarke, Leo Clarke Jr., Charlie Clarke Jr., Kathleen Clarke, Daniel Clarke, and Paul Clarke (Leo Jr.'s son); (front row) Catherine Presant Clarke and Jean Clarke (Leo Jr.'s wife). For many years, Remembrance Day commemorations at Valour Road were a family gathering led by the hero's brother Charlie Clarke and his siblings; Charlie's son, Leo Jr., took up the cause, and now his sons, grandsons, and family continue the legacy. Leo Jr.'s wife Jean passed away in 2013.

accurately portrayed in a photograph taken in Poperinghe during billets in late June. The men who lined up for the group shot included newcomers, such as Lieutenant Strachan, who glowered from the photo's far left. It featured veterans as well: Bill Craw and Fred Tyo, who had both returned to the platoon after brief periods away. Good men were at hand—Dolly Ledgerwood, Chinky Keeling, and, of course, Charlie's brother Leo, who sat cross-legged on the ground. Unsurprisingly, Charlie, who was fast becoming one of the outfit's leaders, stood at the centre. Charlie still considered the Bombers a "sorry lot," but when they took their place at the head of the battalion when the Second officially marched from the salient on August 9, they remained formidable. They would need to be.

The battalion's journey ended in the French village of Albert, located 125 kilometres from the salient, and just north of the slow-moving river called the Somme. The terrors of the Somme would become evident soon enough. But the Second Battalion got a glimpse of their grim future when they climbed down from the train that had taken them on their last leg to this destination.

Clearly visible from every vantage point was Albert's towering basilica, Notre-Dame de Brebières, and the statue on its peak—a gilded likeness of the Virgin grasping the Christ child. But by the time the Second Battalion had arrived, the church had been so battered by shelling that the image of the Holy Mother dangled from her perch, as if about to fall, or, more horrifying yet, "throw her child" to the ground. Soon enough, a rumour spread through the Second Battalion ranks that had already made the rounds of the British army at the Somme: "If the Virgin fell, the War would soon end."

More than one Canadian soldier lay in billets that night silently praying for mother and child to plunge to their deaths. But when morning came, the statue still clung to its precarious perch, as if defying gravity, and the men of the Second Battalion were forced to join a campaign that would prove more trying and terrible even than the Ypres salient had been.

THE SHOW

Charlie and Leo Clarke, September 1916

When the Second Battalion arrived by train in Albert, they knew little of the battle that had been raging for the past two months along the nearby River Somme. Charlie Clarke and his comrades had been too preoccupied with survival during their long summer in the Ypres salient to pay attention to this new battlefield. But on August 30, the day the battalion arrived in this theatre, the Battle of the Somme was still a work in process—a work made up in equal parts of overweening ambition, monstrous miscalculation, and mass homicide.

General Sir Douglas Haig had conceived of the offensive in the Somme River valley as the key to finally breaching the German line and ushering in an Allied breakthrough that would turn the course of the war. In his diary, he envisioned "getting as large [as possible] a combined force of French and British across the Somme and fighting the Enemy in the open!" He hoped to create a sizeable enough gap in the German line to push through mounted troops, which would storm across the front in strength and then form a bridgehead in German territory that would ultimately lead to a German collapse in the west.

At least one of Haig's own generals was skeptical, arguing that the scheme had the potential, at best, to seize two enemy trenches and kill some Germans. But the French endorsed the plan—indeed, insisted on it—because, in their view, it would relieve pressure on their besieged armies at Verdun, where they had been fighting since February 21. (Ultimately, they would lose half a million men in this theatre.) As early as April, during the initial planning stages of the offensive, the French commander-in-chief, Marshal Joseph Joffre, had agitated for the attack to come off as soon as possible. But Haig wouldn't be rushed. As he wrote in his diary, he didn't want "any offensive on a large scale from being made until all is ready." Haig and his planners wanted to attack on August 15. "Papa Joffre" balked. A former military engineer in the colonies who had never commanded an army or soldiers in the field before the Great War, Joffre had nevertheless risen to become the unchallenged generalis-simo of the French war effort, and for many Frenchman its saviour. He declared that "the French Army would be ruined!" if forced to wait until mid-August for relief.

Haig reluctantly agreed to move up the start date by six weeks. By the eve of the offensive on July 1, he had amassed nineteen British and three French divisions, supported by 1,000 field guns, 180 heavy guns, and 245 heavy howitzers, which in the week before the attack had spat one million shells (out of a stockpile of three million) at the enemy's defences. Haig had fielded a host of awesome might, so awesome he at times believed himself to be an instrument of destiny. "I do feel that in my plans," he wrote to his wife, "I have been helped by a Power that is not my own."

But this greater Power did not bring him the breakthrough he yearned for. Churchill would later say that Haig "does not appear to have had any original ideas," and when the starting whistle blew along the Somme front on the morning of July 1, the British commander seemed to lack the vision, talent, and soldierly luck to realize his ambitions. Despite having millions of shells and "the flower of British youth" thrown against them, the German line did not buckle. No gap was created for cavalry to cleave. The German war effort remained unified and formidable. But Haig was undaunted by the failure of his initial plan and by the unfathomable casualties. On August 5, he reported to the war committee in London that the Somme battle was in fact a success because the "pressure on Verdun had been relieved." Haig also claimed his offensive had prevented the Germans from shifting fighting men to the east, and that "Russia would not have got on as she had." He argued that the Somme—where fifty-six thousand men were killed and maimed on the first day—was good for his army's morale. He was not completely wrong. "Our troops were in excellent heart," he declared. Supremely confident, Haig soldiered on, and by the end of August, when the Second Battalion arrived in the theatre along with the Canadian Corps, the battle was still underway. Urged on by Russian demands for another large-scale attack, Haig planned a major offensive for mid-September, in which the Canadian Corps would play a central role.

Charlie and his comrades knew little about the struggle on the Somme before they arrived but they soon had at least a glimmering. Their bivouac in a brickyard on the outskirts of the Albert gave them an unwelcome view of the battlefield and their future. Scout Officer Murray described a horizon of "sterile, shell-packed ridges." Strewn across it was the detritus of Haig's great army—clusters of cannons, ammo dumps, stabled horses and their watering troughs, fuel depots, and, "everywhere khaki-clad soldiers" who hailed from a host of former colonies. They traversed the distant plain and filled the city around them. "Here," observed Murray, "was the Empire, cowed into the narrow, tortuous streets of Albert." They conducted their business to the "deep and steady" drumbeat of artillery fire in the near distance.

The Second Battalion's senior officers must have been aware of the catastrophic turn the battle had taken since the first charge on July 1, but the soldiers would not have known the exact scale of the losses. Casualty figures had been suppressed, and, according to one officer, the "mishaps of the early days of the Somme fighting had not yet been revealed to the troops." For the rank and file, the Somme was just another battleground, albeit mercifully less cramped and claustrophobic than the salient. Getting to the Somme front from Albert entailed a long march through "Sausage Valley," a narrow twisting depression that the Battalion marched to on August 31. As they wound through this canyon, deep enough to escape easy observation from enemy observation balloons, Charlie noted evidence of another offensive in the works. A huge quantity of artillery tubes, guns, and cannons of all sizes and calibres was being set up in the "little gullies and gulches" that adjoined the valley like saps. Scout Officer William Murray said the "guns and the unlimited quantities of ammunition that surrounded them" in Sausage Valley were lined virtually "wheel to wheel." Even for the hardbitten Bombers, this mass of arms was unprecedented. Declared the battalion historian: "Never had such prodigality been dreamed of."

At length, the battalion emerged from Sausage Valley to be shepherded by guides to their new position along the line. The men were immediately struck by the spaciousness of this new battlefield. Instead of creeping along mud-lined subterranean ditches, Charlie and his comrades clambered along "sinuous paths that skirted shell holes" toward and through the community of Pozières, yet another wrecked French village on the Western Front, and then to the cusp of a ridge where the Allied trenches had been dug. The Second settled into the line, relieving a battalion of Australians while occupying the flank alongside another Antipodean outfit. After their exploits in Turkey, the Australians already possessed "a splendid reputation for heroism," according to Murray. But the men of the Second felt a special kinship with them for other reasons. The Aussies were friendly, unpretentious, and strikingly similar to the Canadians in outlook. Like Canada, Australia was a young nation largely peopled by British adventurers. They were Empire, loyal to the bone, but animated also by a strong sense of their own nationhood. As it was for the Canadians, their fight in this Great War was evolving from a defence of the British Empire to a crusade for their own place in the postwar world.

On September 3, the men of the Second Battalion were slated to watch the Australians on their flank battle the Germans for possession of Mouquet Farm, which was part of a larger operation to seize and control this sector's high ground. Haig had not yet abandoned hope for a breakthrough. Throughout the summer, he had schemed with General Ferdinand Foch to join with French forces and push forward to occupy the ridge that included the village "Pozières-Moval-Sailly-Saillisel and to points farther north." A vital element in this plan was a new weapon British armourers had been developing—the tank.

Although members of the Second Battalion were only witnesses to these unfolding events, the Scouts and Bombers had been ordered to take up position on their immediate left flank and to "render whatever assistance the Australians might require." This order came from battalion commander Swift, who knew his men would be fighting on the same battlefield and wanted them to learn as much as possible. But the sentiment came initially from the top.

Haig wanted the Canadians to be acclimatized "before undertaking any offensive operations."

According to Charlie, the Bombers were "thrilled" to participate. Oblivious to the butchery that had preceded their arrival, he considered the Somme to be a fresh venue and opportunity for success—an attitude that seemed to validate Haig's contention that his soldiers saw the Somme as "the way to victory." The battalion's scout officer wholeheartedly agreed. "The Army was obviously going forward," William Murray wrote, "encountering strong resistance it is true, but advancing nevertheless." The Australian battle went off without the Bombers or Scouts having to be involved, except to "shoot down bodies of the enemy" who ranged too close to the line during their inevitable counterattacks. Smoke on the field impeded Charlie's view of the actual charge, but he was impressed by the "terrific bombardment" that opened the attack. The German artillery response was less impressive. During the Australian assault and its aftermath, German shells falling into the Second Battalion trenches killed thirty-four men and wounded fifty-eight others. Still, he was not discouraged. "We were on the offensive," Charlie said, "and it meant a lot to us."

His enthusiasm dimmed after the Second Battalion was relieved at Pozières and marched to a reserve position in Sausage Valley. The Lochnagar Crater lay nearby, the scene of one of the most devastating mine blasts of the war. On the first day of the Somme battle, the British army had detonated twenty-seven tons of explosives near the village of La Boiselle, in yet another ploy intended to bring about a German collapse. The explosion was as devastatingly powerful as planned. An observer watching from a plane reported that the blast created an "earth column" that rose as high as four thousand feet into the air. On the ground, a chasm ninety feet deep and three hundred feet wide was scored into the earth. As with the other man-made craters along the Western Front, this one became the scene of a pitched battle as Allied soldiers charged across this abyss toward the German line. That attack, of course, failed, but the Lochnager chasm remained two months later: a gaping wound in the Somme valley. It was, Charlie admitted, a "horrible sight." But it was not the crater's size that shocked him. What caused Charlie and fellow Bomber Red Barrett to recoil were the dead men who had been left to rot on the floor of the pit.

The boys wondered why the dead hadn't been gathered and buried with honour. Charlie would later call this lapse "one of the greatest tragedies of the war." The tragedy was not just the way the dead were treated, but also the attitude toward the living that this callousness revealed. "The top brass held men's lives of such little consequence," Charlie decided, "as to throw them away...." Charlie never returned to the crater. Few soldiers did. The sight of that place was too demoralizing. It "took a lot of fighting spirit out of the men," wrote Charlie.

And fighting spirit was currency the Canadians couldn't afford to lose. Their turn to take up the offensive was approaching. The Somme was consuming too many lives for the Canadian Corps and Second Battalion to be spared. During the first month of battle alone, one hundred twenty thousand men were either killed or wounded, General Haig told the war committee. And although no single day of fighting matched the butcher's bill of the fifty-six thousand casualties tendered on the first day, the battle still was killing two thousand men and wounding another four thousand to five thousand men every week. How the enemy fared at the Somme was a matter of debate. According to an official report from Haig's headquarters, 1.25 million Germans died during the first month of the battle, a claim that was unsubstantiated and suspect. There was, however, evidence that the enemy was suffering badly. One letter found on a dead or captured German declared the Somme battle "the most terrible days of my life." And a German officer, who had also fought on the Russian front, admitted that the Somme "surpassed in horror all my previous experiences."

On September 9, the Second Battalion received orders to return to the line. The Canadians would be conducting what Colonel Swift called a self-contained operation, which meant that it was their show—their offensive. They would not share the field. The operation was theirs to win or lose. It was also both ambitious and strategically vital to Haig's vision for the war. They were to seize a last section of the strategic high ground along Pozières Ridge that was still occupied by the Germans. And in this offensive, the Bombers would not be hanging back or fighting exclusively at night: they would be going over the top as well. This was unusual. Bombing platoons traditionally supported assaults. Now Charlie, Leo, and the other grenadiers would be fighting over open ground, just like the infantry. Moreover, they had been given a crucial job.

The Bombers had a roster of about thirty-six men, and a new bombing officer: Lieutenant William Hoey was the hero of Hill 60, the man who, with bare hands, had unearthed a dugout of buried soldiers and had been promoted for his devotion. According to the battle plan, the Bombers were to be split into two units and placed on each side of the five-hundred-yard front where the attack would be launched. Charlie, Hoey, and half the squad would charge along the far right of the line. Leo, Bombing Sergeant William Nichols, and the rest of the platoon would advance on the left flank. For both squads, the real work would begin when, and if, the Second Battalion seized the German trench on top of the ridge. Once in the enemy ditch, the Bombers on the flanks were instructed to move fifty yards in each direction and secure the two ends of the enemy line, erect trench blocks or barricades to protect the conquered area, and post sentries in case the Germans attempted to win the trench back.

As for Charlie, he had been given an additional assignment. Once the right block was in place and under guard, he was to lead eight Bombers ahead of the new line and protect a work party that had been ordered to dig a new fire trench. This was to be a cut-off trench located ahead of a long elbow in the German line; its purpose was to shorten the area of the front that would have to be defended from counterattacks. A violent reaction could be expected by the Germans posted there: these were three regiments of the Forty-Fifth Reserve Division, primarily made up of men from the 212th Reserve Infantry Regiment, battle-hardened Flanders veterans drawn mainly from Hamburg and Bremen. The terrible summer of the Somme had steeled some Germans, the devastating British offensive reminding them of the horrors awaiting their homeland should the Allies break through. "One hears far less criticism [among the troops] than in previous months," a German police report stated in September 1916. But many other Germans were at the end of their rope. "I am incapable of giving an account of the battle of the Somme," one soldier lamented. "You could not imagine it."

The Bombers had been given a crucial and dangerous task. Still, Charlie and Leo expressed no undue emotion before leaving the assembly area and making their way down the communication line, Peg Trench, toward the front. "We were not sentimentally inclined," Charlie later wrote, "and we parted without any real thought of what was ahead of us." There may have been a handshake and a parting wish of "Good luck!" but each brother had worries of his own to occupy his thoughts. Charlie had watched men go over the top at Givenchy and Sanctuary Wood. He had also witnessed the aftermath of such battles, such as the dead littering the field at Festubert. But if the battle ahead worried him, he had happy memories to retreat to. Of his home in Winnipeg. And of the homes he found in Europe—the Flagolet family and other welcoming farmhouses where kind men filled his mess tin with fresh milk, and women fed him plates of eggs and chips and slices of home-baked bread. And the brothers had the strong bond between them to sustain them.

When the battalion reached the main trench, they organized themselves for the attack. The men in the assaulting wave filed down five saps and took up position along a forward trench, known as the Jumping Off Line, that had been hastily dug for them. A second wave of men formed up in the main fire trench, and one company—Number Four—waited in reserve in a rear-echelon ditch called Luxton Trench.

The Bombers gathered on each flank of the Assaulting Wave: Leo, Sergeant Nichols and twenty other Bombers on the far left; Charlie, Lieutenant Hoey, and the remaining grenadiers on the right. Between them were three companies of infantry, all awaiting zero hour, which was scheduled for four forty-five. At this precise time, an artillery barrage, fired by three British artillery brigades, was to be unleashed against the enemy. But unlike the practice in previous offensives, this barrage was not to be stopped to make way for the infantry. Artillery officers had been instructed to let loose "a creeping barrage" in which a wall of shellfire would be walked across no man's land toward the enemy line just ahead of the first wave of riflemen. At the same time, a steady rain of hate would be brought down on the enemies' heads to prevent them from taking up rifles and machine guns. This was the theory. In the past, reality had played out differently. The British creeping barrage at Neuve Chapelle in 1915 had killed a good many Tommies who, according to one observer, "went too fast and ran into their own artillery fire." But no matter how controversial, Charlie favoured this "new idea for attacks." Anything was better than charging head-on into a swarm of enemy bullets. But those who feared sharing the field with exploding shells wouldn't have long to wait. Artillery support had been scheduled to last for three short minutes—this was the time the men had to cross no man's land.

The men checked equipment. The twenty-two Bombers on each flank inspected the fuses of their grenades. Those who were carrying them checked their Lee-Enfields and the tools they would use to build the trench blocks. Infantrymen too checked rifles, ammunition, and extra gear such as their masks and box respirators, which had been issued in case of gas. Some men double-checked the rounds in their pistols. Side arms were not regulation for anyone under the rank of officer, but a few Bombers and Scouts carried them. Charlie toted a pistol at Sanctuary Wood, but soon lost it. Leo now packed a Colt automatic revolver and three clips of ammunition, which he had picked up somewhere, and preferred for close-quarters fighting.

By 4:44 P.M., the men stood ready. Soldiers shuffled and stared at the muddy trench wall ahead of them. Officers gazed at synchronized watches and fingered the whistles they would blow to launch the show. But when zero hour struck a minute later, Charlie knew that the attack was on, not from any whistle shrill, but from the deafening artillery fire that descended on no man's land, telling him "all hell was let loose." This opening of the barrage was, for the attacking infantry, like the blast of a dozen starting guns, and with it the men of the Second Battalion scrambled over the parapet and began marching purposefully toward the enemy.

They advanced up a sloping no man's land, cratered and broken, toward the crest of the ridge where the enemy was being savagely bombarded. As planned, the men advanced just behind an uneven wall of explosions that spattered fire, metal, and hot wind in every direction. The problem, of course, was that advancing soldiers didn't know how fast to march or how much distance to keep behind the barrier of fire. In theory, they were to stay at least fifty yards behind the barrage. But who could really tell how far away the shells would fall? And who could account for "shorts"— shells that fell short of their mark? "Casualties were heavy," Scout Officer William Murray said of the charge. And not all casualties came from friendly shells: the Germans bombarded the field with equal savagery.

After three minutes that felt like an eternity, the British creeping barrage ended, and the enemy in the far trench slunk out of their funk holes, bays, and deep bunkers, and scampered back to their firing trench. All across no man's land, the assaulting wave of the Canadian battalion spotted "German forage caps" sprouting up all along the parapet. According to Scout Murray, "the leveled rifles spat a vicious stream."

The Canadians took casualties, particularly on the left flank where the charge ground to a stop, and men dove into craters to return fire while "worming their way forward on their stomachs." Those on the right side of the field fared better. But as in every desperate attack, breakthroughs depended on the bravery and sacrifice of individual soldiers. Platoon leader Major Arthur McLaughlin was a small-town lawyer and community activist in Bowmanville, Ontario, when the war broke out. Despite being an "elderly" forty-four-year-old, McLaughlin enlisted along with cousin, Lorne. On September 9, McLaughlin was leading his men forward, marching with the help of a cane, when a bullet struck him in the stomach. As he fell, he called out to Lorne, the Number 1 Company commander who was advancing nearby, and then waved his platoon forward, shouting: "Go on, boys!" Major Lorne McLaughlin sent a runner to help his wounded relative to an aid station. Arthur lied to the runner about his condition, so not to worry his cousin, and died in a crowded field hospital.

Pozières Ridge was the battle where the padre's son, John Pringle, who had recently been promoted to the rank of lieutenant, met the end of his short, brilliant life. He was guiding his platoon within reach of the enemy trench when he spotted a German squad setting up a machine gun directly ahead. Pringle knew that his men would stand no chance in the face of the machine gun's deadly fire, and so the parson's boy stormed ahead and attacked the position single-handedly. When his men finally reached the trench, they found the bay filled with dead men, and Lieutenant John Pringle's body draped like a flag over the barrel of the enemy weapon. A witness called Pringle's charge the "bravest thing that I ever saw."

Bitter fighting and human tragedy marked the attack on the left. The assailants "worked their way desperately" to the German line, losing in the process a favourite lieutenant, twenty-seven-year-old Henry Cuthbert Stuart, who was shot as the attackers closed within twenty yards of the trench. The company charging at the centre also met with tough resistance. Charlie and his section actually took few casualties on the way to the German line: when they leapt into the enemy ditch, they found it abandoned. Altogether, the Second Battalion reached, seized, and flooded into the enemy trench all along the ridge. At 1708 hours, 23 minutes after the charge began, Major Lorne McLaughlin, the only company commander to reach the trench unscathed, was able to radio this message back to Second Battalion HQ: "The Battalion have captured the enemy's position." "Be sure and hang onto it," he was told.

The length of Pozières Ridge was in Canadian hands. On the right flank, Charlie and his squad immediately set to work. They ran to the right, following the enemy trench for fifty yards and then stopped to build a block with sandbags pulled down from the parapet and whatever else they could find to jam up the channel. As his men laboured on the barrier, Charlie was ordered to move back down the line to the spot where the Bombers had breached the trench. As he waited for his men to return, he reflected on how smoothly the attack had gone, at least on his end of the line. "My party never threw a bomb," Charlie wrote, "or fired a shot." The operation was so quiet, he used the time to scrounge and soon found a treasure trove of souvenirs: "six lovely German Dress Helmets" tucked like trophies on a shell in the trench wall. He was admiring his prize when Lieutenant Hoey marched up, and shouted: "Did you happen to realize that there's a war on?" He ordered Charlie to get to work reversing the parapet, turning the back of the German trench into the new front of the Canadian line. Charlie had just embarked on this task when he spotted movement directly ahead in the new no man's land. Evening light was bleeding away, but he clearly saw a squad of men crossing in front. They were German soldiers, but they weren't attacking. Charlie guessed they had been trapped further down the trench, and were now running away, heading east toward the town of Martinpuich, where the bulk of the enemy was stationed. The men surrounding Charlie noticed the fleeing Germans too. At once, they opened fire. Then a gunner stepped up and mounted a Lewis machine gun on the new parapet and began hosing metal into the fleeing mob. The Germans didn't so much die as fade in the static light. The men "just wilted away," Charlie later described.

But the men of the Second Battalion knew they would soon be facing other Germans who would not be fleeing. When Charlie's men finally arrived, having thrown up the barricade as instructed and posting guards, they climbed out of the trench and crept forward in this unknown territory. Accompanying them was the work party from the reserve company, Number 4, which had been detailed to dig a cut-off above a deep-bowed "snout" in the line. As the sun began to set behind them, Charlie and his men ranged out ahead of these diggers, forming a thin front of eight Bombers to cover three hundred yards of uneven ground. As squad leader, Charlie placed himself at the centre of this line, taking possession of the deepest shell hole he could find. Before long, the sky completely darkened, and Charlie was struck by how "very lonely" he felt so far ahead of this new and precarious stretch of Canadian territory.

Then the shells began to fall. The barrage came from their own cannons, aimed at boxing in the area and keeping the enemy out, and they fell so close to them that the Bombers could feel their heat. When a burning shard struck short and planted itself directly between Charlie's sprawled legs, the burning sensation was the only thing telling him that he still had legs at all. At least one of his comrades was less fortunate. As the exploding shells spouted dirt and stone, Fred Tyo crawled up to Charlie's hole and announced: "I'm wounded in the shoulder. I'm going back to the line." Charlie wished him luck.

Other battered Bombers, wounded and rattled by the barrage, followed Tyo back. One grenadier snaked up to Charlie and began weeping. "I can't stand being alone out here anymore," he said through his tears. Charlie pulled the man into his hole where he spent the night "cringing" at Charlie's feet. But Charlie refused to withdraw early. He would wait it out until morning as ordered, even though he had no idea how many Bombers remained with him, or whether the entrenching party was still digging behind him. The night was too dark and confused for Charlie to be sure of anything except his own mind. The ground churned like a heaving sea, and Charlie and his shell-shocked comrade clung to their crater as if it were a raft in the middle of an ocean.

They hung on until the sun's rays began to seep over the enemy horizon. By then, the shelling had fallen off, and the two soldiers, their duty done, crawled from their hole and slipped back across the gashed and rutted field to the line. When they rolled over the new parapet and fell back into the Pozières Ridge trench, Charlie came face-to-face with an officer. His expression was slack and incredulous. "Good God," he said, "have you been out there all night?"

Charlie checked the time. It was 6:45 A.M. He had been hunkered down in no man's land, riding out the barrage, for almost twelve hours. And he had no idea what had happened along the ridge during the night. He quizzed the soldiers around him. Did they know the fate of the Bombers on the far flank? How was his brother Leo? Was he hurt? Was he alive? No one seemed to know, but later in the morning, a friend appeared who had been fighting on the left all night. The soldier beamed with relief when he found Charlie alive and uninjured. "I'm glad to see you safe," he said.

Charlie repeated the question that was topmost on his mind but his friend had grim news. For most of their platoon, it had gone badly. "They are all gone," he said. But what about Leo? And then his friend told Charlie a shocking story.

POZIÈRES RIDGE

Leo Clarke, September 1916

Fourteen hours earlier, in the early morning hours of
September 9, Leo Clarke stood on the left flank with Sergeant
William Nichols, a Manitoba farmer who had been recently
promoted from lance corporal, and half of the company's bomber
platoon, awaiting the sound of the whistle that would send them
over the top.

Like every man along the line, Leo had much to reflect on
in these minutes before the attack. In the eleven months he had
been with the Second Battalion, Leo had seen action, but in many
ways he was a newcomer. He wasn't an original who had trained
at Valcartier. Nor was he an old-timer who had survived Second
Ypres. Yet, he had proven himself and excelled and had clearly
worked hard to do so.

Throughout his life, Leo Clarke had always striven to do his
best, and had always excelled. He had been a star athlete at Argyle
School in Winnipeg, and among the boys of the West End he
was a natural leader. He was widely admired for his boldness and

confidence. As Leo grew older, women were attracted to him as well. While he was posted in England for training, Leo had found a girlfriend who cared enough to send him a parcel in the trenches. And he encountered another young woman just before he arrived at the Somme. In August, on the long march from Ypres, Leo had been detailed to the battalion's billeting party, which foraged ahead of the marching column and arranged accommodation for the men among the country folk. Leo had found shelter for the Bombers among a cluster of farms in the vicinity of the Belgian village of La Panne, north of Saint-Omer. He had selected a prime spot for himself: the comfortable pigsty of a friendly farmer. Dry, snug, and surprisingly clean, pigpens were coveted shelter. But this billet offered the added attraction of the host farmer's attentive seventeen-year-old daughter.

When the Second Battalion marched into La Panne, Leo guided his fellow Bombers to their billets among the farms down the road from where he was staying. But he declined their invitation to meet that evening to joke or play cards or search out an *estaminet*. Leo said he preferred to stay in, and Charlie understood why when he made an impromptu visit to his brother's billet several days later. He arrived at Leo's pigsty just as his host's daughter was leaving it. But Charlie would only learn the details later: how this sweet girl joined Leo in his shelter at night during the two weeks that the Second Battalion remained at La Panne. Charlie and the other Bombers glimpsed the tender drama when the battalion began its march from town early on August 28. The girl, overcome with emotion, broke into the column where Leo stood with his comrades. Throwing her arms around him, she cried "Oh, Leo! Oh, Leo!" as the Bombers and the battalion adjutant officer and Colonel Swift looked on. Leo had flushed with embarrassment, but the memory had to be a soothing one to carry into battle when the shrill call of an officer's whistle and roar of artillery broke out, and men began scrambling out of the forward trench to attack the Germans of Pozières Ridge. Armed with his newly acquired Colt pistol, Leo scrambled into no man's land and picked his way up the uneven slope toward the ridgeline with his section of Bombers. Thoughts of the girl he had left behind must have been lost as he glanced at the men on either side of him and the danger that lay ahead.

Their flank suffered the worst of the fighting. Leo Clarke watched men fall, and he watched men die. In total, as many as fifty men were killed and one hundred fifty wounded assaulting the ridge. But Leo wasn't one of them. He reached the enemy line, more or less unscathed, with enough of his squad at hand to carry out their assignment. But unlike Charlie's section on the opposite flank, when Leo and his men leapt into the trench they met a dozen or more furious and frightened enemy riflemen on hand. A close-quarters firefight broke out inside the narrow channel, at the end of which Leo and the Bombers drove back the enemy. According to William Murray's account, they brawled and pushed, and when they had battled a distance of fifty yards, Leo and the men with him set to work building the trench block.

It was hard going. Shells, probably enemy mortars, were falling around them. Then, as they laboured on the barricade, a troop of about twenty Germans rounded the traverse ahead of them. The safe tactic would have been to withdraw, consolidate, and then try to drive the enemy back again, but Leo and fellow Winnipegger William Soppitt attacked. Dropping their sandbags and tools, they fisted weapons and scrambled over the partially completed block to meet the enemy head-on. The prairie boys charged forward along that deep, narrow trench, and escaped death from a salvo of enemy grenades that flew over their heads and—as Scouting Officer

Murray wrote—"out ranged them." The German Potato Mashers (stick grenades) went off close enough behind them to bruise and concuss them. One bomb probably wounded Soppitt. Suddenly, he was down. Leo absorbed the brunt of one blast directly behind him, but he was able to fight on. And fight on he did. He lobbed his own grenades down the ditch and stalled the marauding Germans long enough to begin throwing up another temporary barricade to shelter behind. But the Germans rallied and continued their attack. Now utterly alone and staring up into a mob of a dozen or more advancing enemy riflemen, Leo drew and raised the only weapon he probably had left—his Colt automatic.

The record suggests Leo Clarke fired calmly and carefully because every one of his bullets found a target. His only advantage was that, because the space he occupied was so confined, the enemy was unable to overwhelm him en masse. He could engage with the one or two men at the head of the charge; when they fell, he aimed at the next ones scrambling over the fallen bodies of their comrades. In short order, a half-dozen men lay almost at his feet and his Colt's hammer fell on an empty chamber. His clip of seven bullets was empty. He replaced it with a spare he had pocketed and continued firing as more Germans appeared. Leo had no real idea how many men he was fighting, and as more and more riflemen rose up and stormed furiously toward him, he might have wondered if the line would ever end. Would a million men—like the Persians at Thermopylae—press through this narrow pass? Was he, alone, fighting the entire German Imperial Army?

He kept firing as the brawl of angry soldiers rolled nearer. At one point, an enemy officer, perhaps already shot and mortally wounded, took up a rifle and stabbed Leo in the leg with a bayonet. Leo fired again and the officer died, adding his body to the pile of warm, wet corpses on the trench floor. The sight was too horrifying for one German who signalled his surrender. But there were still men behind him who were bent on murder, and Leo had no choice but to fire until he had emptied a second clip, which he quickly replaced. This clip was his last. He fired, and finally, the enemy squad was whittled down to five survivors who panicked. "Turning tail," Murray wrote, "they fled." And Leo limped after them down the narrow, twisting ditch, knowing instinctively that if he did not catch them they would come back. He shot as many as four, and then, when the last one turned and raised his hands, Leo stopped shooting and took the man prisoner.

As they made their way back down the trench toward the Second Battalion sector, Leo and his POW stepped over and around twenty dead Germans: two officers, and eighteen infantrymen, one dead enemy for each shell in his three ammunition clips, save the solitary bullet he now had left. It is not clear how many Bombers from Leo's section were still alive and standing at this stage. Despite being wounded and "bleeding profusely," Leo may have helped finish building the trench block. According to Scout Officer Murray, he was guarding his prisoner when Bombing Sergeant Nichols appeared to check on the barricade's progress. Nichols would not survive the day, but he lived long enough to relieve Leo and dispatch him to a dressing station so that doctors could attend to his wounds. His leg had been lacerated deeply by the bayonet, and his back was wrenched and bruised from grenade blasts.

Minus embellishments and omissions, this was the story the friend told Charlie the next morning. Charlie learned that his brother had single-handedly defeated twenty or more enemy soldiers and in the process spared the battalion a punishing counterattack at a crucial moment in the battle. Charlie's friend also said that news of Leo's exploits was spreading far and wide. There was already talk that Leo would be nominated for a decoration—the ultimate one, the Victoria Cross.

Charlie must have been shocked, impressed, and confused by the harrowing story. But his own writings reveal only one emotion—relief that his brother was still alive when so many other Second Battalion Bombers were not. Later, Charlie walked the length of the trench and took a tally of the platoon. Out of the close to forty Bombers who had started the battle the previous day, only six men remained standing. Bombing Sergeant Nichols was dead, Bombing Officer Hoey was wounded, and four lance corporals were out of action.

But Charlie was alive, and Leo, although wounded, had escaped another close brush with death. Charlie could only wonder how long their luck would last.

PINE STREET

Families of Soldiers, September–November 1916

On September 9, when Charlie and Leo Clarke moved up to the front for the battle of Pozières Ridge, they travelled along communication trenches Munster Alley, Luxton Trench, and Peg Avenue, all named for familiar byways back home. Munster Avenue was a residential street in Toronto, Luxton a school and street in north Winnipeg, and Peg a term of endearment Winnipeggers bestowed on their hometown.

Soldiers named their trenches after the landmarks of home knowing full well that home, despite its distance, was never far away. Every explosion on a battlefield of the Canadian Corps echoed somewhere in the Dominion. On September 9, 1916, the cacophony of fire that thundered across Pozières Ridge was heard loudly and clearly on each street in Canada where a loved one of a fallen soldier lived.

The Great War raged in Canada too, and in Winnipeg, there was no one more brave and dedicated to the war effort than Mary Hall. In 1915, while she awaited word about her three sons in the

British army, she supported them and the other troops by joining the Winnipeg chapter of the Imperial Order Daughters of the Empire (IODE), which raised funds, supplies, and clothing for the boys. When volunteering with the IODE, she worked with women just like herself: widows, wives, and mothers who were either grieving or desperately worried. She knew the agony of receiving a war-department telegram—the government cables that began with the words: "Will you kindly accept my sincere sympathy...." Such a wire had informed her of the death of her son Fred in April 1915.

So tight and efficient were the home front's links to the war, news sometimes travelled faster by informal channels than by official telegram. The Winnipeg-based brother of George Richardson, the hockey star and scion of the powerful grain-trading family, received news of his death in a message sent by one of George's Second Battalion friends. Many learned of the death of a distant relative, old friend, or neighbour through newspaper casualty lists.

Pioneers in northern Alberta who admired Lieutenant John Pringle, the parson's son who was killed saving his platoon at Pozières Ridge, learned of his death in an article in the *Grande Prairie Herald*. And those who knew him best were unsurprised by either his heroics or his passing. "I knew [John] would meet his end in some such manner," one friend said.

Letters from soldiers describing the last moments of a comrade's life often found their way into print. Major Arthur McLaughlin was the old soldier and platoon leader shot in the stomach while marching on Pozières Ridge. His *Toronto Star* obituary included a letter to the dead man's family from his cousin and fellow officer. "He showed no signs of suffering," Lorne McLaughlin wrote of Arthur's last moments, "and was bright and cheerful in the end."

If Lorne McLaughlin had lied about his cousin's suffering to spare the family pain, he needn't have bothered. People at home weren't deceived. News about war was often suppressed and censored. (Immediately after the battle of Pozières Ridge, the Winnipeg *Tribune* published only a vague announcement of an action at the Somme, involving "four Canadian divisions at the front, but which one of them was in Friday's offensive is not yet known here.") Such obfuscation could not obscure the scale of the Great War's tragedies. Casualty lists said it all. On September 14, the *Tribune* listed five Winnipeg boys who had died; the next day, it reported six men dead and twenty-four wounded. The listings rolled off the presses in cities across the Dominion, day after day, with the relentlessness of artillery fire, and people understood the cruel arithmetic implied by these numbers. For every name that appeared on a casualty list, a widow, orphan, or bereaved parent had been created.

Women suffered immeasurably. They grieved as wives, mothers, and daughters, and their pain was compounded by a sense of helplessness. In 1914, Canadian women, like most women everywhere, lacked the right to vote and influence public policy. They lacked the power to stop the war even if they wanted to. And they were barred from participating in the war effort in any direct role, except as a nursing sister. Still, Canadian women fought back. They joined the Red Cross and the IODE. They knitted socks and scarves for the boys in the trenches. They organized fundraisers for war charities such as the St. John Ambulance. Work, frustration, and grief empowered many of them, particularly those who grew to resent the gender inequality of Canadian society and the colossal mess that men had made of things. "Well-kept homes and hand-knit socks will never save the world," one woman told Winnipeg's Nellie McClung after she lost a son at the Somme. "We have allowed men to have control of the big things in life too long." The Great War was the breaking point. By 1916, women in Manitoba, Alberta, and Saskatchewan lobbied for and achieved the right to vote in provincial elections. In 1917, limited women's suffrage became the law of the land across Canada.

Canada boasted a suffragette movement, and Winnipegger Nellie McClung was one of many passionate advocates for women's rights. But during the Great War most of the women who laboured in the IODE and the Returned Soldiers Association did so to support their sons, husbands, and fathers. And like mothers everywhere, the well of their support was bottomless. They waited en masse at the Winnipeg station to meet trains ferrying injured soldiers home, offering help to invalids, mugs of hot tea, and a kind welcome. Harriet Waugh, wife of Winnipeg's wartime mayor, was greeting returning soldiers at the station when she learned that her son had died in combat. According to a local historian, she refused to leave the terminal and continued "pouring tea and answering questions until all the troops were taken care of."

Their activism promoted the cause of women's rights. It also blurred the class lines that had divided Winnipeg and Canadian society. A year into the Great War, class and privilege meant as little in Winnipeg as it did in the trenches. Since the war was wholly democratic when it chose its victims, snatching away sons of both the rich and working class, grief became the great equalizer, particularly among women. No one knew this better than Fred and Harry Hall's mother, Mary. Although Mary lived without money and social connections, few daughters of the IODE had given as much as she had to the Empire. During the first year of the war, three of her sons wore khaki: her oldest boy, Fred; twenty-six-year-old Edmund; and her youngest, Harry. Her late husband Frederick Matticott Hall had served in the army with distinction, as did her father and grandfather. All of her men had given their best years to the Empire. In April 1915, she learned that her family had sacrificed dearly when she received news that her son Fred had died in the battle of Second Ypres. Like all the Halls, Fred was new to Winnipeg. He had lived in the city barely a year before signing up. But the circumstances of his battlefield death were well known. Fred Hall had died trying to help a wounded comrade to safety, and his heroism and sacrifice ultimately earned him a posthumous Victoria Cross, the Empire's most revered decoration for bravery. Mary Hall took possession of her son's medal on August 24, 1915, exactly one year to the day after saying goodbye to her "Freddie" and her youngest son, Harry, at the Winnipeg station.

So now she had two sons left: Harry with the Alberta-based Tenth Battalion and Ted with the Scottish Rifles. She feared for them both, particularly her youngest, Harry, who as a mere boy of eighteen years had no military experience when he volunteered and went to war. In mid-June she learned that Harry had been shot at the Battle of Givenchy. Thankfully, he was alive. The wound was to his arm, and his condition was serious enough for him to be transferred to Britain for treatment. As the summer passed, Harry languished in hospitals and convalescent homes, and Mary feared that the army might deem him fit enough to fight and return to France. This fear was paramount in her mind on the day she sought out fellow IODE sister Marie Steele and pleaded for her help.

Marie was married to Sam Steele, one of Canada's best known and most admired soldiers, particularly in the west where he had based his career. As a young militiaman, Steele had fought Fenian raiders and rebels in Louis Riel's first uprising. In 1873, he joined the newly created North-West Mounted Police force and devoted years to enforcing the rule of law in the Canadian West and the Klondike. After he retired from the Mounties, he accepted a regular army post and when war broke out in 1914, the old rebel fighter oversaw Canada's Military Division No. 10, headquartered in Winnipeg. Steele had wanted a field command, but at sixty-six years he was judged too old. Nevertheless, in early 1915, Major General Steele deployed to Europe leading the Second Canadian Division, and eventually settled into the job as commander of England's Southeastern District.

Mary Hall knew that Steele wielded considerable power in the British army, and she explained her predicament to the general's wife. Mary had already lost a son, one who had done much for the Empire before he died. Now she faced the unthinkable prospect of losing her youngest, Harry, who despite being wounded might again be marched to the front. Hadn't the Hall men given sufficiently? Hadn't she sacrificed enough?

Mary asked Mrs. Steele if she could appeal to her husband, the major general, and seek his help in delivering her maimed youngest boy home. Marie de Lotbinière Harwood Steele was sympathetic to her IODE sister's pleas. The two women, though born on opposite sides of the Empire, had shared similar lives. Like Mary Hall, Marie Steele was a long-suffering soldier's wife who also had a young son named Harry (eighteen-year-old Harwood Elmes Robert Steele was both in uniform and in Europe with the Second Division). Marie Steele trusted her husband to do what he could to safeguard their boy soldier. And because she understood the source of Mary Hall's grief and pain, she promised the widow Hall that she would appeal to her husband.

At that moment, Mary's son Harry was in a convalescent home in the village of Deal near Dover on England's southern coast. He had been shot when the Tenth Battalion went over the top at Givenchy in June 1915. That he hadn't been shot sooner was something of a miracle. By the time he joined the line in the fire trench at Givenchy, Harry was a veteran of the battles of Second Ypres, Festubert, and Plugstreet. He had witnessed scores of comrades die. But strangely he never lost his youthful sense of invincibility. At Festubert, one of the tougher men in his battalion, a big Irish brawler named Jim Foley, had grown sombre and confessed to Harry feeling a premonition of his own death. Harry had told Jim "not to think that way and to be optimistic like I was." Optimism and canny survival instincts had helped Harry and his Scottish friends Duncan and Hector survive when so many hadn't. At Festubert, luck and skill eluded Jim Foley and to Harry's sorrow, big Jim was killed. Harry—who had strained his luck too far—fell during the next engagement at Givenchy. Still, at the end of the day, Harry had been lucky enough. He had been wounded in the arm, and although the limb had turned "black from gangrene," he was in no real danger of dying. After an operation in Glasgow's Stobhill hospital, he was told he had almost lost the arm. But the doctor treating him had been one of Glasgow's top neurosurgeons. "If you had gone to a lesser hospital," a nurse told him, "you would have one arm now."

How lucky had he really been? Although his wound leaked pus and his hand was partially paralyzed, Harry was on the mend and destined to return to the war. By October, at the soldiers' home at Deal, he had recovered to the point where he would soon face an army medical board exam, which would rule on his fitness to return to the front. His mother had explained in a letter that she had appealed to her friend Marie Steele on Harry's behalf. But Harry "didn't think it would do any good." On the other hand, he knew that "some husbands will listen to their wives and try to do what they want." He soon learned that Sam Steele was such a man.

One day in November, the hospital's matron found Harry and announced that two Canadian staff officers had come to visit him. Harry met with them in the matron's office. The men explained that they represented General Steele and had been sent to ask Harry a question. What did he want to do? In light of his general health, did he want to go home or stay? Harry's mother had made her wishes known. Now Steele was giving Harry a chance to make his own decision. Would he prefer to stay and fight on? Or would he return to Canada? In truth, Harry believed he had little choice. "My arm wound is still running pus," he told the officers, "and my hand is paralyzed and I can't grip a gun. I would prefer to go home."

Steele was true to his word. Harry was issued papers and put on a train to Liverpool, where a ship awaited him. On the way, he took a detour to his birthplace, St. Helens, a short distance from the Merseyside port, and visited his father's grave. Tall and intricately carved with floral designs, his father's headstone was a reminder of his mother's grief and love. Harry also visited some old family friends and then boarded the ship bound for Canada. He arrived at Quebec City in late November 1915, and caught the transcontinental train west. When Harry arrived at the CPR station in Winnipeg, his mother, Mary, and his sisters, Ada and May, stood on the platform waiting for him. He was home.

Harry's war was over and Mary Hall would not have to fret over him again. The strain she had endured over Harry and would continue to endure over her son Ted was not uncommon. By 1916, nearly every family in Canada had a man in the trenches, or hospital, or military grave. This included the families of Pine Street in Winnipeg's West End. The Clarke household at 785 Pine had sent Leo and Charlie off to war. Their parents, Harry and Rosetta, wrote to the boys faithfully, sent them parcels of food, knitted clothing, and newspapers. Bob Shankland, now a sergeant major with the Cameron Highlanders, had lived with the Ritchie family at 733 Pine. Annie Ritchie, the only sister in the Ritchie clan, wrote Bob letters and mailed him cigarettes and at least once a tin of fudge candy.

When the families received letters from their kin in uniform, it was a joyous event—confirmation that their soldier was alive and well. But not all the mail that arrived from the trenches brought good news. In late June, Mary Hutchings, who lived 939 Pine, received a wire with word that her husband, Charles, had been wounded. He was one of thousands of casualties of the bitter fighting for Mount Sorrel. In late July, Thomas Mather and his wife Bertha, at 669 Pine, were informed by telegram that their twenty-one-year-old son, Carl, had been shot in the shoulder and face. A serious-minded boy who dreamed of becoming a lawyer, Carl would never plead a case in court. Two weeks later, the Mathers received word that Carl had died of his wounds. The family was posted his personal effects, and the ground he was defending took possession of his body. Carl was buried at Lijssenthoek, a dozen miles west of Ypres, where he remains today.

Before the end of 1916, Robert Quay, whose family lived four blocks away on Strathcona Street, would die at the Somme. The Burnetts, at 872 Pine, and the McKenzies, at 650, would also be in mourning.

When death touched a street in Winnipeg, word spread quickly and quietly. Neighbours responded with visits. They would offer condolences, and true to country tradition they often brought food. Reverend Armstrong of the St. Patrick's Anglican Church, built on Pine just before the war, was on hand to console the survivors. But for many families, there could be no comfort. Before the war, someone strolling down Pine Street's boardwalk might have heard the rush of prairie wind and the chatter of insects. But between 1915 and 1918, if a visitor stopped and strained his ears, he was more likely to hear the keening of grieving wives and mothers.

But some sons did return. On November 21, 1915, around the time when Harry was reunited with his mother and sisters, a special train pulled into Winnipeg's station carrying fifty local boys who were wounded or on leave. Some of these men were maimed for life. Private Peter McPhail had been fighting with Fred Hall's Eighth Battalion at Second Ypres when, according to a newspaper report, "a bullet passed through his left eye, crossed the bridge of his nose and cut the optic of his right eye, totally blinding him." The lungs of Ed Cook, also with the Eighth, had been ravaged by chlorine gas. Private E. Polson limped off the train with a mangled foot. Frank Bristow took in the sight of his home city, which the boys called "Good Old Peg," with one working eye. When a local mother, Annie Greenaway, greeted her son, Tom, he was one limb short, having lost his left leg in the battle for the salient. Yet, Annie must have been delighted and relieved. Her boy was home, and although not whole he was whole enough.

Mary Hall was delighted and relieved to have Harry home. But she was still beset by worries. She was short of money. She and daughters Ada and May were in the process of moving from 179 Spence Street to more modest accommodations. She worried about Ted, who was still in the war. And she grieved for Fred. In quiet moments alone, she went through his papers—the final record of his short life. These files attested to his accomplishments in the British army, his certificates for musketry and telegraph signalling. She reread his last letters to her, written from the trenches. The missives had been so considerate and, she now realized, selfless. They mainly concerned Harry, and Fred's efforts to comfort his mother and ease her worries about her younger child. When Mary had heard that her son had died while trying to rescue another man, she told someone: "That was just like him. He never thought of himself. He did not fear anything."

SWINGING THE LEAD

Charlie Clarke, September 1916

Enemy counterattacks against Pozières Ridge had raged throughout September 9 and 10, particularly on the left flank where Leo Clarke had fought so fiercely. In one assault by German grenadiers, Bombing Sergeant Nichols was killed. But the Second Battalion held the line, and by afternoon it was clear that Pozières Ridge was in Canadian hands.

To understand the enormity of what the men of the Second Battalion had just achieved, all they had to do was turn around and take in the vista from this high ground. "Gazing to the rear from the captured line," declared Scout Officer Murray, "one could see considerable movement all over the area." The ridge was prime territory, and it was theirs—fairly won with the loss of considerable blood. But they would not be given the chance to continue the offensive and "turn this position into a cauldron again." The next day, the Second Battalion was relieved. Charlie Clarke and the surviving members of the battalion left the ridge "section by section," limping down the holed and gutted battlefield they had stormed the day before.

Exhausted, the various sections assembled at La Boisselle behind the lines and began the march to Albert with a regimental band leading the way. The band was headquarters' way of congratulating the men, an acknowledgment that they "had done everything that was asked of them, had fulfilled every requirement." This nod was no empty gesture. Word of the victory at Pozières Ridge had spread among the troops of other imperial outfits. As the Second Battalion continued their limping march to billets, passing soldiers applauded, shouting: "Good Old Second."

Once the battalion reached Albert and "we dragged our feet along the cobble stones," Charlie's platoon seemed to swell in size and the future didn't look quite as bleak. Bombers whom Charlie had presumed dead straggled up. Two of them explained that they had been concussed in the artillery barrage of the night before and put temporarily out of commission. The other two had helped wounded comrades to the dressing station. And then another Bomber caught up with the platoon the next day, and Charlie was both relieved and shocked by the sight. Leo Clarke looked raw and ragged after his desperate battle at Pozières. Charlie inspected his brother's back, which had absorbed the force of a grenade blast. Flesh and muscle were tender and bruised, and Leo moved with difficulty. He belonged in the dressing station he had just "skipped out" from because he couldn't abide the ambulance's food—rock-hard biscuits, canned bully beef, and tea without milk or sugar.

"I can eat better here with you," Leo said. It seems unlikely that this was the real reason for his premature return. Most wounded soldiers who discharged themselves from hospital did so because they yearned to be with comrades. That night, the assembled Bombers celebrated the reunion and their survival by feasting on delicacies from home culled from the backlog of parcels that had been waiting at Albert. Many of the packages were addressed to dead, missing, and wounded men. Since these packages almost always contained food and perishables, the soldiers had devised a policy to deal with them. All parcels were opened without delay. All food would be devoured and enjoyed by the men at hand. Photos, letters, and non-comestible gifts were put aside for any wounded soldiers who were expected to return. Gifts addressed to dead soldiers were shipped back to their family. After Pozières Ridge, there were a lot of gifts for the dead to be shipped home.

But there was little time to dwell on loss. On September 12, the battalion was mustered and marched out from Albert. The Bombers occupied the place of honour at the head of the column, but Leo, too injured to walk, rode on a horse-drawn limber at the rear of the procession. It was fortunate he was not on his feet: the column crawled along. The narrow roads of the Somme were clogged with troops and supply wagons heading to the front. Incoming reserves enjoyed priority, so the Second was forced to give way and trudge along on the side of the road.

After two days of marching, they stopped for twenty-four hours at the quaint village of Ferme de Rozel, on flat high ground one Canadian soldier called France's "bare uplands." Rozel possessed an ancient stone church with a tower as squat as a battlement. Although they had put some distance between themselves and the front, it was obvious that the war was being fought without them: they could see "the flash of guns by night" as the full might of the British army pounded the enemy. For some of the men, the flashes, lovely as summer lightning, were a comforting reminder that they were safely out of it. For others the distant fire simply proved that the war was inescapable. No matter how far away one marched, the glow could still be glimpsed and its heartbeat heard.

The Bombers received a further reminder of the war's proximity when a tall, heavy-limbed officer rode up on horseback. The visitor was the commanding general of the First Canadian Division, but to some men he didn't look the part. With a long, soft face devoid of moustache or hollowed cheeks, Arthur Currie lacked the severe countenance of many of his fellow commanders. Moreover, different from the many preening taskmasters in the Allied armies, he had the rare habit of giving orders in a "quiet, decisive way," according to one of his officers. But Currie needed neither a martinet's features nor his demeanour to intimidate his subordinates. His size was enough. Currie seemed always too large, even for his horse. And when he was on foot, he loomed above his fellow commanders and just about everyone else. Charlie saw the general as "a big impressive man." But on this occasion, after Currie dismounted and lumbered up to the men on parade, nothing he said impressed.

"Most of you have seen long service in the line," Currie began, his stare fixed on the Bombers, "and have distinguished yourselves, and in the recent attack have performed brave deeds, and I congratulate you. But I must say this to you: You cannot live on what you have done. You must go back up the line again into another attack and live up to the good name you have made for yourselves."

The general's speech sent "cold chills" through Charlie's bones, and after Currie strode away, a few of the Bombers griped about his remarks. But Charlie saw the justice in their leader's words. With the exception of Winston Churchill, Currie was perhaps the truest talent to emerge during the Great War. And he was too insightful and war weary to ply the men with platitudes. He spoke the truth. There would be more battles to be fought, and no one was going home until they were won.

Currie knew that the end was not in sight. But to Charlie, the Canadian general also seemed to be warning the troops of impending misery. "There was something mysterious going on," he realized. Whispers about another big push spread through the ranks. Then on September 15, while in billets fourteen kilometres from Albert, the men awoke to a deafening artillery barrage raging at the front, and Charlie wondered if another "show" had begun. It had. That morning, the Allies had launched a major attack toward the village of Courcelette, which featured the conflict's newest innovation—the armoured tank. To his credit, Haig had been briefed on the tank before and had immediately recognized its potential in tipping the balance of the war. He had requested a thousand be made available for the Somme offensive. He was told that just sixty-two would be ready by mid-September, but when the British infantry clambered from trenches that morning, they were supported only by twenty functioning "Mastodons," as the men called them.

The iron beasts lived up to Haig's high hopes. Within two hours of the battle's start, a British pilot spotted British armour as far forward as the village of Flers, and the usually circumspect Haig rejoiced in his diary that the "tanks have done marvels." But the offensive sputtered on the right flank and might have failed entirely had it not been for the Second and Third Canadian Divisions, which attacked in tandem with the village of Courcelette as their objective. The Third Division laid the groundwork for the main attack by engaging the enemy at Mouquet Farm and Fabeck Graben trench. The Third couldn't overrun these positions, but by restraining the Germans there, they allowed the Second Division to push toward the village.

All along the way, the fighting was savage and bitter. Despite the introduction of modern weapons, including the tanks and airplanes, the infantry on the ground wielded old-fashioned bayonets, and innumerable Germans were gutted as the men of the Second Division poured into the enemy trenches. One soldier said he killed by hacking and cutting "the same as if I was making logs." But the new instruments played a role as well. The twenty wobbly tanks involved in this late-hour skirmish at the Somme changed warfare forever. A single armoured vehicle saved the men of the Twentieth and Twenty-First Battalions, who had been pinned down ahead of a landmark known as the "Sugar Factory." After a "bitter struggle," the Canadians rallied and battled their way into Courcelette. The village—crushed, burning, and the target of furious German shelling—may have been a dubious prize, but it was a prize that the Allies intended to keep, with the help of the Second Battalion.

Charlie and his comrades had left Rozel and were standing in reserve in the village of Harponville. On September 16, they were mustered early from their billets and marched back along what officer historian Murray called "the foyer of the great theatre"—the Somme—where they would assist in the defence of Courcelette. The bulk of the battalion stopped just outside of Albert, bivouacking on the familiar ground of the Brickfields under what its commander called "sullen, wet skies." When the Bombers marched on to the front, Charlie was now serving as acting sergeant, while Leo, still too sore to fight, remained behind.

The Bombers slipped into the ruined village on September 20 under the cover of darkness and an impenetrable rain that "deluged the area, turning the low-lying grounds into quagmires and inundating the shelters." But neither rain nor the night hid Courcelette's devastation, which shocked even the battalion's hardbitten chief scout, who described it as a "synonym for all the destruction that could be concentrated in any one area." The

Bombers were shocked when they spotted the carcass of a British tank that had been put out of commission and lay, according to Charlie, like a dead beast "[t]ipped crazily to one side and straddling the trench." Courcelette was on the verge of falling to the enemy. Enemy flares traced the sky like omens, casting shadows and illuminating wreckage. Their frequency told Charlie that the Germans were as nervous as they were.

The Bombers set up headquarters in what had been a deep German bunker, and Lieutenant Hoey ordered Charlie to organize the men for the main operation of the night—manning two outposts ahead of the new front line on the far side of the village. Charlie went out with the first detail to settle them in and ensure that they were properly positioned. When Charlie returned to headquarters, Hoey announced that he wanted someone to fetch rations, which meant that one of the Bombers would have to travel to the rear on "a long weary road" that all considered extremely perilous. Charlie wanted to send a reliable and cool veteran, but Hoey chose a new man. The Bombers were still being sent dregs for replacements, and a recent addition was a Second Battalion man named Little Bill. The tiny man's "blue shoulder straps" revealed he was a Second Battalion original, one of the few men who had arrived in France in early 1915 and had survived all that had happened since. But Little Bill had "lost all interest in the war" along with his nerve, and was no good to them.

Hoey had a theory about dealing with troubled men: he argued that if given responsibility, they would rise to the challenge. So Hoey insisted that Little Bill be sent to fetch the rations. The man protested, and Hoey, betraying his own frayed nerves, shocked Charlie by drawing his sidearm, and repeating the order while brandishing a gun. With shells detonating in the distance, Little Bill reluctantly left the bunker and headed to the rear. But, of course, he didn't return that night, and part of the platoon went hungry until the next day when an old friend appeared. Bill Roe had left the Bombers after too many scrapes with death and had taken on the job of company cook. But "Good Old Billy," as Charlie called him, was still a Bomber at heart and braved a "poisonous" war zone to deliver the grenadiers' rations and a "big Dixie of tea still piping hot." "That was just the kind of thing [Roe] was always doing," Charlie later reflected. "It was all above and beyond the call of duty. He had been one of us for many months and knew what we would appreciate."

That evening, Little Bill, the soldier originally detailed to fetch the rations, finally stumbled back to the Bombers' bunker with what Charlie called a "sad tale of how he had lost his way." Lieutenant Hoey was livid. He sought to punish the miscreant by having him spend the night in the forward outpost along "Sunken Road," a desolate lane crossing no man's land that led directly to the nearby German lines. Manning this outpost was a crucial job, as the position was intended to provide early warning of a German attack. And because this post was so important to the platoon's survival, Charlie again thought that detailing Bill the job of standing sentry there was a bad idea. But Hoey insisted, Little Bill howled in protest, and Hoey again drew his pistol to enforce the order.

Charlie struggled to make the best of a bad situation. He chose "a good man," a Bomber veteran who was steady under fire, to stand sentry with Bill at Sunken Road. And Charlie personally guided the two men to the outpost. Still, when Charlie left them Bill was weeping. And not without reason. The cloud cover had broken and a full moon was shining down on them, lighting up the destroyed village more effectively than a hundred flares. Their visibility made it a particularly dangerous night to guard an outpost. In the morning, a mist settled across no man's land, which was, if anything, even more menacing. When Bill and his mate heard men moving on the road ahead of them, they "felt the hair raising on their backs," as they imagined a full-blown German attack storming down Sunken Road. But instead of gunfire, they were met with whispers of "kamerad, kamerad." A pair of war-weary Germans had crept forward to surrender, and Bill marched them back to the Bombers' headquarters and proudly presented them to Hoey. Charlie could see that the act of taking these prisoners had emboldened and transformed Bill. The little man was suddenly the soldier he had been before. The old colonial warrior Hoey had been right all along.

But Hoey himself would soon chafe and stumble under stress. That night the Bombers were relieved and began withdrawing from Courcelette in a long file. They had just started their march when an errant German shell fell onto the road beside the column and exploded. When the dust cleared, Charlie took in a grisly and grim scene. "One minute there were men intent on going their way," he later noted, "and the next minute a shambles with smoke and fumes of bursting shells, cries of the wounded and the last twitch of the dying." Ground zero of the blast was now a crater and a man lay at the bottom, with more bodies of wounded and dead Bombers sprawled around it. Others like Charlie had emerged relatively unhurt, but strangely two Bombers vanished, as if atomized by the blast. After taking stock of the platoon, Charlie realized that Hoey and Little Bill were nowhere in sight, alive or dead. After calling for stretcher-bearers and marshalling the surviving Bombers back into file, he led the platoon's remnants back to Albert where Hoey and Bill were waiting. And despite Hoey's protests that he had been scouting ahead and hadn't known about the barrage, Charlie knew the old officer had panicked. "Sometimes, it didn't take much shelling," Charlie observed, "to set a man off."

Of course, some men could not be set off. They were as steady as cannon fire, and Charlie's brother Leo was one of them. Leo, still recovering from the blow to his back, was waiting for the Bombers in billets in Albert, and he was desperate to join them the next time the Second Battalion was sent to the line. He was restless and fretfully worried that he wasn't doing his bit. He tried to contribute by keeping the Bombers supplied with tasty provisions. He had been filling in time by gambling, playing crown and anchor and dice. He won regularly and used his winnings to buy delicacies for the boys, such as "canned fruit, fancy biscuits, sardines and chocolate bars" from the YMCA canteen. There was little time for the brothers to speak in private. But Charlie did hear one piece of humbling news. In recognition of his bravery at Pozières Ridge, Leo had been officially nominated for a Victoria Cross. And during a rare moment when they did discuss that battle, Leo admitted to being troubled. He could not forget the Germans who had tried to give themselves up during the mad firefight in the trench. "I had to shoot some of the men that were surrendered," Leo had confessed to Charlie. But when Leo described the desperate encounter, how the Germans behind the men who wanted to capitulate were attacking him with grenades, rifles, and bayonets, Charlie understood why it had been impossible to spare anyone. "He had to keep shooting," Charlie realized, and he told Leo so. Still, Leo was unsettled, and again disappointed when he was denied permission to join the Bombers when the platoon was ordered back to the line.

During the Bombers' absence, the situation in Courcelette had become even more desperate. On the far side of the village, the Germans had stormed and occupied Regina Trench, which had been dug along high ground and as such represented a key position. Allied counterattacks hadn't been able to dislodge the enemy, and frustration and fear settled over the area. Chaplain

Frederick Scott called this zone a "region of gloom and death," and Charlie noted how "casualties had been mounting in a terrible way." Reinforcements, in the form of the Fourth Canadian Division, had been summoned and were on the march. But until they arrived, a brigade was thrown together from local units, including the Second Battalion, to hold the battered position. Charlie was returning to the front. Leo, despite his protests, was forced to remain behind.

On this trip to the line, they passed familiar territory—Pozières Ridge, the scene of the Second Battalion's greatest battle, now was nothing more than a muddy cemetery. When they reached the front, there was no line to take over. With Regina Trench in enemy hands, Charlie and the Bombers took cover in shell holes ahead of the German wire and quietly fashioned a new line by digging channels and traverses between the holes. The men hunkered low and remained quiet so not to invite shelling. The next day, they were relieved and marched back toward Albert.

On the way to billets, they again crossed their old battleground at Pozières Ridge where, ironically, Charlie almost died, as if the ghost of some frustrated enemy had risen up and lashed out at him. An artillery shell fired from a nearby gun exploded prematurely, and Charlie was bowled over after being struck in the chest. His comrades ran to him. Charlie "took stock of [him]self," and realized that, although banged up, he had not in fact been eviscerated by a hunk of shrapnel. He wasn't dying. Apart from a severed equipment strap, Charlie merely had a bruise on his chest. He was dazed and shaken, however, and so the men stopped to brew tea over a small fire. And then, with a sense of relative well-being restored, they continued on their way. Charlie found that he was more affected by the sight of a shell hole they came across presently. After recognizing the pit, he stopped, stood at the crater's rim, and gazed down at the bottom. He was standing just ahead of the trench the Second

Battalion had conquered on September 9. Enemy corpses lay at the bottom of the hole, and suddenly Charlie found himself overcome by sadness. These bodies were the reason this place was so familiar. Charlie remembered watching them die. Now, all these weeks later, their corpses remained, unburied, dishonoured by neglect.

Charlie eventually summoned his resolve, and the Bombers kept moving. When he and the others finally arrived at Albert, Leo was at hand and he was visibly upset. Although still injured and limping, Leo told Charlie that he was more determined than ever to rejoin the Bombers on their next deployment. "But why the hurry when you are still wounded?" Charlie wanted to know. Leo replied that he was afraid some of the men might "consider him a coward." As proof, he said that he had overhead the battalion doctor mutter that Leo was "swinging the lead"—army jargon for malingering. Leo Clarke would not have people calling him a shirker. "I'm going with you," Leo declared, "if I have to crawl."

UNBURIED DEAD

Charlie and Leo Clarke, October 1916

Leo Clarke would not have long to wait. The battalion was recalled to the fragile line ahead of Regina Trench, and Leo limped along with the battalion, which was part of an "emergency" force that would hold out until the reserve units arrived. Charlie didn't consider his brother fit for duty. But he realized that Leo's determination to return to the platoon "was getting to be an obsession." Charlie thought it "ridiculous" that he feared being branded a shirker. Hadn't he just been nominated for the Victoria Cross? But there was no dissuading him.

The battalion set out on October 12, passing across old familiar battlefields and dreaded Somme landmarks, such as Mouquet Farm, the scene of Canadian determination and misery. As they advanced, Charlie, still ranked as acting sergeant, marched at the rear of the Bomber column. Leo marched at the head. He too had been promoted to sergeant in recognition of his leadership and initiative at Pozières Ridge. The column wound into Courcelette, a sprawling ruin that was as haunted, dark, and derelict in daylight as at night. The stench of cordite attacked the men's nostrils, and the drumbeat of artillery echoed on relentlessly as shells passed overhead like "freight trains" that had taken flight. As they advanced closer to the front, Charlie worried about his brother, leading the platoon. Leo was not only wounded, he was also hamstrung by his newness to the theatre. The other Bombers had endured several tours in Courcelette and knew roughly the lay of the land. Leo was experiencing this terrible place for the first time.

As far as Charlie was concerned, Leo belonged in hospital. His wounds were a Blighty, and Leo would probably "have been over in England instead of here" had he not fled from that dressing station after he was hurt. But his decision to return to the platoon was understandable. The battle for Pozières Ridge had been cathartic for many in the Second Battalion—its trauma creating an adhesive that further cemented the men to each other. The battle had affected Charlie deeply, a fact he recognized when they had come upon the corpses in the crater at Pozières Ridge. Charlie had been brooding about the sight ever since. "Their skin was all wizened up," Charlie later reflected, "and I thought how like monkeys they looked." But even more unsettling than their appearance was the memory of how they had died.

Early on September 10, the morning after the attack on Pozières Ridge, Charlie had scrambled back to the main trench after spending a harrowing night in no man's land. Shortly after he arrived, these same German soldiers had wandered out of the mist. They were nonchalantly walking directly in front of the Canadian-held trench. Charlie guessed that they were a work party dispatched to shore up the German line somewhere, and had lost their way. Sentries shouted out, and the Germans froze and raised their hands. Standing beside Charlie was another Bomber. They had shared a shell hole in no man's land together during the previous night, and the entire time this man had sobbed, unhinged by the shells falling like hail around them. The sight of the Germans turned his timidity to fury. He stuck his head above the parapet, and began cursing at the confused enemy—hurling invectives and abuse at them, quieting only when one of the men, a single rifleman who had taken cover in a shell hole, shot the ranting Bomber in the face. The man fell back, mumbling, "I'm dead, I'm dead," and the Canadians along the line opened fire on the would-be prisoners. The enemy work party literally melted before Charlie's eyes, crumpling into the shell hole where Charlie later found them.

When the guns fell silent, the only German left alive was the soldier who had shot the Bomber. He was tucked into a crater, impervious to fire. So Charlie took up a rifle with a grenade clasp on its barrel, mounted an explosive, made a quick calculation, and fired. Both Charlie and the German target stared skyward and watched the grenade fly through the air. The man was gazing up in fascination just as the device detonated above him. When the smoke lifted, the defiant rifleman lay dead and Charlie realized that he had seen "his first and only victim of the whole war." He later explained: "I had fired thousands of grenades back at Wulvergham. We had heard of groups of wounded being taken out of the German trenches, but I had never seen a man fall to one of my shots." Charlie hadn't been "very proud." In fact, as much as he admired him, Charlie had been angry with the dead man. But when he stumbled upon these unburied remains weeks later and gazed down at their "shriveled skin and shrunken features," he felt only pity and a strange kinship with them. Charlie thought of "their homes and their families" and he silently cursed the war. Each dead man represented a grieving mother, wife, or child. Each one left a family that would never be whole again.

But the Clarkes were whole and reunited as the Bombers filed into the mouth of "Murray Avenue," the main communication trench at Courcelette, which snaked to the front line just ahead of the German-occupied Regina Trench. Like most communication trenches, Murray was a tight, claustrophobic ditch. They trod on wooden mats ("two by fours with slats nailed across") that elevated them from the mud and ducked beneath a canopy of razor wire strung like netting over the top of the trench to keep out grenades when possible. Frayed strands of the barbed ceiling hung down in spots and men called out "wire overhead" to warn those coming behind them.

The Bombers crept along, forced to stop when approaching troops squeezed past, or when the guides at the head of the column stopped to consult trench maps. "Some waits were often fifteen minutes," Charlie recalled, "and we chafed under the delay." The end of the Bomber line stalled at an intersection, which to Charlie was like a city street at rush hour: "stretcher-bearers would come by carrying a wounded man, men would come carrying boxes of bombs, and runners with messages to God knows who squeezed past and went on their way."

The Second Battalion line seemed stalled indefinitely. Charlie grew impatient, left his position, and pushed his way to the front of the platoon. He had just sidled up to his brother when a cluster of shells detonated on the side of the trench, spraying the men with dirt and smoke. As the men buckled over, Charlie heard Leo grunt in pain and saw him claw at his shoulder. Had he been hit? Together they tore open Leo's shirt and found the wound. The laceration was not life-threatening, but a sliver of metal had pierced the skin. Charlie helped his brother bandage it and then said: "Go to a dressing station."

But Leo scoffed at the thought. The wound was minor, he

protested, and when the column continued on, Leo was at the head of the Bombing platoon, guiding the men into the reserve trench where the battalion was ordered to take up position. The Bombers settled into a cluster of shelves, bays, and dugouts immediately off Murray Avenue. Lieutenant Hoey had ordered a pair of young runners to man the first bay along the trench and then stationed his subaltern next to them. Hoey claimed a spot in a deep funk hole dug into the trench wall around the first traverse, and Leo took the funk hole directly across from the lieutenant. Charlie found a comfortable hole further down the trench, which was on the far side of another traverse. Hours later when the relief was completed and the battalion settled in, most of the men curled in their holes and struggled to sleep, serenaded by the white noise of the front: the whistle and thunder of falling shells, the crack of rifle fire, and the hiss of Very lights crossing the sky.

But there was no sleep for the Clarkes. As sergeants, they roamed the line, keeping tabs on their platoon, making sure all were accounted for, equipped, and ready should they be needed. The battalion was scheduled to man the trenches for only two days and the thought of a quick tour in this awful place bolstered their spirits, as did the warm sunlight that flooded the trenches the next day. The Bombers rose for morning stand-to, the dawn ritual when combatants on each side of no man's land lined the trenches awaiting a potential attack. They breakfasted on "extra rations" they had brought with them, mainly bread and jam. Then the Bombers, given no special assignment, either sunned themselves or tried to get some "badly needed rest."

Leo Clarke, nursing his fresh shoulder wound and aching from the punishment he had endured at Pozières Ridge, retreated to his bunk in the trench wall and tried to sleep. But the funk hole offered little comfort and he was in pain. And just as the night had been uneventful, the new day was fairly quiet, except for—as the war diary complained—"a brisk artillery duel" that lasted for hours and kept the men on their toes. Most of the shelling seemed to come from the Allied side, and the battalion recorded no casualties. When October 14 dawned, the men hoped that they would be relieved before nightfall, as promised. Another fine morning had broken, and Charlie had just begun the routine of another day in the trenches when a commotion echoed down the line. He rounded the nearest traverse to investigate and saw that a gaggle of senior officers from the Fourth Division, "with red tabs on their shoulders and brass on their caps," had invaded their trench.

The Red Tabs, as soldiers called the brass, chatted noisily and held up maps, which they bickered over. The Fourth Division, of course, was the reserve force that the defenders of Courcelette had been waiting for. Made up of the Tenth, Eleventh, and Twelfth Infantry Brigades, the division drew its recruits from across Canada. Among them were two Manitoba battalions: the Forty-Fourth Manitobans and the Seventy-Eighth Winnipeg Grenadiers. And, as it appeared, they were led by a coterie of noisy officers. The division's commander was, coincidentally, the Second Battalion's first leader, the "dashing, charming … self-promoter" David Watson who, according to a later historian, had lobbied for this "plum job." His intelligence officer, Captain Allan Aitken, was the keen son of a Scottish Presbyterian minister whose brother, Max, would later become the Fleet Street press baron, Lord Beaverbrook. Aitken's eagle-eyed observation of the German line led him to conclude that an enemy dressing station, protected by "at least two M.G. [Machine Gun] positions," was, in fact, a "Strong Point."

William St. Pierre Hughes commanded the division's Tenth Brigade. An old rebel fighter and lifelong militiaman, he also happened to be the brother of the minister of militia. Victor Odlum, a fearless front-line officer, Bible thumper, and non-drinker, whose temperance earned him the nickname "Old Lime Juice," commanded the Eleventh. Leading the Twelfth Brigade was a British aristocrat, Boer War vet, and former Reuters correspondent who went by the title Lord Brooke, perhaps to avoid being addressed by his Germanic-sounding real name, Leopold Greville. Which of these martinets, if any, numbered among the divisional staff crowding the Second Battalion trench is not clear. Charlie never identified them in his later writings, suggesting only that his former CO was not one of them. (He would have recognized Watson and commented if he had been present.) But Charlie edged close enough to the officers to realize they were debating the location of Regina Trench, which supposedly lay directly opposite this point in the line, although no landmarks other than a vague horizon of ruination were visible.

The commanders squinted at their maps and continued to argue. But Charlie grew concerned when the brass began to peer over the parapet with binoculars. Charlie knew that enemy sentries always watched for the flash of sunlight on glass lenses, because binoculars were used exclusively by officers, and officers were prime targets. In the past, lens flashes had brought on artillery fire. On this sleepy morning one could almost assume the German lookouts would not notice. So Charlie wasn't apprehensive until three of the officers actually climbed onto the parapet to study the German line.

Charlie stepped forward. "Sir, do you know you are in full view of the Germans?" he asked. But they shot him "filthy looks," and continued their reckless reconnaissance. Charlie knew from experience that they were in danger of an artillery strike, so he called Lieutenant Hoey. Hoey also warned the brass not to show themselves, but they ignored him as well. The officers soon finished their scouting expedition and then filed into Murray Avenue on their way back to headquarters. They had only just left the Second Battalion trench when the shells started to fall.

Charlie and the others (the platoon's runners and a new Bomber, Private Moore) were ready for it. They knew that the sight of brass hats above the parapet would invite a strafing. So they hunkered down or retreated to their funk holes. Leo, who had witnessed the officers' antics, was tucked in his shelf in the main trench wall when Charlie bolted for cover. By the time the first salvo exploded, Charlie was ensconced in his small bunker. But he knew from the violent shudder of the earth behind him that the strike had been "a direct hit" at the exact spot where the officers had exposed themselves, and a hit on the trench where his brother, Leo, had taken cover.

Charlie rolled out of the trench wall and staggered toward the explosion. When he rounded the corner traverse, he could barely see ahead of him. Smoke hung in the air and clumps of dirt fell from the sky. But through the haze it was clear the trench had collapsed and was filled high with earth. Then Charlie spotted a man limping away. It was Lieutenant Hoey, wounded, perhaps badly, hobbling at full speed to a dressing station.

"Where's Leo?" Charlie shouted.

"He's down the trench," Hoey called out over his shoulder. He was telling Charlie that Leo was already retreating down Murray Avenue toward the rear. But Charlie knew this was impossible. He had just seen Leo curled in his funk hole in a length of trench that was now completely filled with mud and clay. Charlie stumbled forward. The trench had imploded right up to the junction of Murray Avenue, and one of the Bombers, Private Moore, was buried up to his neck. His grime-covered head stuck up from the dirt like the top of a carrot, and his wide eyes were "staring in shock." Charlie clawed at the earth with his fists and managed to free Moore. Then he glanced around at the carnage becoming visible as the haze cleared. He could see the platoon's two young runners sprawled nearby. They weren't buried, but they were both dead—their skulls cracked open by either shrapnel or the concussion. There was no sign of Leo.

Charlie spotted a spade (ironically, a German one), grabbed it, and began shovelling at the spot where he dead-reckoned Leo had been hiding. Working the spade "like fury," he soon heard a clank, and knew the tool's blade had struck the metal of Leo's helmet. He tossed the spade and began moving soil with his fingers. Moments later, his brother's face took shape in the earth. Charlie cleared dirt away from his nose and mouth so that he could breathe. To his relief and delight, Leo's eyelids opened. His eyes, two white balls in this great mound of clay, flickered with recognition, and Leo smiled. Leo was alive, and conscious.

Charlie continued scraping and scooping away the dirt, stopping to cover Leo when the incoming shells spat up geysers of earth around them. Soon more rescuers arrived. A Bomber, Red Barrett, ran up, and helped clear away the last of the earth entombing Leo. Together, they lifted him from the hole they had dug around him and lowered him onto a stretcher that had been brought up, all the while using their bodies to shield him from the spray of dirt and debris. When he was safely on the litter, Charlie and Red ran Leo down Murray Avenue until they came to a stretch that was narrow and more secure, and where the barrage seemed lighter. They found a deep funk hole in the ditch wall and slipped Leo's stretcher onto it. Here they stayed until the artillery fire stopped. Charlie knew that a run for a dressing station would be suicidal while the shelling continued, and this moderately sheltered spot was the wisest place to wait it out. He sent for a medical officer and remained at his brother's side.

Charlie looked over Leo's damaged body. He stared into his brother's eyes and recalled how "boyish" and innocent Leo had looked when Charlie had first unearthed him. Ostensibly, Leo was whole and sound. All limbs were accounted for. There was no blood or open wound, and Leo, conscious and speaking, was in no noticeable pain. But Charlie knew instinctively that his brother was fading. Dying. Charlie had seen enough death to recognize the signs.

And so did Leo. He told Charlie to take his Colt revolver and his wallet from his pockets, instructing him to "spend his money on treats for the boys." They remained together until the shelling subsided two hours later, and it was safe to make a run to a dressing station. While they waited, the surviving Bombers appeared in the trench, one by one, as if drawn by some invisible force to their two sergeants. They huddled around Leo as family encircles a loved one in a hospital bed. Charlie chose his six "biggest and best men," and ordered them to carry Leo to the aid station. Although not the nearest facility, the Bombers decided to deliver Leo to the ambulance at Pozières Ridge, which was a larger medical facility and would have fewer wounded to treat. Charlie, of course, wanted to go along. But with Hoey absent and Leo wounded, he was the platoon's only leader. Ever the good soldier, he would remain at his post.

Charlie bid his brother goodbye and watched the six faithful Bombers bear Leo down the narrow, ugly slash in the Somme known as Murray Avenue.

THE LAST PARADE

Charlie Clarke, October 1916

After Leo was taken away, Charlie gathered together the surviving Bombers, and "kept close to our own part of the trench." They warmed themselves in the sunlight that filtered into their narrow ditch, and prayed there would be no more direct hits.

Their prayers were heard. No more Bombers fell that day. The Manitoba boys of the Eighth Battalion began arriving along the line in late afternoon, and by 10:35 P.M. they were in place. Officially relieved, the Second Battalion limped down Murray Avenue in a long column. The tour at the front had been brief, but exhausting. "We were tired," Charlie later admitted, "and still numb with the shock of loss."

The bulk of the Second Battalion headed for a reserve trench but Charlie slipped from the column, skirted the wreckage of Courcelette, and ran the six miles to the First Field Hospital at Pozières. There he found the squad of Bombers that had delivered Leo, but not Leo himself. His brother had been evacuated to a larger hospital. But how was he? The men didn't know much other than Leo had been unconscious when they staggered up to the hospital. His condition had been both serious and hopeful enough to warrant a transfer. Charlie absorbed the news. Leo was alive. This was something.

Charlie and the six men rejoined the Second Battalion in its reserve position at Candy Trench, just behind the line. The next morning, they led the column on its march toward its billets in Bouzincourt, a village of a few hundred souls nestled in ancient woods just northwest of the Somme. On their weary slog, the battalion wove through Albert with its great cathedral and the gilded statue of the Virgin above it. The Madonna and Christ child still dangled from the turret "in a despairing gesture," according to one soldier, but refused to end the war by falling to the ground. In fact, British commanders, determined that the war not end under any conditions other than their own, ordered army engineers to fasten the relic to the church. There it would stay until early 1918, when the British lost Albert and blew down the cathedral's steeple to keep this vantage point out of German hands. According to a British Tommy, one morning "when the smoke cleared after the explosion of one big shell the statue was missing." The war was out of the Virgin's hands. For the Second, entering Albert and leaving it was a sign. Although they didn't know it, the men were withdrawing from the Somme. Charlie and his comrades would never return, although something of the Second Battalion would remain in this gruesome place—namely, many of its best and noblest men (18 officers and 601 soldiers) who had been wounded or killed there. The maimed would carry the Somme's scars indefinitely. The dead would spend eternity either swallowed up by its mud or at rest in one of the plethora of cemeteries around Albert.

These casualties weighed heavily on the men as they marched away. "It was a sad journey," Charlie thought. As he marched Leo was in his thoughts, and the more he considered him, the more convinced Charlie became that Leo's grave wound had been evitable. "I felt his life in France had been just one narrow escape after another," he later wrote, as he took into account the numerous times Leo had been forced to leave the line due to illness or injury. Even more heartbreaking was the realization that Leo's last wound had been utterly avoidable. If he had not returned to the battalion as a walking wounded, he might still be in the care of doctors. "If he had only stayed in hospital," Charlie lamented.

But Charlie Clarke was not the only Second Battalion soldier ruing the past. For the outfit's commander, Lieutenant Colonel Swift, the Somme itself was regrettable, and he dismissed the campaign as a grind of "sudden downpours, knee-deep mud, long marches over narrow country roads, picturesque French villages, and always the Second Battalion … trudging doggedly along." But Swift took it as a matter of pride that his battalion had met all its challenges. Swift later wrote: "The Somme also reminds us that the Second were the first Canadian unit to go into the front line there and also the first to participate in an attack and to stage an attack."

From Bouzincourt, the Second Battalion marched to Warloy, La Vicogne, and to Montrelet. With each passing mile, Charlie was painfully aware of the "missing faces" from the Bombers' ranks. There were now only four men who had been original members of the platoon. The rest were replacements and transfers. A few served with the Bombers reluctantly, but even the originals were weary. "We tried to be proud and kept our heads up, but we were tired and sadly depleted," he said of his comrades. "The whole battalion was the same." Heavy losses had infused the men with a sense of fatalism. They grew to believe that they had little power to determine whether they would live or die. A man's fate was preordained,

Charlie believed. "If your name was on the shell, you would get it," he said. "C'est la guerre."

Such a shell had been etched with his brother's name, and Charlie knew that he had a duty to inform his parents. He resolved to write and comfort them as best he could. But there was little time as the battalion continued its advance north from Bernaville to Le Meillard, Frohen-le-Petit, and across the meandering Authie River into Frohen-le-Grand. They marched to Remaisnil, and spent the night in Barly on the outskirts of Picardy. They would soon pass into the region of Pas-de-Calais, leaving the Somme far behind. On October 22, the Bombers, looking "seedy" and drained, rose from their billets for the march to Frevent where First Division commander Currie awaited. The battalion fell in at 8 A.M., and Charlie had just taken his place at the head of the platoon when the adjutant officer, Captain Edmond O'Flynn, brought his horse alongside the Bombers, and called out to Acting Sergeant Clarke.

O'Flynn, a twenty-nine-year-old lawyer from Belleville, Ontario, dismounted, and Charlie approached. Then O'Flynn in a kind voice gave Charlie the news. It was news that changed everything. Charlie learned that his brother Leo had been conferred a great honour. He had been granted the Victoria Cross for his service in defending the Second Battalion's left flank at Pozières Ridge. Charlie, of course, was not completely surprised. He had always said Leo would distinguish himself. "Didn't I say there at Wulverghem," he later declared, "that the Second Battalion would be proud of him?"

And Charlie was not surprised by the other news that O'Flynn delicately imparted, even though his words brought him more pain than pride. They spoke a few more minutes, and then Charlie stumbled back to the ranks, taking his position at the head of the Bombers. The order was given to march and Charlie, feeling dizzy, led the platoon from the village of Barly, an otherwise forgettable commune in France that would be permanently etched in Charlie's memory.

In many ways, Charlie's war ended at that moment. There would be more marching, and fighting, and despair. Charlie Clarke would be one of the first Canadians to enter the line in front of an obscure stretch of high ground known as Vimy Ridge. He would see the bomber platoon disbanded, and would watch more friends die. But Barly was a watershed in his war. After leaving it, nothing would remain as it was. Even home would never be the same again.

PASSCHENDAELE

Robert Shankland, October 1917

The war changed men, and not just through death and maiming. As a later historian, characterizing Europe's next worldwide conflagration, wrote: "War, that merciless revealer of character, uncloaked these men as precisely as a prism flays open a beam of light to reveal the inner spectrum." Some men buckled and broke while others discovered unsuspected reserves of strength and initiative. Many soldiers discovered themselves in the mayhem and violence, and Lieutenant Bob Shankland of the Forty-Third Battalion, the diminutive, soft-spoken, and earnest young Scot who lived at 733 Pine Street, was one such man.

When Bob Shankland shipped to Europe in June 1915 wearing the *Hielan* bonnet of the Winnipeg Camerons, he was officially a member of the Forty-Third Infantry Battalion. And he thrived in the company of Canadian patriots and Scottish expatriates just like himself. Smart, thorough, and energetic, he rose through the ranks while in training in England and was tested in battle shortly after the Forty-Third Battalion set foot in France in 1916. Sergeant

Shankland led a squad of stretcher-bearers into the conflagration that would be remembered as the Battle of Sanctuary Wood. His boldness and initiative earned him a Distinguished Conduct Medal. Bob displayed similar pluck and leadership at the Camerons' two actions at the Somme, first at Zollern Graben on September 20 and then in the attack on Regina Trench on October 8. As they had been at Sanctuary Wood, Bob and the Forty-Third Battalion were neighbours to Charlie at the Somme. The two men might have passed each other along Murray Avenue or in the rubble of Courcelette, but they never knowingly met. Just as they never met before the war, when Bob Shankland lived on Pine Street, just a few doors away from the wind-pelted, family house where Charlie grew up. But as with Charlie and Leo, Bob Shankland's stature grew with every engagement with the enemy. By the end of 1916, he was a lieutenant.

The Somme had been as devastating for the Winnipeg Camerons as for Charlie's Second Battalion. In the October attack on Regina Trench, the Highlanders charged across no man's land only to find that their artillery had failed to destroy the German wire. Hundreds of men became tangled in barbs and were cut down by enemy fire. Lieutenant Colonel Robert MacDonald Thomson, the old warhorse who had co-founded the Camerons and had served as its only leader, was wounded in the fiasco. Dispatched to a dressing station by ambulance, the forty-seven-year-old commander was expected to live until a shell landed on his horse-drawn carriage, killing him and an irreplaceable piece of the Winnipeg Camerons' past. Thomson's brother-in-law and the battalion's chaplain, Charles Gordon, presided over his funeral in a "soldier's cemetery just outside of Albert." Most of the other members of the Forty-Third Battalion who bade Thomson goodbye were Winnipeg Scots who had worked, played, and worshipped together at the same kirk back home. They were, wrote Padre Gordon, "the pathetic little remnant of the battalion which had been the pride of their colonel's heart."

After the Somme, William Grassie, an Aberdeen-born realtor and investment manager from Winnipeg, took command of the Forty-Third. The Camerons were too depleted to play a leading role in the battle for Vimy Ridge in April 1917. However, after being bolstered by replacements and brought back to fighting form, they joined the Allied offensive that would later be known as the Third Battle of Ypres. Launched on July 31, 1917, the offensive revealed how Commander-in-Chief Haig still sought the breakthrough—and the enemy collapse—that had eluded him throughout the war. But attacks by the British Second and Fifth Armies in August brought neither a breakthrough nor progress, despite the extraordinary expenditure of some four million shells against the Germans. By the end of September, Haig had exhausted his reserves, but remained undaunted. The "enemy is faltering," he assured subordinates, "and a good decisive blow might lead to decisive results." On October 12, he threw New Zealand and Australian troops against the German line, and despite the formidable toughness of these soldiers, they were chewed up and severely mauled. It was the turn of the Canadians. The Corps commander was now Arthur Currie, whose leadership and tactical insight earned him the ultimate promotion when General Byng was elevated to lead the British Third Army. Although new to this command, Currie knew his mind and had little confidence in the strategic soundness of Third Ypres. Currie too was later accused of butchering his own troops, and it is true that Currie was not averse to sending his men to their death. During the war's dark hours he would caution his soldiers that "there was to be no retreat for Canadians, and that, if need be, we should fall where we stood." But he abhorred wasting lives and he viewed Third Ypres as a pointless exercise. His intellect, which one historian would blithely describe as a "precise, school master's mind," told him the attack on their assigned target, the pulverized Flanders village of Passchendaele, would bring about sixteen thousand Canadian casualties, and he protested at the waste. But Haig remained adamant. Currie prepared for the attack by taking every step he could conceive of to avoid disaster—to no avail. As Currie predicted, thousands would die in this battle. More would be wounded, and few would escape without a scrape. Lieutenant Bob Shankland was about to face the greatest test of his life.

That test began early on the morning of October 26, 1917. Shankland and one hundred eighty soldiers of the Forty-Third Battalion lay sprawled on the muddy banks of Ravebeck Creek awaiting the offensive's zero hour, which was scheduled for 5:40 A.M. The Cameron men had shivered and brooded in the trenches all night, although there were no real entrenchments to speak of. As one Tommy pointed out, the front mainly consisted of "a series of shell-holes that had been reinforced with sandbags so you could hide inside them." The men urinated in empty cans and shivered through the worst weather to befall Flanders in decades. "It had rained and rained and rained," a British lieutenant reported, and the downpour transformed an already inhospitable landscape into what an artilleryman called "a sea of filthy oozing mud." The muck insinuated its way into everything. "It was mud, mud, everywhere," the artilleryman declared, "mud in the trenches, mud in front of the trenches, mud behind the trenches." Rifles became clogged with it. Men were drenched in it. The muck drowned wounded men, swallowed artillery pieces, and became a dangerous and debilitating new element the soldiers had to contend with. Corps commander Currie understood the unique dangers the sludge posed to his men, and to combat it ordered the construction of roads, duckboard paths, and artillery gun pits. Currie was worried that he couldn't fight both the extreme weather and the Germans. But as historian Tim Cook pointed out, he tried "at least to give the infantry a fighting chance."

On the morning of October 26, a fighting chance was all Bob Shankland and his platoon could hope for as they huddled in the doubtful shelter of the crude front line and awaited the order to attack. Soaked and shivering, some of Shankland's men were fortified by their last rum ration. Bob may have gained energy by nibbling the fudge candy stowed in a tin box that he carried in a jacket pocket. A gift from his old friend Annie Ritchie, the sweets were a fine souvenir to bring into battle. He had left his childhood home of Ayr and journeyed to Canada with Annie's brother George and then shared the Ritchie house on Winnipeg's Pine Street when Annie lived there, and the other Ritchie siblings who followed. If Annie Ritchie, twelve years older than Bob, wasn't a surrogate mother to him, she was certainly a sister. Her thoughtfulness in mailing Bob fudge candy proved her affection.

Annie might not have recognized Bob Shankland now. He had worked in Winnipeg as the cashier in a dairy. Now, on this October morning, two years after they had said goodbye, he was an officer and decorated war hero, caked with the bloody grime of the Ypres salient and focussed like a rifle's sight on the battalion's objective in the upcoming battle: a hill adjoining Passchendaele Ridge known as Bellevue Spur. The job given to Shankland and the Winnipeg Camerons was brutal in its simplicity. Moving in concert with the Fourth Canadian Mounted Rifles and the Fifty-Eighth Battalion, they were instructed to storm up the slope of the spur and clear the enemy from the high ground. But conquering this prominence posed a unique challenge. The Germans at Passchendaele were not defending a uniform line as they had along the Somme. They now were employing a different approach.

By 1917, Imperial Germany had a new Chief of Staff. The old Prussian war horse, Erich von Falkenhayn, was cashiered after the German army's failed offensive at Verdun in 1916, which cost the Germans almost one hundred fifty thousand dead. Falkenhayn's fall made way for the two rising stars of the German war effort, Paul von Hindenburg and Erich Ludendorff, whose success in the Eastern Front against Russia had made them public icons and earned for them the confidence of the kaiser. Hindenburg, the senior partner, was promoted to chief of staff in late August 1916, and Ludendorff joined him in Berlin to oversee the war effort. The defences at Passchendaele reflected Hindenburg and Ludendorff's new defensive strategy. The bulk of the German infantry would be kept in reserve, poised and ready, while the approach and the hill itself were guarded, not by entrenchments, but by a series of fortified, concrete pillboxes. These bunkers, which sheltered machine gun crews and infantry, were strategically positioned so that each one stood in the protective line of fire of another. According to one soldier, they loomed menacingly "like still, gray, humped raccoons watching and waiting for anything to move." Bob Shankland and the Forty-Third Battalion massed on the right flank of the Canadian line, with the Fourth Mounted Rifles on their left. Directly ahead of them lay fourteen or more of these concrete emplacements. Currie had wished for his men a fighting chance during their day at Passchendaele. They had barely that. As October 26 dawned, the Canadians shivered and prayed along the Allied lane and contemplated the coming fight of their lives.

At 5:40 A.M., the whistles blew and the Winnipeg Camerons rose up from their shallow cover and leapt into the field. For many, the charge was like running into a swamp or a great shallow lake.

Some men sank up to their waist in dung-tinged muck, but they plodded forward just behind an advancing artillery barrage spat out by the vast arsenal of guns supporting the attack. Currie was a proponent of the creeping barrage, and according to witnesses, the dance between artillery and infantry worked, despite the sea of mud the men plodded through. "Men advanced with such practiced skill," reported a soldier with the Fiftieth Battalion, "as to be almost touching the hem of the steel cloak as it alternately moved, and halted, and moved forward again." The artillery, said this soldier, an Albertan named Victor Wheeler, rang like a symphony, "a polyphony of carefully orchestrated sounds, like the majestic Ninth Symphony of Beethoven, even more overpowering when performed on the battlefield."

The enemy lashed back with a barrage of shells that screeched like Valkyries as they fell. Ironically, the only protection from the rain of metal was provided by the sea of mud, which swallowed some projectiles whole and cushioned the blast and shrapnel spray of others. Exploding shells drove the sludge up in fountains. But shells and mud were far from the worst of it. Enemy machine gunners in the pillboxes and enemy snipers nestled on the ridge rained down fire as the Canadians approached. Headshot soldiers died before falling. Wounded men drowned in the sludge. According to a later report in the Winnipeg *Tribune*, the men braved bullets and shrapnel and struggled onto the face of the ridge just to escape the "very awfulness of the situation" on the low ground.

The Mounted Rifles' attack on the left bogged down, but the Camerons fared better. The Forty-Third crossed the swampy field, mounted the slope of the spur, and was advancing toward the crest when they marched into the sights of three German pillboxes. Fire from these bunkers was concentrated and devastating. Those who were not cut down into neat windrows slipped into shell holes and depressions on the side of the hill. The Camerons had attacked in two waves: Companies B and C leading the surge; Company A and Bob Shankland's D followed. The first wave, the kilties of B and C, took the brunt of the pillbox metal, but after shaking off the shock and licking their wounds, the survivors soldiered on. C Company managed to edge around the flank of one of the nests, and an enterprising sergeant in B Company led an attack against the other two, clearing them of the enemy and neutralizing them as a threat. By the time the two companies reached the top of the spur, they had been reduced to twenty exhausted and wounded riflemen and one machine gunner. They took cover in a vacated trench just ahead of an enemy reserve line, which was coursing and flexing with furious German infantrymen. The enemy reserves rained fire on the Canadians, which were barely hanging on when Bob Shankland and about twenty survivors of D Company, including a machine gunner, scrambled to the top of the hill and joined the diehards in the captured trench.

Shankland was shocked by what had become of the battalion. Artillery, machine-gun, and rifle fire had reduced it to a ragtag, limping, but fiercely angry unit of about forty men from three separate companies, and apart from Bob, not one officer had made it to the top of the spur. Now this small force faced hundreds of German infantrymen who were laying down fire from their trenches and adjoining bunkers and clearly preparing for a counterattack to drive the Camerons back down the slope. They were facing annihilation and the prudent move would have been for Shankland to withdraw his men to a more defensible position and await reinforcements, particularly from C Company. But if the Forty-Third gave up their position on the spur, the objective and the day would be lost, and the survivors might be wiped out as well. The offensive faced failure. The attacks by the Mounted Rifles on the far left, and the Fifty-Eighth Battalion on the far right had stalled, and along some stretches of the Canadian front, the attackers had been pushed back to their jumping-off line. Now in this trench on the top of the spur, Shankland and his forty comrades were the remnants of the Highlanders. They represented the offensive's last best hope.

From Bob Shankland's perspective, hope was far from lost. His men, though few and shaken, were well stocked with ammunition and most were in fighting form. The fact that the Germans had not attacked their position on the spur immediately revealed, perhaps, the enemy's uncertainty. They didn't know how many Canadians they faced. Shankland understood poker well enough to seize on this advantage. He knew that the hand he held—the size of his force—was not as strong as the Germans feared it was. But he did not order a retreat. He had every able rifleman and both machine gunners lay down a vicious field of fire on the enemy trench. As it turned out, his timing was fortuitous: a line of Germans chose that moment to emerge from their position and storm forward to counterattack. The Camerons' wall of metal beat them back and may have fooled them into thinking that their thunderous defence was greater than just forty guns. Bob Shankland ordered the men to continue their fire, but he knew that they couldn't hold this position much longer. They needed ammunition and reinforcements, and with German shells pounding the approach behind them, he also knew that moving up reserves through this deluge would be nearly impossible. They might lose most of the reserves just getting up the hill.

But Bob had noticed an anomaly in the course of the barrage. As intense and relentless as it was on much of the slope, enemy shells did not appear to be falling on the left side of the spur, near a cluster of houses designated Waterloo Farm. This gap was either an oversight unspotted by enemy observers or an opening for German infantry. Whatever its inspiration, the hole created a tunnel up the hill for reinforcements. Shankland told his men to hold the position. And then he scrambled out of the trench and ran down the hill, probably following the shell-free route to test whether it was, indeed, clear of fire. He landed at the foot of the spur alive and unwounded and then waded through the mud to the Forty-Third Battalion Headquarters, where the Camerons' commander, Lieutenant Colonel Grassie, paced his bunker, depressed and confused by the day's terrible events. As far as Grassie could tell, the attack was failing bitterly. He would later call the initial phase of the battle the "worst show we had had," a stunning indictment, given the horrific "show" they had endured at the Somme. But when Bob Shankland, caked in mud, presented himself at HQ, he brought news that all was not lost. In his "broad Highland brogue," Bob Shankland reported that forty Camerons were installed at the summit of the spur and tenaciously holding their own. Although Grassie had to be heartened that stalwarts had reached the crest, this was not exactly great news. Indeed, the report was sobering. These men could not hold out much longer against German infantry and the network of enemy bunkers that supported it. The good news, the reason that Shankland had braved sniper fire and errant shells to report in person, was that a unique opportunity had presented itself: the artillery gap on the left side of the spur offered a chance that could, if quickly exploited, alter the battle's course. If reserves moved immediately, they could reach the summit and use the Forty-Third's position on the crest as a new jumping-off point for the offensive. Grassie was amazed. This lowly lieutenant had just presented him with a second chance. Grassie later declared: "Shankland converted what looked like a bad day into victory."

Grassie issued orders to get reserves to the summit by way of the left slope. According to one account, Bob led a reserve force up the hillock. According to others, he forged ahead alone, anxious to return to the summit as quickly as possible, in order to oversee the defence of the Forty-Third's new line. When he reached the top, he found that his men were still hanging on. But the situation had deteriorated. The Germans continued to pour on fire and had made several attempts to range out and encircle the Forty-Third's position. In each attack, the flanking parties rounding the hilltop were spotted early and picked off. But the Winnipeg Scots were in danger of being enveloped. Shankland knew that reserves were on the way. The only question was, would they arrive in time?

Grassie had started the battle that morning with the Fifty-Second Battalion, fellow Canadian Scots from the shores of Lake Superior, earmarked as a reserve force. As soon as Shankland made his report, Grassie ordered the Fifty-Second to be deployed and passed on intelligence that the left slope was open. The Ontarians leapt into action. Acting Captain Christopher O'Kelly, also a Winnipegger, led a reserve force into the field and mounted the spur. O'Kelly, just twenty-one years old, was young to be in command during such a crucial battle, but he had earned his stripes. When the war broke out, O'Kelly had been a student at Winnipeg's St. John's College, an old Anglican school that dated back to the epoch of the Red River settlement. Instead of militia experience, he brought a sharp intelligence and loyalty to the army when he joined up in 1915, first with the Winnipeg Rifles of the 144th Battalion, and later with the Ontarians of the Fifty-Second Battalion, where he was ultimately transferred. Infused with commitment, daring, and a God-given ability to lead, O'Kelly had already earned a Military Cross and a captaincy by the time he and his men scrambled the crest of Bellevue Spur, tasked with salvaging a Canadian offensive that teetered on the cusp of disaster.

And O'Kelly and his men arrived just in time. When they reached the spur's summit, the Forty-Third was still hunkered down in its trench, exchanging fire with a line of German infantry and as many as six enemy pillboxes ranged across the hill and adjoining ridge. What they hadn't yet noticed was another flanking party of Germans edging around the prominence to the Canadian left. O'Kelly and his men opened fire on this force, breaking them up and driving them back to the German line. Then the men of the Fifty-Second turned their wrath on the pillboxes. According to the *Official History of the Canadian Army in the First World War*, O'Kelly and his fighters worked southward and engaged the bunkers one at a time. The bulk of O'Kelly's force laid down a "diversion with their rifle grenades and Lewis guns" while a handful of soldiers circled around behind and cleared each concrete hut with grenades. They began their assaults at around noon and before long they had overrun the six pillboxes and taken an astonishing one hundred prisoners.

As O'Kelly and his men neutralized the bunkers and their machine-gun nests, Bob Shankland led a charge against German infantry. He and his Camerons rose from their position and stormed forward, wiping the enemy from the spur and trans-forming a potential fiasco into a Canadian victory that would soon become legendary. The battle had been desperate. The Forty-Sixth Battalion on the right had fought tenaciously right up to the Ravebeek Swamp, where they established a defensive position. On the far left, the Fourth Mounted Rifles had rallied and captured another ruined forest called Wolf Copse and bolstered their end of the line. The official history described the Fourth CMR's ordeal as payback—"a rebuke for Sanctuary Wood." But like everywhere along the Canadian front, its soldiers ultimately won through inspired acts of almost inconceivable selflessness.

At one point, when the Fourth Mounted Rifles were stalled in the mud and raked by murderous machine-gun fire, a "feisty" private from Owen Sound, Ontario, named Tommy Holmes, who looked even younger than his nineteen years and "wore a perpetual grin on his face," single-handedly charged through the muck at a line of enemy gun nests, and managed to get within a grenade throw of each, handily eliminating the crews with skillful bomb tosses. History has not recorded how many youthful summers Tommy spent on a country baseball diamond, honing his throwing arm. However, in Flanders that day, his accuracy and verve were astounding. At one point, his grenade cache spent, he raced back to his stunned comrades along the main line for more bombs, which they readily gave him. He then returned to the field and continued his solitary battle, this time capturing a German pillbox and nineteen reeling gunners. A witness called his rampage "unadulterated bravery." Holmes later said: "I thought everybody did that sort of thing."

Enough did exactly that sort of thing to win the day. Captain O'Kelly and his Lake Superior Scots continued ranging out along the spur just below Passchendaele and seeking out enemy to destroy. Over eighteen hours of attacks, forays, ambushes, and raids, O'Kelly and his troops captured a total of 284 enemy soldiers, and overran twenty-one machine-gun nests. Bellevue Spur was fairly won, as was Passchendaele village a week later. The cost of the battle was steep, 15,634 Canadian casualties, which was roughly what corps commander Arthur Currie had predicted when asked by Haig to join the fray at Third Ypres. The victory almost wiped out the Forty-Third Battalion. The Winnipeg Camerons had attacked the spur with slightly fewer than five hundred men. At the end of the first day, approximately one hundred fifty men were left standing. These numbers, although jarring, scarcely encompass the horror of a battle in which men literally drowned in the sludgy earth or were eviscerated by fire as intense as any preceding Great War engagement. One veteran called it "the most ghastly attack in which I ever participated." But as intense as it was, the offensive's ultimate success had hinged on the exertions of a handful of men.

For their role in bringing about victory, both O'Kelly, the Anglican student, and Holmes, the smiling kid from Owen Sound, were nominated for the Victoria Cross. But the first VC nomination went to the day's foremost hero, Bob Shankland, the one-time cashier from Pine Street, Winnipeg. He had not so much initiated the victory on Bellevue Spur as he had imagined it. Trapped in a trench on the objective's crest with a bedraggled band of survivors, Shankland had possessed the acumen to glimpse opportunity where a sober man would have seen only annihilation. Perhaps, as Shankland said years later, the cunning card player in him took hold and told him that in a pitched battle a good bluff could be as decisive as any weapon. Or perhaps Shankland had simply been a true Cameron who had resolved that the Forty-Third "can never yield." But whatever the inspiration, Lieutenant Colonel Grassie was clear about the result. "It was undoubtedly Shankland's good work that won the day," he later stated, and recommended him for the Empire's most prestigious award for bravery.

Bob Shankland survived the battle and accepted the Victoria Cross in person. But only he knew how close he had come to perishing on October 26. Late on that day, after the Germans on the spur's summit had been killed, captured, or driven back, Bob hobbled off in the direction of a dressing station. He was bleeding from a gunshot wound. He had been hit directly in the chest during combat, and when he stuck his fingers inside his tunic, he felt wetness. But after probing the laceration, he realized he wasn't bleeding badly. His breathing was even and he seemed not to be succumbing to shock. Bob understood why he wasn't dying when he pulled from his pocket the tin box of fudge that he had been carrying, a gift from his surrogate sister, Annie Ritchie. The box was now marked by a gaping hole, a bullet or sliver of shrapnel having glanced off the tin. The projectile had wounded Bob, but not mortally, as might have been the case if the tin box were not in the way. If any soldier in the trenches understood the importance of home, it was Bob Shankland on the evening of the Canadian victory of Bellevue Spur. For him, Annie Ritchie's Winnipeg kitchen, four thousand six hundred miles away as the crow flies, was not far away at all. It was close enough to save him.

And home received word of Bob Shankland's exploits soon enough. His VC was officially bestowed in an audience with King George V on December 1917. The editor of the Manitoba *Free Press* learned of the news by wire and ran the story in the paper's December 22 edition. The reporter described Bob's feats at Passchendaele, how "he rallied the remnants of his own platoon and men of other companies, disposed them so as to command ground in front and inflicted heavy casualties upon retreating enemy." It described how he "dispersed a counter-attack" and enabled "supporting troops," commanded by fellow Winnipegger Christopher O'Kelly, to mount the summit and join in the battle. But most importantly, the *Free Press* quoted the passage from the citation that captured the true essence of his feat: "His courage and splendid example inspired all ranks and coupled with his great gallantry and skill, undoubtedly saved a very critical situation."

Annie Ritchie, reading Bob Shankland's VC citation in Winnipeg, knew him too well to be surprised. But she may have been shocked by the sight of the dignified man wearing a captain's "glistening" insignia who stepped from the troop train at Winnipeg's CPR station on March 24, 1919. The date was less than two years after the Battle for Bellevue Spur had been fought and won, and now the survivors of that battle—the Winnipeg Camerons of the Forty-Third Battalion—had returned home. In response, the city, according to the Winnipeg *Tribune*, went wild. Declared the paper: "Whistles shrieked, bells jangled, and thousands cheered." The welcome was jubilant and thunderous, but in terms of intensity and pure happiness, the collective response paled in comparison to the warmth of each individual greeting between a soldier and his mother, wife, or child. "The scenes of reunion were indescribable," wrote one witness. "Women laughed hysterically, and tears coursed down their faces as they embraced their dear ones and held them tightly, as if afraid that they would be torn from them again." In the first moments after the men and their families were rejoined, "a strange quiet settled down over the station." The pause was the city uttering a gasp of relief and surprise. From the station, the men paraded through Winnipeg in a "cold rain" that they happily ignored (no Manitoba downpour, no matter how frigid, could equal Flanders in misery) and one returned soldier spoke for all when he quipped: "I wouldn't give a hoot if it was hailing brickbats. We're home again and that's what counts."

Wearing their steel soup-bowl helmets and toting field weapons, they marched into the auditorium of the Board of Trade Building on Main Street, which had been transformed for the occasion into "a mass of color [with] flags of all nations, bunting and flowers." A Union Jack, as immense as a battleship's standard, draped the wall ahead of a platform where seats had been set out for battalion officers, local politicians, and VIPs. Among these dignitaries, recorded the Winnipeg *Tribune*, "Capt. Robert Shankland, V.C., also occupied a seat of honor."

For those like Annie Ritchie who had known Bob before, gazing at him on that podium was a heady experience. Like so many other men in that room, he was no longer what he had been. Bob Shankland could go back to being a cashier at the Crescent Creamery dairy. Indeed, many of these men planned to return to their old lives as farmers, clerks, carpenters, bricklayers, railroad men, streetcar drivers, police officers, and, of course, family men. But, like Bob Shankland, they were now different. In many cases, they were scarred and hollow, nurturing traumas they would carry with them for the rest of their lives. But in the best of cases they were substantially greater than they had been in 1914. And every soldier who returned home on Bob Shankland's train, and the trains that arrived before and after, understood that they and their world had been transformed.

HOME

Charlie Clarke, December 1918

Charlie Clarke certainly understood that the world had changed when his train pulled into the CPR station in Winnipeg four months earlier. Like so many other survivors, Charlie had been away a long time. It was six weeks shy of four years since he had left the same station for the battlefields of Europe. Four years.

The time away might have seemed longer to Charlie; so much had happened since he had left. A world war had been fought and won. An armistice had been signed between the Allies and the Central Powers of Imperial Germany and Austro-Hungary, and an hour before noon on November 11 (the eleventh hour of the eleventh day of the eleventh month), the war had officially ended. Now twenty-three-year-old Charlie Clarke was home, and his family—his father, Harry, his mother, Rosetta, and his brothers, sisters, and friends from the neighbourhood—were gathered on the platform to meet him. For Charlie, his homecoming was filled with "many tender moments," as his long-suffering parents rejoiced in his return, and marvelled at the subtle but telling changes in him.

Charlie had left as an innocent teenager. No innocence marked him now. He had seen, endured, and survived things that would take him and his fellow veterans a lifetime to make sense of. Although inexplicable, these trials were subtly etched onto Charlie's young face, forged into his lean form, and as readily recognized as any scar to those who knew and loved him best.

Charlie's father Harry eventually asked about Leo. Whenever he summoned memories of his brother, Charlie's thoughts returned to Barly, that sleepy French village situated a hard five-day march from the Somme. While billeted at Barly, Charlie had been pulled from the ranks by the battalion adjutant and informed that his brother, a newly recognized hero of the Empire, had died of his wounds.

After being crushed by the collapsing trench just outside Courcelette, Leo had been carried by stretcher to the medical station at Pozières. He was then bundled into an ambulance train and sent to the No. 1 General Hospital in the coastal city of Etretat. During that interminable trip, Leo had shared a rail car with his wounded officer, Lieutenant Hoey. They barely spoke. Leo, Hoey later recalled, was in "terrible agony all the time." When they arrived at the field hospital, he was "very weak, restless, and groaning." Although conscious, Leo had difficulty speaking to the attending doctors and nurses, and a medical inspection confirmed what Charlie had determined on the battlefield, that Leo's "lower limbs [were] completely paralyzed." That first night in Etretat, Leo rested, "passing a fair night with some sleep." He awoke early, and according to hospital staff, he was restless and even spoke. But the next morning, his skin took on a bluish hue as his body, for reasons not yet clear to medical staff, became starved for oxygen. Leo rapidly grew weaker and, according to his doctor, "much worse." Then at 11 A.M. on October 19, 1916, Leo Clarke died. He was twenty-three. That same day, the British army announced that Leo had been awarded the Victoria Cross.

Perhaps because of Leo's stature as a VC recipient, the hospital performed a post-mortem examination and found "blood everywhere" within his chest cavity, which of course indicated severe internal injuries, and great damage to his lungs. As Charlie had feared, Leo's wounds had been mortal. "I felt that this was the end," he wrote after inspecting Leo's broken body shortly after he was wounded. "I couldn't see him getting over this." And so, despite Charlie's frantic efforts to save him, Leo never truly had any hope of surviving. He was buried in the village's main churchyard, not far from the hospital. By the end of the war, his body would rest alongside those of 546 other Allied soldiers.

Ironically, Harry Clarke in Winnipeg had been the first family member to learn of Leo's death. He received a cable with the grim news and immediately wired his brother Arthur in Hertfordshire. Had Arthur heard from Charlie? Did he know what could have happened? Charlie learned of his brother's death later, the announcement travelling slowly, as it struggled to catch up to the Second Battalion on the march. Notwithstanding his earlier forebodings, it had been a shock to hear the news from Captain O'Flynn. But the officer had been kind. After informing him of Leo's death and his Victoria Cross, which was news the adjutant probably hoped would be consoling, O'Flynn asked Charlie if he preferred to forgo marching and ride on the supply wagons. Charlie declined with thanks, saying, "If I march with the Bombers, I'll be among friends and pals. It will be better for me."

As the Bombers' only sergeant, Charlie took his place at the head of the platoon and led the march from the village. He was surrounded by comrades, but desperately alone. He grieved for his brother and agonized for his parents. He resolved to write them as soon as he could. Barely three hours later, while the men ate their lunch in a clearing near the road, he discovered that they already knew. When mail was issued, Charlie received a letter from his Uncle Arthur, explaining how his father had wired him, pleading for details about Leo. Charlie answered his uncle, telling him everything he knew. He would do the same in a letter to his father. And apart from that, he realized, he had no option but to keep marching. "There was nothing else I could do," he later reflected. "Soldiers were losing brothers somewhere every day. That was war."

Charlie and the Second Battalion wound their way north, passing a solid "stream of supplies and fresh troops" headed in the opposite direction. These men and materials were destined for the cauldron of the Somme while the Second Battalion was bound for the salient, which didn't seem to bother the boys. Perhaps, after a season of horror and loss on the Somme, a tour of Ypres was almost a relief. But in truth, Charlie had witnessed so much loss that the endless cycle of war was becoming clear to him. When they skirted the tiny village of Houdain, eighty kilometres south-west of Ypres, they passed a pocked and devastated building that predated the destruction beginning in 1914. The building had been ravaged during the Franco-Prussian war of 1870. "It seemed strange," Charlie would later reflect, "that disaster and ruins had been left from so long ago." War, death, grief, and ruin, it was now clear, were perpetual. The only way to escape the cycle was to survive, and eke out as much satisfaction as one could during the time remaining in a man's life.

When the Bombers billeted in "Extra Cushy"—Estrée-Cauchy on maps—Charlie and the boys had been on the march for days. "We were wet," he declared, "and tired and muddy, but not down-hearted." Charlie was, after all, alive, which was for a soldier in

France in late 1916 a gift. Charlie, his good friend Bill Roe, and fellow Bomber Freddie Harrison slipped from their billets and hitched a ride on military transports to the bigger town of Bruay to forage for a friendly *estaminet*, and the inevitable heaping plates of chips and eggs. They arrived to find the city pleasingly devoid of other soldiers and, for one evening, they escaped the war. In a clear affirmation of life, they marched into a photography studio and commissioned a group portrait. With the grime of the Somme still on their boots, the three friends stared pensively into the camera's lens. Of the three young men, Bill Roe looked the most solemn, and Fred Harrison, probably anticipating a drink and hot meal, the most cheerful. Charlie's expression, though far from cheery, was nonetheless hopeful. Life was too precious for an afternoon in Bruay to be squandered on sadness. He would not be downhearted.

He would be a leader.

With no bombing officer appointed or planned, Charlie assumed command of the platoon, and a short time later was ordered to accompany a pair of the battalion's senior officers on a horseback reconnaissance. In the Great War, officers still travelled on steeds, and in a nod to Charlie's reputation as a front-line fighter, he was brought by his commanders to inspect the trenches and bomb depots of the battalion's next posting—broken ground soon to be considered sacred. "We then went down the road to the floor of the valley that led to the village of Souchez, which was just a pile of rubble," he later recalled. "Then onto the path of trench mats that led to the Zouave Valley and onto Death Valley." Finally, they arrived at their destination. "There in front of us was Vimy Ridge! We were probably the first Canadians to see this—the sight of Vimy rising high before us with Notre Dame de Lorette rising almost at right angles over to the left."

Charlie and the battalion held the line ahead of Vimy in the autumn of 1916, many months before the offensive and victory that would make history and forge a new identity for Canada on the world stage. Despite the short life expectancy of bombing platoon commanders, Charlie would live to participate in this offensive, albeit in a support role. The decision was made to pull Charlie from the line and install him as a bombing instructor at the Brigade Training School at Château de la Haie. The tactics of the war were changing. Grenades were being introduced to the general infantry and seasoned grenadiers were needed to train the men. From the brigade school at the château, Charlie became the brigade bombing sergeant and oversaw a program that schooled all personnel in the finer points of bombing. Charlie even instructed headquarters staff, "who used to avoid our men at all costs if we came around carrying a bag of bombs!" As a result, "the war was to go on for two more years," he would later note, "but I did not see a great deal of the Front Line." There were exceptions. One, of course, was Vimy Ridge, the great victory in which one hundred thousand soldiers of the Canadian Corps swept over and seized this redoubt in a series of pitched battles, in April 1917. Charlie would remember Vimy as a collage of images, or what he called "vignettes": the daffodils "pushing up through the snow" in a moonlit clearing, the German dead stacked like cordwood along the road to Fresnoy, and a German pilot drifting to earth under a silk canopy after an air duel over "9 Elms." Not all his memories were horrible. There were the

fine baths we had at Noeux-le-Mines, white tiled shower rooms, lots of hot water. The little old lady I was billeted with who gave me my first taste of horsemeat. The shell that landed in the horse lines in the village square, and all the housewives with their baskets and big knives cutting up the dead horses before the smoke had cleared

away. The Estaminet at Bully-Grenay, the blond at
Gouy-Servins, the young farm girl Juliet at Barlin, Are
you going to marry Juliet, Sergeant?

These vignettes softened the true legacy of Vimy, which for
him was anything but glorious. What Charlie Clarke held close
to his heart when he remembered Vimy Ridge was its dear and
dire cost—the 13,477 Canadians killed and maimed there. Vimy's
heritage "is the memory of our comrades," he later wrote, "who
left their blood, and a good many their lives there in the mud and
shell holes that were soon to be covered with the snow that fell
making everything look so clean, and brought out the Daffodils
that bloomed in abundance in the clearings around Farbus Woods."

After Vimy, the other great effort Charlie joined was the
crossing of the Canal du Nord at Nord-Pas-de-Calais in 1918, a
preliminary attack on a strong point in the German line during
the last great Allied campaign of the war—the Hundred Days.
Ironically, given that the end was so near, Charlie incurred his first
wound at Canal du Nord, a shrapnel injury that put him out of the
show for good. But, in many ways, Charlie's war had really come to
an end in 1916. His brother's death had been a closing, of course.
But if war for soldiers has always been a struggle among comrades
for whom their devotion and allegiance truly lay, Charlie's war
came to a close when he bade goodbye to the Bombers. And true to
their history, the platoon parted with a bang. Their last gathering
was on Christmas 1916.

They were in billets in the village of Burton, near Bruay, and
had resolved to organize a special Christmas dinner. There was
much to celebrate. There was still no end in sight for the war, but
the Bombers had survived the Somme, and this alone was reason
to give thanks. Furthermore, a circle of Bomber originals was now

back together, no longer separated by wounds or transfers. Charlie's old friends Billy Roe, Fred Tyo, the farm boy Dougie Ledgerwood (whom they called "Big Dolly"), Winnipegger Harold "Chinky" Keeling, and Little Freddie Harrison were all on hand. Present in spirit were all the absent friends, the comrades and leaders they had fought beside and watched die. But for this dinner, the old-timers did not dwell on their losses. They tore open the parcels from home and distributed the delicacies—mainly a "good supply" of Christmas pudding. Then battalion cook Billy appeared with the main course—a roast suckling pig replete "with an apple in its mouth." The men feasted, and for those who imbibed (Charlie still didn't) there was beer and wine, the one advantage of warring in France being the wine. The evening was unforgettable. The men laughed, suppressed their terrible memories, and recalled the highlights: Bill Craw's poetry and the Hielandman's griping and Fred Tyo's skill at pole-vaulting during the battalion games. They were revelling in life and hopeful about the future. Still, Charlie Clarke's description of this dinner decades later was tinged with sadness. The men knew they soon would be parting ways and the extraordinary bond they shared was about to be severed.

In a bid to preserve that moment, the following day, as some among them nursed hangovers, they journeyed to Bruay to have their portrait taken, just as Charlie, Bill Roe, and Fred Harrison had done before. The friends assembled in a local studio, and the photographer stole their shadows. Afterwards the friends retired to a café for chips and eggs and hair of the dog for those who needed it. They felt relaxed and nostalgic and imagined themselves returning home as victors. And with home in mind, someone asked: "What's the first thing you'll do when the war is over?" All the men piped in, and every man had a different answer. But Charlie liked Fred Tyo's quip the best. "The Royal Alec Hotel in Winnipeg with a girl in every room and a bottle of whisky with her." The Bombers erupted into laughter, told more lies, and at the end of the afternoon reluctantly left Bruay to go their separate ways. Only later would Charlie understand how permanent this goodbye was. Some of these friends would not survive the war. Big Dolly would die on July 29, 1917, on the eve of the Battle of Passchendaele. Fred Harrison would also die at Passchendaele, but in November, during the final hours of the offensive. Chinky Keeling would survive 1917, but not the war. He perished on September 27, 1918, six weeks before the Armistice.

Charlie had developed a philosophy about life and death in the trenches. "Some men," he decided, "seem fated to have things go wrong." Charlie came to this conclusion after watching a soldier die in a training accident long after his brother's demise. But the insight applied to Leo as well. Despite his bravery and large heart that ached for fallen foes and fascinated at least one farmer's daughter, his death was fated. He was just one of a staggering multitude of victims of the Great War, a body count so large that years later the world's survivors were still reeling. During the 1,566 days of the conflict more than 16 million people died. Among the uniformed combatants, the French lost 1.4 million soldiers, the Russians approximately 2 million, the Germans 2 million, and the British Empire 1.1 million. Of the 619,636 Canadians who enlisted, 60,000 died, and 172,000 were wounded, many maimed for life.

Winnipeg too gave up a disproportionate number of its young to the war. In late July 1918, marking the war's fourth anniversary, the *Tribune* reported that seventy thousand soldiers had departed Winnipeg for the killing fields of Europe, and while "all of these men were not from the city itself, the great majority were, and all the others spent at least a portion of their period of training here."

Of those men, 1,658 never returned, leaving many to mourn their loss. And because the vast majority of the war's soldiers were young men—boys, really—parents dominated the bereaved. When Major Charles Gordon, chaplain of the Cameron Highlanders, returned home, he looked up the mother of a sergeant, "Aleck," he had watched die. Aleck had ignored Gordon's entreaties to rest after he was wounded. "But, Major," Aleck had insisted, "I must make my report of the wounded." Gordon described to his mother her boy's devotion to duty. "She listened," Gordon recounted, "with the tears quietly running down her cheeks. When I had finished she said quietly: 'Major, I dinna grudge my boy, I wadna hae him back.'"

Harry Clarke did not grudge his boy, Leo, either. But he mourned him, finding solace, or a measure of it, in the one aspect of Leo's war that had survived him—his bravery, or more precisely the small bronze medal with the crimson flash and the embossed words "For Valour" that symbolized it. Harry had been presented with his son's Victoria Cross in the spring of 1917 in a sombre ceremony at the corner of Portage and Main Street in Winnipeg. The Governor General, a bullish-looking politician and aristocrat—the Ninth Duke of Devonshire—had travelled to the Manitoba capital and placed the son's medal in the father's trembling hands. A photo survives of the event. Harry and the Governor General stand in profile in the forefront. Their heads are slightly turned, but one can glimpse Harry's clenched hollow face etched with grief that had aged him beyond his forty-eight years.

Leo's medal was "treasured" by his father—eventually framed and mounted on the wall of the parlour in the family's Pine Street home. Also framed was a letter from King George V to the Clarkes, in which the King confided his sincere regret that "the death of Private Leo Clarke ... deprived me of the pride of personally conferring upon him the Victoria Cross." In a bid to keep the memory of his son alive, Harry Clarke erected other personal memorials. He commissioned a bronze plaque, which he had posted at the front of St. Patrick's Anglican Church. The plaque read:

THIS PULPIT
IS SACRED TO THE MEMORY OF
SERGT. LEO B. CLARKE, V.C.
WHO DIED IN FRANCE OCT. 19TH 1916 FROM
WOUNDS RECEIVED IN ACTION
AWARDED VC SEPT 9TH 1916
THY WILL BE DONE

He would also erect a scroll of names of the West End boys who had served in the Great War, denoting with a cross each young man who did not return. He was not alone in acting on this impulse. Within five years of the war's end, a local association of "soldiers' relatives" would erect a monument, a giant likeness of a Great War soldier exuding what historian Jim Blanchard called "happy informality" as he "seems to wave good-bye to his loved ones." So many memorials to honour so many dead.

When Charlie slipped from the family house at 785 to reacquaint himself with his neighbourhood, he might have been comforted by how unchanged it seemed. Pine Street was still lined by austere wooden houses with their open terraces. And beyond the neighbourhood lay the snow-covered prairie where Charlie and Leo had played as boys. Home looked the same, but it wasn't. There were too many missing men, and as Charlie spoke to people to catch up on the fate of neighbours he heard an incredible story—two other men from Pine Street, Fred Hall and Robert Shankland, had also been awarded the Victoria Cross. Leo had not been the only one.

Three VC heroes from little Pine Street. It was a startling revelation. And unprecedented. There was no other street in Canada, Great Britain, or the wide Empire that had distinguished itself in such a way. As word of this spread throughout the West End, some wondered: How could this be? Why was this street so special? Charlie and any returning veteran from the trenches knew the answer. These men had seen too many examples of selflessness, sacrifice, tragedy, pathos, stubbornness, misery, and resolve among boys just like Leo Clarke, Fred Hall, and Bob Shankland. Pine Street was unique—exactly as unique as every other street, alley, lane, and road in the country that had made comparable sacrifices during the Great War.

And the young country's sacrifice had been staggering. Placing the Great War generation's commitment in a modern perspective: had the same percentage of Canada's population gone to war in 2014, the total men in uniform would have been 2.6 million, and the number of dead at the war's end would have reached 250,000. In Canada and across the western world, the Great War was not so much a conflict as a catastrophe. Pine Street was one of hundreds, perhaps thousands, of communities across the Dominion that had paid dearly.

Yet, Pine Street was inordinately special. Many fine sons of Canada had called it home, and among others these men included Leo Clarke, Fred Hall, and Robert Shankland. But these three heroes would not return to Pine or the gentle Winnipeg West End to live. Both Leo and Fred Hall were resting in the ennobled soil of France and Flanders, and Robert Shankland would spend his postwar years elsewhere. But Charlie would not stray far from this place. The war taught veterans like Charlie innumerable lessons, most of which would take each man a lifetime to understand. But for Charlie one thing was clear. He knew, after years of wanderings and war, where he belonged. It was along this stretch of solid houses and good people hard on the Manitoba prairie.

When standing on the frozen boardwalk of Pine Street, Charlie Clarke was home. And here he would remain for the rest of his life.

EPILOGUE

The Great War Generation

For surviving members of the Great War generation such as Charlie Clarke, Harry Hall, and Robert Shankland, the march of life was not easy in the postwar world. This was particularly so in Winnipeg, which faced inordinately hard times. The price of wheat plunged on the prairies between 1919 and 1921, and because Winnipeg, as historian Jim Blanchard observed, was "so dependent on prosperity in the agricultural sector, the fall in prices was a disaster." Hard times fell on the city. And the country.

The sacrifices Canadians had made in the war emboldened them to demand more from society. Workers across the nation began to collectivize. Strikes broke out. And despite the euphoria of the war's end, the unrest spread. One of the largest and most important general strikes erupted in Winnipeg in early summer 1919, and although the agitation was forcibly put down, it changed labour and politics. The Great War generation would leave its mark on the country and the world by marching into the future with the same ferocity they took into battle.

Fred Hall's younger brother Harry recovered from his wounds in Winnipeg and waited for his Tenth Battalion comrades, Duncan Cross and Hector McIvor, to return from the war. They never did. Harry eventually learned that his two friends had fallen at Vimy Ridge. Harry also sought the company of other veterans. Frustrated that Riel Rebellion and Boer War survivors dominated veterans' groups, Harry and a few other vets created the Great War Veterans Association, which spread across Canada, merged with other organizations, and eventually became the Royal Canadian Legion. True to the Hall family's passion for music, Harry sang in his spare time, and while studying voice with his sister Ada, was attracted to one of her students, a petite auburn-haired beauty named Ann Reid. Harry Hall married Ann on April 16, 1924, and after a brief musical career became a chiropractor, spending a portion of his life in the United States. They had two daughters—Gail and Joan. Both children perpetuated the Hall family's tradition of devotion to the military and music. Gail would serve in the US navy in the Second World War, and Joan became a prominent singer, operatic performer, and founding member of the Canadian Opera Company in Toronto. Harry Hall died on November 25, 1985, at the age of ninety-one. One of his last great projects was authoring a long series of letters to his granddaughter, also named Gail, which recorded the family history and his Great War experiences.

Harry's brother Ted survived the war, but died young in 1928. His mother, Mary, however, remained a casualty, grieving for her eldest son and for her husband for the remainder of her life. Mary returned to Great Britain after the war and visited her former home of St. Helens where her husband Frederick Matticott Hall was buried. She arranged for the name of their son, Fred, to be added to her husband's headstone. After her death in Toronto in 1955 at the age of ninety-one, the family added her name to this stone. In the end, all three rest together.

After the Armistice, Robert Shankland would make a home in Winnipeg. But he first went back to his ancestral home in Ayr, Scotland. Throughout the war, he had visited there while on leave. Ever modest and probably reluctant to worry his family, Bob didn't tell his father, William, about the Victoria Cross he had been awarded. The elder Shankland first heard the story from a Canadian chaplain whom he happened to sit beside on a train in Scotland. Bob's exploits eventually became famous and when he stopped in Ayr in early 1918, he was presented with the Freedom of the Town award. In 1920, he returned again to marry Anne Haining, who might have been a childhood sweetheart since her father, like Bob's father, had been a "popular stationmaster" in nearby Prestwick. Bob brought his new bride to Winnipeg where they raised a family—two sons, William ("Billy" for short) and David. Bob prospered and became a community leader, serving as a member of the Winnipeg Board of Trade. He later moved the family to Vancouver and entered the stocks and securities business. But his life as a soldier would never be left entirely behind. When the Second World War broke out, Bob returned to Winnipeg and enlisted again with the Seventy-Ninth Camerons. Considered too old for a field commission, Bob Shankland was eventually appointed camp commandant of the Canadian Army HQ in England. His oldest son, Billy, earned his wings and served with the Royal Canadian Air Force. Robert Shankland made his last trip to Ayr in 1964 at the age of seventy-seven. He was shown around the "auld toun" and hinted at the strategy behind his daring at Passchendaele. "I played poker with the Hun," he confessed when asked about the battle of Bellevue Spur. "That's a game of bluff." Bob Shankland died in Vancouver on January 20, 1968. He was cremated and his remains scattered over the grounds of Mountain View Cemetery.

Despite Winnipeg's postwar economic and social upheaval, Charlie Clarke did not leave, at least for any length of time. He settled back into the Pine Street house where his younger siblings still lived, taking a job with the Winnipeg office of the Metropolitan Life Insurance Company, which his father had managed. In time, he noticed that a new family from Scotland had moved in down the street. They had a young daughter, Amelia, whom Charlie admired from afar. One wintry evening during a snowstorm in 1921, Amelia Birney trundled toward home, her head bowed to escape the wind, when she almost collided with someone. She looked up, only to realize that the figure she had bumped into was her neighbour Charlie Clarke. As a prairie wind whistled around them, Charlie asked Amelia if she would accompany him to a dance on Friday at the local community club. She agreed. Four years later, the two young people were married in a service in the neighbourhood church, St. Patrick's Anglican.

That same year, Charlie lost his mother, Rosetta. Life marched on. In 1928, Charlie and Amy Clarke had a child, a boy, whom they named Leo Clarke Jr. They had a second son, Richard, and the arrival of George later completed the family. The Clarkes eventually settled into their own home on Pine Street, which now bore a different name. In 1925, the City of Winnipeg, recognizing the neighbourhood's special legacy, voted that this street be officially known as Valour Road.

But life on Valour Road, or any other in Canada, did not grow easier with the passage of time. The malaise that overwhelmed the Manitoban economy enveloped the world after the collapse of the U.S. stock market on September 4, 1929. The Great Depression was the first major calamity to confront the Great War generation in the postwar world. And a calamity it truly was. Canada's gross national product dropped by almost half, and within four years unemployment would reach 27 percent. But across all Canada's regions, the prairies suffered the most, as wheat prices continued to plummet and farming communities survived only on the produce they grew to feed their families.

Heroes who had survived the gas attack at Ypres were forced to live on government relief, stand in bread lines, or ride the rails across the country in a quest for work.

Charlie lost his job at Metropolitan Life. For most of the Depression, he worked where he could, and like millions of hard-strapped men struggled to put food on the table. But during these trying times, veterans stuck together. Periodically, Charlie's old friend from the trenches, Bill Roe, rumbled into Winnipeg, driving a truck filled with farm produce that he gave to his friend. Just like the morning at Courcelette when he arrived with rations and hot tea, William Abraham Roe was a loyal Bomber, coming to a comrade's aid. Like Charlie, Bill had survived the war relatively unscathed. He returned to his father's farm, and within a year married a local girl, Jessie Maude Duncan. The Soldier Settlement Board, the postwar program that rewarded surviving warriors with farmland, allotted the couple the southwest quarter of plot 25-15-11 near Neepawa, Manitoba. During the Depression, Bill and Jessie made cash by selling cream and eggs, and ate well on the produce and grain he shared with Charlie.

In time, another old soldier stepped forward and paid a visit to the Clarke home. Jim Murray was a prominent citizen, a former major in the Canadian Corps, and an "army friend" of Charlie's. On that memorable visit, Murray brought news of a job at Winnipeg's Standard Dairy that was Charlie's if he wanted it. "There was a very happy buzz the night of his visit," remembered son Richard

Clarke. After years of struggle, Charlie had a permanent position delivering milk and cream each morning. But as much as friends like Bill Roe and Jim Murray had helped him, Charlie also gave back. As a milkman, he became a fixture of the community. Patient and ever helpful, Charlie became the man everyone went to when in need. And there was much need in Charlie's lifetime. The Great Depression ended with the start of another great war, the Second World War. Both Charlie Clarke and Robert Shankland returned to uniform, but of course not to the field. Their generation led the Allies to victory, ushering in a new age of prosperity and technological advancement.

After the Second World War, as nature took its course, more and more of the Great War veterans began leaving the world they had moulded, led, and endured in for so long. As Bill Roe got older, he stopped travelling to Winnipeg and he and Charlie Clarke lost touch. But Charlie knew when his old friend died. Charlie kept a booklet containing the names and addresses of members of the Thirty-Second Battalion association, the outfit that he had shipped out with. The name W. A. Roe is followed by the brief but tender notation "RIP 1961."

Over time, Charlie's eldest son, Leo Jr., became better acquainted with his family's role in the Great War. Charlie was reluctant to talk about his own exploits, but Bill Roe had shared his memories of what Leo Jr. called "Dad's outstanding accomplishments." Once, while on business in the town of Manitou, Leo met a banker named Bill Rankin who recognized something in him and asked if he was related to Charlie Clarke. Rankin too had served with Charlie in the trenches and told Leo stories of his father, cautioning him "not to say anything about them, as Charlie would have told them if he wanted them known." But eventually Charlie decided that he did want his war to be known. Over the years, he sat down and wrote several short memoirs, entitling them "Incidents & Anecdotes," "Leo Clarke, V.C., Autobiography by Charles E. Clarke," and "One Man's Warfare," among other articles and letters.

In his later years, Charlie's mind remained alert, and his body strong, his years of physical work with the dairy having paid off. Surrounded by family (his son Leo, his siblings, and nephews and nieces), Charlie Clarke enjoyed a tranquil old age. Any demons that had followed him from the Great War were driven away, and when he died in 1974 at the age of seventy-nine, he was a man at peace with himself, his family, and his legacy. After his death, and burial in Winnipeg's Brookside Cemetery, his eldest son, Leo Jr., took custody of the Victoria Cross and the war relics he had guarded since 1918. His generation would be the last to hold this priceless decoration. In 2010, the Clarke family donated Leo Clarke's VC to the Canadian War Museum (CWM), along with other heirlooms including Leo's pistol and war-era photos. Soon after, Fred Hall's family came to the same decision. In 2012, Fred's nieces, Gail Cargo and Joan Hall Paulseth, also donated Fred Hall's VC and various family papers and photos to the museum. Because the CWM had purchased Robert Shankland's VC in auction in 2009, the Hall donation completed the Valour Road collection and brought almost a century of history full circle.

But this legacy could never be removed from the proud Winnipeg street where the story began. Every year, Leo Clarke Jr. and his family continued to observe Remembrance Day in the neighbourhood, just as the Clarkes had been doing since 1925. And each year, interest in their home, their story, and their past grew. In 2005, the city constructed a plaza at the corner of Valour Road and Sargent Avenue, replete with a statue depicting three Great War soldiers silhouetted on a horizon. This plaza became the new destination for patriots and pilgrims, and the site for the crowded Valour Road Remembrance Day observance where the Clarke family—Leo Clarke Jr., his son, grandchildren, nieces, and nephews—continued to stand front and centre.

The Clarke family's devotion to this shrine was and is understandable. Valour Road is their legacy. But why do so many others without a direct link to the neighbourhood brave the cold to stand in this plaza on November 11? Men like Charlie Clarke understood that everyone touched by the Great War and the conflicts that followed holds his own personal memorial. Charlie had his. Every Sunday when Charlie attended church at St. Patrick's Anglican, he would gaze at the scroll hanging just left of the altar, which his father had commissioned. The honour role was inscribed with names of the neighbourhood boys who had gone off to war—all friends Charlie had grown up with. "As I read the list of names," Charlie once wrote, "mental pictures form in my mind of them swimming in the old Brick pond or in the river between the two railway bridges, the fights we had, the races we ran, and those who did not return."

Asterisks marked the name of each boy who fell, West End boys like John Quay and Roy Hatfield and George Cooper and, of course, Leo Clarke. These boys had raced in track meets at Argyll school and on the prairie behind the Clarke house. "All the other boys that did not return, their names go flying through my mind," he once recalled, and perhaps Charlie was so moved by this simple monument because in his memory these boys were perpetually running, not through the cratered terrain of no man's land where they had died, but across a vast prairie on the edge of a frontier city, running as if they believed they could reach the end, but knowing, like all sons of Manitoba do, that the plains, like life's possibilities, are limitless.

ACKNOWLEDGMENTS

I offer special thanks to Al Zuckerman and Mickey Novak of Writers House, and my editors, Penguin Publishing Director Diane Turbide and freelance editor Jonathan Webb. I thank my old friend Nick Garrison of Penguin for his initial interest in this book.

My quest for details on the lives and background of the Valour Road heroes ultimately reached the doorsteps of their families. The descendants of both Clarke and Hall were thoughtful and generous, and this book could not have been written without their consent and help.

Leo Clarke Jr., of Winnipeg, nephew and namesake of the Valour Road hero, was my first contact. His brother, Richard Clarke of Sechelt, BC, was involved in a genealogical project while I was researching this book. As a result, we were able almost daily to compare notes and share findings, although Richard provided me with far more than I was able to give him.

I also thank Leo Clarke Jr.'s sons, Paul and Eric, for their help. Gail Cargo and Joan Hall Paulseth provided a wealth of information on their father, Harry Hall, and their uncle, Fred. Through correspondence and conversations with Gail and Joan, I developed a greater understanding of the two forces that guided the Hall family—duty and music. Gail served in WWII and her son, Doug Cargo, spent a career in the military. Joan Hall Paulseth's dynamic career as an opera singer, performer, and music teacher gave me a taste of the passion with which the Hall family pursued music. Joan Paulseth's daughter Gail Burton kindly shared both correspondence and photos of her grandfather, Harry.

Researching this book was an enterprise that spanned two continents. While I conducted research in Europe, Ben Dearing collected essential information for me in Winnipeg. In Winnipeg, I also thank Royal Canadian Legion curator Bruce Tascona; Hugh O'Donnell of the Queen's Own Cameron Highlanders of Canada association; Gerry Woodman, manager of the Royal Winnipeg Rifles Museum; and Manitoba historian Duff Crerar. For my research into the Second Battalion, I thank Brian Boyd of Ottawa, son-in-law of battalion officer and historian W. W. Murray; the legendary officer's son Ian Murray, of Hilton Head, South Carolina; and the staff of the Governor General Foot Guards Museum in Ottawa.

As in all meaningful projects, one's own history inadvertently plays a role. While conducting research in Ottawa, I was reacquainted with a childhood friend, Floyd Low, a retired Canadian soldier and military researcher. I thank him for his help. When considering the mettle of the Manitoba and Ontario men central to this story, my thoughts returned often to university friend Malcolm Campbell of Kenora. Not only was Malcolm a fine metric with which to understand Kenora men like Arthur Clarkson, Malcolm's sister, Elizabeth Campbell, kindly allowed me access to her research site, *The Kenora Great War Project*. The associated site, the *Canadian*

Great War Project, was also an invaluable resource, and Elizabeth's Kenora-based bookstore, Elizabeth Campbell Books, is an excellent source for rare and out-of-print titles. I must also thank my niece Pauline Nadler-Smith of Manitoba for her help.

For research into Robert Shankland's early life in Scotland, I thank John Hope and Pam Ellis of St. Nicholas Church; John Inglis, who provided information on the Ayr Boys' Brigade; Sheena Taylor and the staff of the South Ayrshire Council, Scottish & Local History Department; Kenneth Neill, captain of the Fourth Ayr Boys' Brigade Company; and Scottish writer Jennifer Robertson.

Joan Robinson kindly shared information and photos on the life of her ancestor, William Roe.

As always, I offer thanks to my constant collaborators, Erika Papp and Gusztav Nadler.

NOTES

PROLOGUE

3   "Victoria Cross isn't really much to look at": Jean Sangwine, broadcaster, "Manitoba's Men of Valour," CBC Radio, November 11, 1964.

4   Valour Road Remembrance Day ceremony: *The National*, CBC Television, November 11, 2012, www. cbc.ca/player/News/TV+Shows/The+National/Canada/ ID/2303456384/.

4   Description of ceremony and the Valour Road ceremony tradition: Leo Clarke Jr. and Paul Clarke, in discussion with the author, September and October 2013.

A CITY ON THE EDGE OF THE WORLD

7–8   Description of Clarke home on Pine Street circa 1914 and Henry Clarke profile provided in interviews. Clarke family genealogical material provided by Leo Clarke Jr.

of Winnipeg and Richard Clarke of Sechelt, BC. Clarke ancestor Edward Daniel Clarke is a well-known historical personage whose bio can be found in online sources including this Wikipedia entry: http://en.wikipedia.org/wiki/Edward_Daniel_Clarke.

9   "Prosperity": Blanchard, *Winnipeg 1912*, 4.

9   "Progress": Ibid.

9   Winnipeg's population: Ibid., 9. The 1911 Census placed Winnipeg's population at 136,035. Population figure of 166,000 rounded down from Blanchard's 166,533.

9   The *Chicago Tribune*: Ibid., 5. Blanchard attributes this to the *Tribune*, but the original source appears to be the September 1911 *Record-Herald*, William E. Curtis.

9   Rosetta Clarke's full maiden name: Rosetta Caroline Nona Bodily, b. Feb. 24, 1892.

10   Description of Winnipeg's West End: Clarke, "Autobiography," 2.

10   "a tar paper shack": Ibid., 3.

10   "Pine Street had no road": Clarke, "Omands Creek," 1.

10   Like most in the West End: Amelia Birnie Clarke, "Autobiography," 5. Memories and a brief profile of Henry Clarke also came from the personal writings of Mrs. Charles Clarke.

11   "the most peaceful century": Keegan, *Warfare*, 22.

13   "powder keg": Ferguson, *Pity of War*, 8.

13   That fateful summer: Keegan, *Warfare*, 22.

13   "partial mobilization": Keegan, *First World War*, 76.

14   If Harry Clarke were among the crowds: Blanchard, *Winnipeg's Great War*, 13, 14.

15   "the old world": Gordon, *Postscript*, 193.

15   "When news of the war came": McClung, *The Next of Kin*, chap. 1.

15   "War! That was over!": Ibid.

15   "consider what it had to do with me": Gordon, *Postscript*, 193.

16   "World Conflagration": Ibid., 192.

16   "[F]illed with the war spirit": Currie, *"Red Watch,"* chap. 4.

16   The mob didn't seem to care: Winnipeg *Tribune*, August 6, 1914, 5.

17   Borden considers: Borden, *Memoirs*, 214.

17   "buckle on his harness and get busy": Cassar, *Hell in Flanders Fields*, 18.

17   "Every mother's son is spoiling for a fight": Winnipeg *Tribune*, August 6, 1914, 5.

17   "Canada Ready to Strike Blow": Ibid., 3.

17   "parades, martial music and flags": Blanchard, *Winnipeg's Great War*, 19.

17   "on Main Street": Ibid., 20.

18   "cream" of western Canadian manhood: Winnipeg *Tribune*, August 6, 1914, 5.

18   "He would go": McClung, *In Times Like These*, chap. 2.

18   "a desire to see the world": McClung, *Three Times and Out*, chap. 1.

18 "He would go": Ibid., *In Times Like These*, chap. 2.

18 "I was proud of my battalion": Gordon, *Postscript*, 193–194.

18 "Nations can't go to war": McClung, *Three Times and Out*, chap. 1.

18 Prime Minster Borden's cabinet agreed: Borden, *Memoirs*, 214.

18 "The world is changed": Gordon, *Postscript*, 194.

THE PINE STREET BOYS

21 Frederick William Hall and Frederick Matticott Hall early life: Harry Hall letter to Gail Burton, 1979. Private collection.

22 "feature of social functions," "painful internal complaint" come from an unidentified newspaper obituary for "Bandmaster F. Hall," dated January 27, 1905.

22 The family moved to London: Harry Hall to Gail Burton, June 9, 1979. Private collection.

22 Peter Stanton's relationship with the Hall family: Ibid., July 15, 1979. Private collection.

23 "He gave up the prospect": Manitoba *Free Press*, August 26, 1915, 16.

23 "conducting, arranging, harmony," "I respected and admired Fred": Harry Hall to Gail Burton, October 13, 1979, private collection.

24 "Mother, I have always had the feeling," *Free Press*, August 26, 1915, 16.

25 On August 7: Blanchard, *Winnipeg's Great War*, 20. No documented evidence places Hall in this parade. However, he was by this time a member of the militia's regimental band, and for this reason I have placed him here.

25   Fred Hall's enlistment: Manitoba *Free Press*, June 24, 1915.

26   "a boozy celebration": Blanchard, *Winnipeg's Great War*, 34, 35.

27   "There was the screaming of sirens": Curry, *From the St. Lawrence*, chap. 5.

27   Fighting at Mons: Arthur, *Forgotten Voices*, 29–30.

28   "Enemy Renews Struggle": Winnipeg *Tribune*, December 1, 1914, 1.

28   "British Casualties": Manitoba *Free Press*, December 5, 1914, 3.

29   William and Jane Shankland information comes from the 1891 Scottish census.

29   "quiet and retiring," Shankland academic record: Winnipeg *Tribune*, December 21, 1918, 51.

29   "sallow" and Shankland height: Robert Shankland attestation paper, Collections Canada.

30   "Sure and Steadfast," "Our object still remains the same": Inglis, *The Steadfast Way*, 6.

30   "He was aye a game yin," Shankland early life: Winnipeg *Tribune*, December 21, 1918, 51.

30   Fought like "madmen": Grant, *Lion*, 325.

31   Shankland's neighbourhood of Church Street no longer exists in Ayr, but according to an 1855 city map found in the National Library of Scotland, Church Street intersected John Street south of Elba Street in present-day Ayr.

31   "weeded out": *Cameron Highlanders of Canada Memorial Site*, http://www.cameronhighlanderscanada.com/43pg1.htm.

32   "man among other men": Keegan, *Warfare*, xv.

33   "It would be all right": Clarke, "Warfare," 1.

33   101st Edmonton Fusiliers: Charles Clarke attestation paper, Collections Canada.

33–34   Twelfth Manitoba Dragoons: Background on the Dragoons can be found at *National Defence Canada and the Canadian Forces*, http://www.cmp-cpm.forces.gc.ca/dhh-dhp/his/ol-lo/vol-tom-3/par1/arm-bli/12MD-eng.asp. And also at *Canadian Expeditionary Force Study Group*, http://www.cefresearch.ca/phpBB3/viewtopic.php?f=39&t=8005.

35   "We were off": Clarke, "Warfare," 2.

35   Charlie stood between his mother and father: This description is based on a photograph provided by Richard Clarke.

35   "And my heart falls back to Erin's isle": "The Girl I Left Behind," Irish folk song, 1791.

35   "God, isn't it a shame": Blanchard, *Winnipeg's Great War*, 81.

35   the Winnipeg *Telegram* agreed: Ibid., 82.

36   "pea soup," "handy with his fists": Clarke, "Autobiography," 2.

37   "fights," "races," "he was ashamed to take home so many": Ibid., "Omands Creek," 3.

37   "lurid gleam": Winnipeg *Morning Telegram*, October 12, 1904.

37   "It was an event always remembered": Clarke, "Autobiography," 3.

38   "good to be alive," "Enjoy your life now": Clarke, "War-fare," 3.

39   In Clarke's diary-based account, he identifies the troopship as the "Massanabee." HMS *Essex*'s logs available at http://s3.amazonaws.com/oldweather/ADM53-41086/ADM%2053-41086-036_0.jpg.

40   "A new world": Curry, *From the St. Lawrence*, chap. 5.

40   "pioneers and backwoodsmen": Ibid., chap. 6.

40   "Canadians were not ordinary soldiers": Murray, *2nd Battalion*, 32.

40   "The thatched cottages": Curry, *From the St. Lawrence*, chap. 6.

40   "brought back memories": Clarke, "Warfare," 5.

41   "big blowsey looking woman": Ibid.

41   "mighty rumbles," "very exciting and fearful": Ibid., 7.

THE GOOD SERGEANT

43   The brothers endured: Harry Hall to Gail Burton, July 8, 1979. Private collection.

44   "the halcyon days": Murray, *2nd Battalion*, 81.

44   "would soon be in a position": Haig, *War Diaries*, 73.

44   The Eighth Battalion war diary states that this mobilization began on April 14, and that it was completed on April 15. Some histories state the Eighth left billets on April 15.

44   "an eternal memorial": Beckett, *Ypres*, 233.

45   "We would be terrible traitors": Graves, *A Crow of Life*, 184.

45   Rubble and carrion: Murray, *2nd Battalion*, 33.

45   "still functioning": Reid, *Named by the Enemy*, 79.

46   "naked, flat, and oozy": Beckett, *Ypres*, 226.

47   Barbed wire in no man's land: Tenth Battalion War Diary, April 15, 1915, Collections Canada.

47   Trench conditions: Ibid.

47   The Germans had turned their attention: Lee, *Gas Attacks at Ypres*, 9.

48   April 22 shelling: Tenth Battalion War Diary, April 15, 1915, Collections Canada.

48   "Houses were seen to collapse": Lee, *Gas Attacks at Ypres*, 7.

48   "quiet": Eighth Battalion War Diary, April 21, 1915, Collections Canada.

48   It was a "beautiful" spring day: Arthur, *Forgotten Voices*, 79.

48   It was a "beautiful" spring day: Lee, *Gas Attacks at Ypres*, 7.

49   Falkenhayn poison gas strategy: Keegan, *First World War*, 213.

49   "peculiar" clouds: Lee, *Gas Attacks at Ypres*, 19.

49   that to some looked like: Arthur, *Forgotten Voices*, 77–78.

50   "There's something funny going on": MacDonald, *Death of Innocence*, 193.

50   "grey-green": Keegan, *First World War*, 214.

50   "Open immediate rapid fire!": Arthur, *Forgotten Voices*, 78.

50   "fat was pouring": Ibid.

50 the gas was a "vesicant": Keegan, *First World War*, 214.

50 "This is not war": Ibid., 223.

50 "Asphyxie! Asphyxie!": Curry, *From the St. Lawrence*, chap. 8.

51 "The men came tumbling": Arthur, *Forgotten Voices*, 80.

51 "got orders to shoot": Ibid., 79.

51 6 killed, 33 wounded: Eighth Battalion War Diary, April 22, 1915. Collections Canada.

51 Tear gas: Reid, *Named by the Enemy*, 81.

52 "sixteen 75-mm [cannons]": Lee, *Gas Attacks at Ypres*, 21.

53 "exhausted and gasping": Holland, *Tenth Canadian Battalion*, 8.

53 "looked the picture," "refugees," "fugitives": Urquhart, *Sixteenth Battalion*, 56.

53 "hydrochloric acid," "confusion of transport wagons": *Calgary Herald*, 1, 15.

53 Harry spotted "kilted" warriors: Harry Hall to Gail Burton, May 24, 1979. Private collection.

54 "I may be killed": *Renfrew Mercury*, May 21, 1915.

54 "Let me tell you": *Toronto Star*, April 26, 1915.

54 Boyle briefs Tenth Battalion: Harry Hall to Gail Burton, May 4, 1979. Private collection. Hall states that he learned of the attack from Boyle. "The Colonel told us that at 12 P.M. we were ordered with the Sixteenth Battalion to attack the Germans."

54 "cold steel": Urquhart, *Sixteenth Battalion*, 57.

54 Kitcheners Wood visible as "a dark blur": *Calgary Herald*, May 28, 1915, 1, 15.

54   When advancing, keep to the right: Ibid.

54   "We've been aching": Lee, *Gas Attack at Ypres*, 28. Lee does not attribute the quote. Its source may be the National Defence site for the Calgary Highlanders, http://www.calgaryhighlanders. com/history/10th/personalities/commandingofficers.htm.

55   "A great day," "thrilled": Urquhart, *Sixteenth Battalion*, 58.

55   Boyle's position, pale "waning moon": Holland, *Tenth Canadian Battalion*, 9.

55   "The lines went steadily ahead as if they were doing a drill maneuver," "a joke," "Hell broke," "spitting flame," "blinding vortex of dust," "roar": *Calgary Herald*, May 28, 1915.

55   "like the blows of a hollow hammer": Urquhart, *Sixteenth Battalion*, 58.

55   "lost confidence": Ibid., 59.

56   "tropical storm": Lee, *Gas Attack at Ypres*, 29.

56   "fear of their own gas": Ibid., 22.

56   four thousand metres: Tenth Battalion War Diary, April 24. Collections Canada.

57   "cotton bandoliers": Reid, *Named by the Enemy*, 82.

57   For Harry, the coming days were a blur: Harry Hall to Gail Burton, May 24, 1979. Private collection.

57   At the first opportunity: Harry Hall to Gail Burton, May 4, 1979. Private collection.

POISON

58   Eighth Battalion C Company: Fred Hall's company is also referred to in some histories and reports as No. 3 Company.

59 "bluish haze," "paralyzing effect," "advancing unchecked": Lipsett report, 8th Battalion (90th Rifles) Narrative of Events, April 30, 1915. Collections Canada.

60 "renewed twice": Ibid., 2. "The garrison of the trench had to be renewed twice during the morning to enable it to be held."

60–61 "waning moon," "gully": "VC Winners from Manitoba," by N. Anderson, Manitoba *Free Press*, July 6, 1940, 5.

61 "They [the Canadians] were mown down" "one after another the officers were killed or wounded": "Awarded Victoria Cross for Bravery," Manitoba *Free Press*, June 24, 1915.

62 "one of the largest gatherings of the townspeople": unidentified newspaper obituary for "Bandmaster F. Hall," January 27, 1905.

62 "Waving his arms feebly": "Mother Receives Victoria Cross," Manitoba *Free Press*, August 26, 1915, 16.

64 "Sergeant Major Hall was killed whilst trying to put a wounded man under cover": Lipsett report, 8th Battalion (90th Rifles) Narrative of Events, April 30, 1915. Collections Canada.

64 "No greater love": John 15:13. Quote appears in untitled letter found in the online post for Frederick Hall, *Canadian Virtual War Memorial*, Veteran Affairs Canada, http://www. veterans.gc.ca/eng/remembrance/memorials/canadian-virtual-war-memorial/detail/1592737?Frederick%20 William%20Hall.

64 The King James Version of John 15:13 reads: "Greater love hath no man than this, that a man lay down his life for his friends."

64 "Freddie went away with the troops from the C.P.R. depot":

"Mother Receives Victoria Cross," Manitoba *Free Press*, August 26, 1915, 16.

65   Hall Festubert recollections: Hall letter to Gail Burton, June 17, 1979. Private collection.

65–66   "We knew we would never make it," "This is crazy," "If the forward men get mowed down, I'm ducking into a shell hole," "I'll be there before you," "I've lost my platoon," "You can go to Blighty": Harry Hall to Gail Burton, June 9, 1979. Private collection.

A DEAD MAN'S MEAL

67   "pitched and rolled": Clarke, "Warfare," 7.

67   "one continuous stream," "to all practical purposes": Gass, *Clare Gass*, 16.

68   "pitch dark," "what I didn't imagine," "puffs of smoke": Clarke, "Warfare," 7.

68   "the first shots fired": Ibid., 8.

69   Make up of Second Battalion: Murray, *2nd Battalion*, 4 and 5.

69   Second Battalion's movements on April 22: Ibid., 38.

69–70   "Fighting was in progress": Ibid., 39.

70   "ditches, soggy and choked with weeds": Ibid., 38

70   "sagged, crumpled": Ibid., 44.

70   Remaining W. W. Murray quotes and description of Second Battalion at Kitcheners Wood: Ibid., 44–57.

70   "We were young and healthy" "full packs, overcoat, blankets, and rifles": Clarke, "Warfare," 8.

71   "Old Timers": Ibid., 8.

71   "louder," "star shells," "I took my rum isue," "heart breaking," "We wondered," "full packs, overcoat, blankets, and rifles": Ibid., 8 and 9.

72   "decisive victory": Keegan, *First World War*, 207.

72   Munitions figures: Ferguson, *Pity of War*, 259 and 260.

73   "confusion": Cook, *Sharp End*, 179.

73   "The Canadians are blown to hell": Ibid., 180.

73   "worst one-day loss": Ibid., 148.

73–76   Clarke Festubert narrative: Clarke, "Warfare," 9, 10, and 11.

75   "There they were, the flower of the British army": Clarke, "Incidents," 1. Original passage: "My section commander, thought there might be some of his friends amongst the dead, and suggested that we go up and see. This was my first morning up in the trenches, and he was an old timer. I thought it would be fine. I had never seen a dead body before. We jumped up and over the parapet, and there they were, the flower of the British army, and must have been hit as they went over the top some one had stopped and placed a small flag over the face on one man...."

75   "I don't know what I expected": Ibid., 2.

75   "it was so much cleaner than my own," "I ran, and a good runner I was," "in a daze": Ibid.

76   "Look, he still has": Ibid., "Warfare," 11.

BOMBERS

77   "son of a bitch," "raged": Cook, *Sharp End*, 189 and 192.

77   "splendid men," It was their generals who were "sketchy": Haig, *War Diaries*, 126.

77–78   "rushing sound": Clarke, 3.

78   "breath," "blown to smithereens," "a miss is as good as a mile": Ibid.

78   a "quiet tour," "The feeling generally was that the abortive operations at Festubert": Murray, *2nd Battalion*, 64.

78   "[Festubert] had served to initiate us into trench warfare," "Ah Oui": Clarke, "Warfare," 9 and 11.

79   French newsboys; two-day mail deliveries; "It is extraordinary": Fussell, *Great War*, 76 and 77.

79   "what a great part [these letters] played in our lives": Clarke, "Warfare," 11.

80   "express train travelling at the rate of 65 to 70 miles an hour": Rawling, *Surviving Trench Warfare*, 25.

80   bomber history and strategy: Ibid., 209–212.

81   "black art": Cook, *Sharp End*, 209.

81   Life expectancy of "16 days" for bombing officers: Ibid., 210.

81   "sensitive head," "dooser," "slab of wood," "jam tin" bombs: Clarke, "Warfare," 12.

81–82   cans jammed with guncotton primers: Rawling, *Surviving Trench Warfare*, 24.

82   "bayonet men," "bays," "affect my life": Clarke, "Warfare," 12 and 13.

ROSE OF GIVENCHY

83   12,000 miles of trench: Fussell, *Great War*, 44.

84   "pure bloody mess": Cook, *Sharp End*, 214. Cook quotes Brigadier General Richard Turner.

84   "Cornflowers," "Roses of Picardy": Fussell, *Great War*, 309 and 311. Fussell devotes a chapter to the symbolism of "Roses and Poppies" and quotes soldier poet Wilfred Owen who called "Roses of Picardy" "the favorite song of the men."

85   The battalion's No. 2 Company manned the bill's fire trench: Second Battalion War Diary, June 10, 1915. Collections Canada.

85   "one of the keenest and most competent officers": Murray, *2nd Battalion*, 67.

85   "very quiet": Second Battalion War Diary, June 11 and 12, 1915, Collections Canada.

85   "short strokes": Clarke, "Warfare," 13.

86   "masters with their tools": Arthur, *Forgotten Voices*, 149.

86   "big cheeses": Ibid.

87   Bombers order to take the field: Murray, *2nd Battalion*, 68. According to Charlie Clarke's account, this operation was never executed due to the attack's failure.

88   According to Captain Richardson: Ibid., p. 66. Richardson's first estimate was 25 men taken out by the mine; he later revised this number to 50.

88   "appeared to suffer only slight losses," "70 yards": Ibid., 66.

88   "blue flag": Ibid., 67.

89   "The flag was then seen to be slowly withdrawn": Ibid.

89   "This attack seemed" and casualty numbers: Murray, *2nd Battalion*, 68.

89   "sound men": Ibid., 67.

90   "lined with Germans": Ibid.

91   "I sat up and leaned forward with my elbows on my knees," "Smoke and fumes filled the air," "Just dead men": Clarke, "Warfare," 14.

92–93   Clarke's experiences at Givenchy: Clarke, "Warfare," 13, 14, and 15.

93   That the flowers could flourish: Murray, *2nd Battalion*, 64.

THE HUGE PICNIC

94   Flanders rain flowed: Clarke, "Incidents," 11.

94   "nitrates, potash, and bacteria": Graves, *A Crown of Life*, 183 and 184.

95   Plugstreet's trenches were sound: Clarke, "Warfare," 15.

95   Plugstreet remained quiet: Second Battalion War Diary, June and July 1915. Collections Canada.

96   Plugstreet Wood: Murray, *2nd Battalion*, 69 and 70.

96   To prepare, the men were told to "get busy": Curry, *From the St. Lawrence*, chap. 18.

97   "full of surprises": Clarke, "Warfare," 22.

97   Poem "My Dugout": Ibid., 22 and 23.

98   Bomber Fred Tyo: Ibid., 20 and 66.

98   "nimble of foot": Ibid., 20.

98   By the summer of 1915: Ibid., 27.

98   E. Moody family history: 1891, 1901, 1911 Great Britain census records.

98   Moody passage to Quebec: Cunard Line ship manifest, Southampton–Quebec, July 1913.

98   "beloved" member of the Bombers: Clarke, "Warfare," 25.

98   "lull in activity," "esprit de corps": Murray, *2nd Battalion*, 69.

98   "The original 2nd had been virtually destroyed at Ypres," "Davie," "martinet," "competent," "able": Ibid., 69 and 71.

99   Watson "disturbed" by losses: Haig, *War Diaries*, 455.

99   "our great friends": Curry, *From the St. Lawrence*, chap. 18.

100   "on the look out": Clarke, "Warfare," 16.

100   "If he never got back": Ibid., "Incidents," 16.

100   "live and let live": Rawling, *Surviving Trench Warfare*, 47.

100   Poem "Early every morning": Curry, *From the St. Lawrence*, chap. 17.

101   "short afternoon of hate": Cruttwell, *Royal Berkshire Regiment*, chap. 3.

101   "grim and formidable": Curry, *From the St. Lawrence*, chap. 18.

101   "every night the picks": Cruttwell, *Royal Berkshire Regiment*, chap. 3.

101   "The summer of 1915": Clarke, "Incidents," 8.

102   "few followers," "They had a packing case" "I did them well," "life of Riley," "cut out to be a cook," "wind vane": Ibid., "Warfare," 17 and 18.

102   "bricked and covered": Cruttwell, *Royal Berkshire Regiment*, chap. 3.

103   "admirable," "huts well-built": Ibid.

103   "bathing parade": Second Battalion War Diary, September 21, 1915. Collections Canada.

104   Canadian and British casualty figures: Great Britain War Office, *Statistics*, 255.

104   7,000 average casualties: Fussell, *Great War*, 47. Fussell's casualty calculation of British "wastage" is challenged by other scholars. See Leonard Smith, "Paul Fussell's *The Great War and Modern Memory*: Twenty-five Years," *History and Theory*, 2001, Vol. 40, issue 2, 241–260.

BROTHERS-IN-ARMS

105–107 The arrival of the Second Canadian Division: Clarke, "Warfare," 21.

106   fourteen months: Ibid., "Incidents," 9.

106   "someone from home": Ibid., "Soon enough we had to go," "Warfare," 21.

107   Twenty-Seventh at Locre: Twenty-Seventh Battalion War Diary, September 27–30, 1915. Collections Canada.

107   Haig at Loos: Haig, *War Diaries*, 153.

107   "with that heroic vigor": Murray, *2nd Battalion*, 73.

108   "muddy and wet": Clarke, "Warfare," 21.

108   "wretchedness": Murray, *2nd Battalion*, 75.

108   Twenty-Seventh Battalion at Tea Farm: Twenty-Seventh Battalion War Diary, October 16, 1915. Canada Collections. Brimble's burial site is now the Loker Churchyard, plot I.F.3.

108   The Second Battalion deployed in the Wulverghem sector: Second Battalion War Diary. Collections Canada.

109 "Wulverghem to Kemmel and St. Eloi," "Had the Germans," "as thinly held as our own": Holland, "Formation of the Corps.," *Tenth Canadian Battalion.*

109 Messines town and church steeple: Clarke, "Warfare," 23.

109 "feel naked": Ibid.

109 "eyeballs": Urquhart, *Sixteenth Battalion*, 105.

109 "This was something new to us": Clarke, "Warfare," 23.

109–110 Lt. Pym's background and appearance: Pym attestation papers and military personnel file, Collections Canada. Attestation papers were consulted or sought for every CEF serviceman depicted in this book. In some instances, such as the case for famous soldiers such as Fred Hall and Leo Clarke, etc., the personnel records, consisting of pay, hospital, and transfer records, were available online in digitally scanned format.

110 "lead us on a merry dance": Clarke, "Warfare," 24.

110 Raids to obtain snips of wire: Ibid.

110–111 "bloodthirsty," "show off": Clarke, "Incidents," 14.

111 "When you were laying out in no man's land": Clarke, "Warfare," 23 and 24.

111 "lived in a murderous world of their own": Murray, *2nd Battalion*, 76.

111 The Germans had perfected a new hazard: Clarke, "Warfare," 23.

112 "real lumberjacks": Clarke, "Incidents," 9.

112 Description of Flanders's farms: Ibid., 10.

113 "her nimble fingers": Ibid., "Warfare," 27.

113 "home away from home": Ibid.

113–114 Description of Bombers' bombs: Ibid., 25 and 26.

114 One night, Bill Craw: Ibid., 22.

114–115 "doggo inside the wire for upwards of two hours": Murray, *2nd Battalion*, 76.

115 Sergeant Moody's death: Clarke, "Warfare," 27.

115 "Shot my first German at 3 P.M.": Leo Clarke diary transcription, Winnipeg *Tribune*, August 21, 1918, 12. Charlie's brother Leo, who had volunteered to be a sniper, registered his first kill, making a terse entry in his diary.

115 On October 11: Murray, *2nd Battalion*, 73.

116 "a crazy mutt," description of November 11: Clarke, "Warfare," 28. Concerning Leo Clarke's motivation for joining the Second Battalion, Charlie Clarke writes: "After missing me in Winnipeg, when his telegram had been delayed, he had just one thing on his mind and that was to catch up."

A NEW YEAR OF SLAUGHTER

118 "Will this ever end?": Arthur, *Forgotten Voices*, 110.

118 New Year 1916 at Wulverghem: Clarke, "Warfare," 32.

118 "sentry duty and going out for rations," Ibid., 29.

119 "D" frame shelter: Ibid., "Incidents," 15.

119 "Lots of bombs and hand grenades for both sides": Leo Clarke diary transcription, Winnipeg *Tribune*, August 21, 1918.

119 "baths," "artillery duel" at Wood Camp: Second Battalion War Diary, December 1, 1915. Collections Canada. The entry reads: "Balance of Battalion at Baths. Artillery duel in afternoon on our front. Commanding officer inspects billets."

120   gunshot-wound: medical notes from Leo Clarke hospital file H.Q. File No. 649-C-1609, Collections Canada. Leo Clarke's diary entry for December 9 states: "Hit in three places. Wounds do not hurt. Shell hit dugout. Slight wounds on right side."

120   Second CCS evacuation concerns: No. 2 Canadian Casualty Clearing Station, War Diary, December 1–10, 1915. December 7 entry notes: "Confidential letter received from Headquarters Boulogne asking for quantity of our stores to be moved in case Boulogne were evacuated."

120   Leo Clarke's discharge on Dec. 11, 1918: Charlie Clarke's wartime account "One Man's Warfare" states on page 30 that his brother remained in hospital until after January 1, 1916. But Leo Clarke's medical records and diary entries published in the Winnipeg *Tribune* list his release as December 11, 1915. C. Clarke may have misremembered the date of his brother's release at the time of writing either his original diary or the "Warfare" account.

121   "monster Christmas Dinner": Murray, *2nd Battalion*, 77.

121   "white cloths and silverware": Clarke, "Warfare," 30 and 31.

121   "a very hot place": "The Late Private Harty," *Renfrew Mercury*, January 21, 1916, 1.

122   "eventually silenced": 8th Battalion War Diary, Dec. 30, 1915, Collections Canada.

122   "Two of my men killed": Leo Clarke diary, published in part in the Winnipeg *Tribune*, Aug. 21, 1918.

122   There had been a truce: Arthur, *Forgotten Voices*, 55.

123   Sixth Black Watch sergeant shot: Fussell, *Great War*, 309.

123   British unit defies orders: MacDonald, *Death of Inno-cence*, 599.

122–123 "lovely and clear," "The shouts of joy": Clarke, "Inci-dents," 14.

123   "The screams could be heard": Ibid., "Warfare," 32.

123   "a year of slaughter": Ibid.

THE RAID

124   "new fad": Clarke, "Incidents," 16.

124   "show off": Ibid., 14.

124   "dominate no man's land," "irruptions into enemy positions": Keegan, *First World War*, 198.

125   "Canadian toughs": Rawling, *Surviving Trench Warfare*, 47.

125   "Raids were to be the thing": Clarke, "Warfare," 33.

125   Sports and war: Fussell, *Great War*, 29.

125   "brave, noble, and generous": Murray, *2nd Battalion*, 81.

125   "gold in the heels": "Col. Richardson Left $30,000 for War Orphans' Education," *Toronto Star*, March 4, 1917.

126   "expect to return alive": Richardson obituary, *Ottawa Journal*, February 14, 1916, 12.

126   "honour," "tubes," "O.C. Raid": Murray, *2nd Battalion*, 78 and 79.

126   "to stir up," "didn't want to miss": Clarke, "Incidents," 16.

127   "privilege," "relieved," "looking for trouble": Ibid. "I didn't see much sense in looking for trouble, but didn't want to miss anything, so I put my name down. The next thing I heard was that my name had been taken off the list, because my brother Leo had put up the argument that two brothers should [not] be on the raid together and that as he was the eldest it should be his privilege. Well I was relieved to tell the truth."

127 "Special Duty Party," "Anti-Aircraft Farm": Murray, *2nd Battalion*, 78 and 79. Raider Oliver Denman was a signaller assigned to establish radio communication in the German trench during the incursion.

127 "flanking parties": Clarke, "Warfare," 34. "Out on each flank there was to be a flanking party out in 'No Man's Land' to intercept any German patrols that happened to be out."

127 "heard so much of the Bomber's exciting lives": Clarke, "Incidents," 17.

128 "light snowfall," "brilliant, moonlit night": Murray, *2nd Battalion*, 79.

129 Preparing Mills bombs: Clarke, "Warfare," 34. "Out in billets, we prepared some 300 Mills bombs; checked them over and put in the detonators, ready for the raid."

129 "straining our eyes": Clarke, "Incidents," 17.

129 "fizzle": Ibid., 16.

130 "heavily manned": Second Battalion War Diary, February 8, 1916. Collections Canada.

130 "slithered": Murray, *2nd Battalion*, 79.

131 Murray, Denman, "conscious, but that's all": Ibid. W. W. Murray identifies Richardson's rescuers as "J. H. Murray," who appears to be James Hugh Murray, originally of Meadowville Station, Nova Scotia; and "R. O. Denman," who appears to be Oliver Denman, a New Brunswick-born clerk living in Sault Ste. Marie before the war.

131   "well-built": Ibid., 80.

132   "muddle": Clarke, "Incidents," 17.

132   "We had no ginger in us": Clarke, "Warfare," 35.

131–132 Rudyard Kipling poem "For All We Have And Are," first published in *The Times*, London, on September 2, 1914. If Richardson had read and committed this verse to memory, he may have received the words from another soldier. Collecting, recording, and sharing verse was common in that era, particularly among educated Great War soldiers. Note that the diary of Canadian nursing sister Clare Gass contains transcriptions of numerous poems including an early reference to John McCrae's "In Flanders Fields." See Gass, *Clare Gass*, 76.

132   trust to educate orphans: "Capt. Richardson's Generous Bequests," Toronto *Globe*, March 6, 1916.

PADRES

133   *minenwerfer* attacks on Second Battalion, "Stokes mortar": Clarke, "Warfare," 35.

135   bombers' late morning naps: Charles Clarke, "Warfare," 30. "There were three of us in our dugout that didn't take their rum issue. That gave the others a real good shot and they would have a good sleep after breakfast each morning."

135   Pringle characterization, "stick his head," "huge hands could span your head," "almost lift you up with one hand," "talk of joining the bombers": Clarke, "Warfare," 36.

136   "lumberman": Pringle attestation papers and military personnel file, Collections Canada.

136   John P. Pringle background: "Canada," London *Times*, October 7, 1916. Also, "Lieut. Pringle Charges German Machine Gun Single Handed," *Grande Prairie Herald*, October 10, 1916.

136   "gamblers, robbers," text of Thanksgiving Day poem (author unknown): Aitken, *In Memoriam*, 13 and 14.

137   chaplains and Riel rebellion: Crerar, *Padres*, 13.

137   Charles Gordon enlists, "no fighting man": Gordon, *Postscript*, 193 and 194.

138   Frederick Scott, "I have got to go to war"; Scott, *The Great War*, 15. Frederick Scott's father was respected poet F. R. Scott.

138   Scott and Pringle: Crerar, *Padres*, 33.

138   Alexander Gordon family: Reid, *Named by the Enemy*, 52.

138   "the most stirring appeals," poem "O Canada! A drum beats through": Gordon, *Postscript*, 196 and 197.

138   "friends and guides," "windy": Crerar, *Padres*, 34. From notes made by C. F. Winter.

138   "six hundred men": Scott, *The Great War*, 15.

139   "I had the feeling": Ibid., 50.

139   "There was something uncanny": Ibid., 57.

139   The poem "Requiescant": Ibid., 75.

139   "great joy": Ibid., 146 and 147.

140   Few had enlisted: Crerar, *Padres*, 164.

140 "the war'll be over by Christmas": Murray, *2nd Battalion*, 77.

140 "You know boys": Clarke, "Warfare," 33. Clarke's account refers to the village as "St. JansCappelle."

140 Plugstreet wit: "Tommy's Humor," Winnipeg *Tribune*, June 14, 1916, 6.

140 "dreary, sodden": Scott, *The Great War*, 157.

141 "that his son was gone": Clarke, "Warfare," 36.

141 Pringle commendation: Pringle military record, Queen's University Online Archive.

141 "with trembling lips": Aitken, *In Memoriam*, 18.

141 "it ends right": Crerar, *Padres*, 165.

141–142 learning of son's death: Scott, *The Great War*, 147.

142 "horses upon horses," "a lonely white cross": Ibid., 156.

THE LAST LARK

144 grenade attack at Wulverghem: Second Battalion War Diary, March 1–14, 1916. Collections Canada.

144 McCrae's poem "In Flanders Fields."

145 "favourite billets," "blood in their eyes," "Heard first Lark," Newton Pippin barrage: Clarke, "Warfare," 37. "So we got busy and got a box of Newton Pippins and went straight to work, firing them over our shoulders like we did the Hales."

145 "spell of hate": Gordon, *Postscript*, 225.

146 "We went after Fritz again in the morning, then again [in] the afternoon and again at night," "Things were working up to something": Clarke, "Warfare," 37.

146 "Leo had felt the pressure too": Clarke, "Warfare," 37. March 14's diary entry was: "Beautiful day, Aircraft busy, Minenwerfers in afternoon. No Mail." Leo Clarke's diary entry, as described by the November 23, 1918, Winnipeg *Tribune*, stated: "Three narrow escapes." On March 15, Leo Clarke wrote: "Within 10 yards of a Minnie Werfer—Ha! Ha! Almost covered with dirt, but not hurt."

147 "something," "our dugouts had heaved": Clarke, "Warfare," 37 and 38. "We sat the bombardment out in our dugout. There had been a line of shells land just about ten feet away from us and they had made a continuous shell hole or trench for over a hundred yards."

147 "We beat it from our dugouts": Winnipeg *Tribune*, Nov. 23, 1918, 43 and 44. Leo Clarke wrote: "March 16—First heavy bombardment I was under; 995 shells went over; 200 did not explode; was not scared, but a little nervous. We beat it from our dugouts to the Signaller's dugout at D 3...."

148 "Looking back, I believe," "Worse trip": Clarke, "Warfare," 38. Clarke wrote: "Our grenade fire must have harassed them much more than we had realized and they had made an all out effort to put an end to it."

148 "old boys": Ibid., 40. "Then the next day I found that the Battalion were in the trenches in the Ypres Salient; the dreaded Ypres Salient. Even since we had been in France, the old boys spoke with dread of Ypres."

149 1916 origins of Spanish flu: J. S. Oxford, A. Sefton, "Outbreaks of Influenza," 155–161.

150 No. 3 ambulance attacked in Ypres salient: Handwritten field report Ref. A.M.D.8. 24-3-2 to Lt. Colonel, A.D.M.S., Medical Historical Recorder, London, England. Attached to No. 3 Field Ambulance War Diary for April 1915.

150   "it is almost impossible": Gass, *Clare Gass*, 227.

150   "They come in such numbers": Purdom, *Everyman*, 252–259.

150   "Some of these new patients": Gass, *Clare Gass*, 26.

151   April schedule at No. 3 Field Ambulance: No. 3 CFA War Diary, April 1916. Collections Canada.

151   "passes," "holding camp," "ration limbers": Clarke, *Incidents*, 19.

152   "had breakfasted": Fussell, *Great War*, 74.

152   "England looked strange": Graves, *Goodbye*, 188.

152   "never seen anything at all like it before": Fussell, *Great War*, 49.

153   "All good things": Clarke, "Warfare," 39. Charlie Clarke's leave and Leo Clarke's hospitalization did not run concurrently. Charlie Clarke was on leave between March 27 and April 6, 1916. On page 40 of "Warfare," he wrote: "On Thursday April 6th, I arrived in Poperinghe." Leo Clarke, according to records contained in his army Personnel Records Envelope, was admitted to hospital on April 10 and "rejoined his unit" on May 2.

153   Leo Clarke leave in England, May 1916. Letter from Arthur Clarke to Harry Clarke, May 11, 1916. This leave is not recorded in Leo Clarke's military personnel file and may have been approved by the medical CO at the hospital in which he was convalescing.

SHIFTING GROUND

154   "evil reputation": Urquhart, *Sixteenth Battalion*, 125.

155   "grim ruins on either side": Scott, *The Great War*, 50.

155   The battalion was posted, description of Hill 60: Clarke, "Warfare," 40.

155   "the most hated position": Urquhart, *Sixteenth Battalion*, 132.

155–156 "history of trench warfare at its worst," "calibrating point": Murray, *2nd Battalion*, 85.

157   "Jackson Street," "Larch Wood": "Report of German Attack," Second Battalion War Diary, April 1916, Appendix 1.

157   "barbed wire, corkscrew stakes," "ordinary strafe": Murray, *2nd Battalion*, 86.

157   "Gods joined in": Clarke, "Warfare," 42. "Then the gods joined in. A continuous bombardment plus a whale of a thunderstorm."

157   Late in day on April 26: Clarke, "Warfare," 42, "Incidents," 20. Charlie Clarke reported that the explosion occurred at 6:25 P.M. The Appendix Report for the Second Battalion War Diary states 6:30 P.M.

157–158 Sergeant Dick Reynolds's description of the mine blast: Murray, *2nd Battalion*, 87.

159   "The Germans are in our trench": Clarke, "Incidents," 20.

159   a lunar-sized crater 130 feet long, 85 feet wide, and 30 feet deep: Second Battalion War Diary, Appendix 1. Collections Canada.

160   "We had better get those men": Clarke, "Incidents," 21.

160   "He scared me more than anything": Clarke, "Warfare," 43.

160   "safest place": Clarke, "Incidents," 21.

NOTES

161   "explosive similar to 40% dynamite": Second Battalion War
      Diary, Appendix 1. Collections Canada.

161   "catastrophe," "avalanche of metal": Murray, *2nd Bat-
      talion*, 6.

162   Hoey exploit in unearthing buried soldiers: Second Battalion
      War Diary, April 1916, Appendix 1. Collections Canada.

163   "Out of the four men squeezed inside," Clarke, "War-
      fare," 44.

164   "heavy going," The tour was, as Charlie said, "uneventful":
      Ibid., 45.

164   An unusual quiet: Murray, *2nd Battalion*, 90.

SANCTUARY WOOD

165   "charred, jagged": Bennett, *The 4th Canadian Mounted
      Rifles*, 19.

165   "orange, red, and green" Very lights: Urquhart, *Sixteenth
      Battalion*, 137.

165–166 "a scene of indescribable desolation": Gordon, *Postscript*,
      235 and 236.

166   description of Maple Copse before attack, "Hell": Charles
      Savage, "Post-War Memoir."

166   "calm, beautiful": Bennett, *The 4th Canadian Mounted
      Rifles*, 19.

166   "harmless as a bottle of milk": Douglas, *Captured*, 23.

168   "form a new line": Fraser, *Private Fraser*, 144.

168   "biggest we had ever been in": Douglas, *Captured*, 29.

168   "jelly": Cook, *Sharp End*, 350. "'The ground shook like

jelly,' recounted Lawrence Rogers, a thirty-eight-year-old sergeant."

168   "cloud of steel": Bennett, *The 4th Canadian Mounted Rifles*,18.

168   "every conceivable type of gun": Ibid.

169   "our front line was practically destroyed": Douglas, *Captured*, 30.

169   "gone to heaven," "like a ship on a rough sea": Ibid., 34.

169   Mercer's death: "Gen. Mercer's Death," *Medicine Hat News*, June 26, 1916, 1. In a postcard to his parents mailed as a POW and published widely across Canada, Gooderham stated: "He lay in the field suffering no pain and next day he was killed by shrapnel instantly."

170   "paying the penalty in full for their rashness": Fraser, *Private Fraser*, 146.

170   "matted welter of trees": Gordon, *Postscript*, 238.

170   "with heavy rifle and M[achine] Gun fire and commenced an attack": Fourth Battalion War Diary, June 4, 1916. Collections Canada.

170–171 "We'll hae nane but Hielan Bonnets here": Sinclair, *The Queen's Own Cameron Highlanders*, 74.

171   "withering enemy fire": Fraser, *Private Fraser*, 147.

171   "shell it from three sides," "stretcher bearer!": Urquhart, *Sixteenth Battalion*, 140.

171   petrol cans: Forty-Third Battalion War Diary, June 5, 1916. Collections Canada. "Water was delivered to men in front line in petrol tins."

172   "should never have been": Fraser, *Private Fraser*, 147.

A SADLY DEPLETED BUNCH

174   "grueling tour": Murray, *2nd Battalion*, 89.

174   railway dugouts: Clarke, "Warfare," 46.

175   "several thousand," "He had a good Blighty": Ibid.

175–176 Harry Lukka's death: Clarke, "Incidents," 25. "The boys had been too busy to take his body out, he had been a mess, his head blown off, so they had put his body over the back, till it could be looked after."

176   The German position: Murray, *2nd Battalion*, 95. "It was established that on the left the Germans were about 400 yards away; but on the right they occupied the whole of Armagh Wood." This report made by the Second Battalion scouts.

177   "take over a special job," "torn up with shell holes," "on the edge of Sanctuary Wood": Clarke, "Incidents," 21.

177   "in the dark of night," "face to face": Clarke, "Warfare," 49.

178   "landed in with the Germans," "My eyes followed the bayonet," "We had found the 43rd," "You came at a hell," "Hurry up," "Up went the German S.O.S. signals": Clarke, "Incidents," 27.

179   "clumps of mud," "make ourselves as small as possible," "badly shaken": Clarke, "Warfare," 50.

180   "scorched": Clarke, "Warfare," 50.

180   "born lucky": Clarke, "Incidents," 28.

180   "Big Dolly": Clarke's "Warfare" identifies his comrade as "a young farmer from Hamiota" (page 52). His "Incidents & Anecdotes" (page 21) identifies the man as "Big Dolly," which in his annotated platoon photo is further identified as

"Dolly Ledgerwood." Elsewhere in his memoirs, he calls this man "Dougie." Doug Ledgerwood was born April 26, 1894, in Virden, Manitoba, and enlisted in the army in December 1915.

180–181 "leapfrog," "stepping stone": Clarke, "Incidents," 21 and 22.

181 Thirteenth Battalion charge: Clarke, "Warfare," 52.

181 "sorry sadly depleted": Clarke, "Warfare," 51.

181 "it just goes to show": Ibid., 55.

182 "loose livers," "would find them in a ditch": Ibid., 57.

182 "and a little child shall lead them": Charles Harris, "And a Little Child Shall Lead Them," 1906.

182 "timid little man": Clarke, "Warfare," 56. "The trenches were in a terrible state and moral was very low. I went out for rations just after we got settled. It was a long hike. I had another man with me. He was a timid little man who had a tenor voice like an angel.… In September 1918, I met him back with the Battalion and questioned him about his disappearance. He told me that he had been wounded by a ricochet bullet."

184 "an old woman": Clarke, "Warfare," 57. Clarke does not name Strachan in this account. But Strachan is identified in a group photo of the Bombers taken at that time. "We had a new Bombing Officer. He had been Company Sergeant Major of No. 1 Company and had received his commission in the field. We thought he was an old woman. He used to fuss a lot. I think he was prewar militia."

184 promotion to Lance Corporal: Ibid., 58.

184 "mortally wounded," W. S. King's death: Murray, *2nd Battalion*, 105.

184   "even the old timers had expected": Clarke, "Warfare," 60.

185   "throw her child": Fussell, *Great War*, 45–46.

185   "If the Virgin fell": Clarke, "Warfare," 62.

THE SHOW

187   "mounted troops," "bridgehead": Haig, *War Diaries*, 182 and 183.

187   "getting as large a combined force": Haig, *War Diaries*, 184.

188   "any offensive on a large scale from being made until all is ready": Ibid., 185.

188   "kill Germans": Ibid., 184.

188   Allied artillery at Somme: Keegan, *First World War*, 313.

188   "I do feel that in my plans": Haig, *War Diaries*, 195.

188–189 "does not appear to have had any original ideas": Ibid., 221.

189   "flower of British youth": Keegan, *First World War*, 369.

189   Haig report to War Committee: Gilbert, *Somme*, 145.

189–190 "sterile, shell-packed," "here was the Empire," "deep and steady": Murray, *2nd Battalion*, 113. "All around were the evidences of what was involved in a great offensive—artillery parks, ammunition dumps, horse lines, watering troughs, stores of gasoline, engineering material, and, everywhere khaki-clad soldiers."

190   "mishaps of the early days of the Somme fighting had not yet been revealed": Ibid., 115.

190   "gullies and gulches": Clarke, "Warfare," 61.

190   "guns and the unlimited quantities of ammunition that surrounded them," "wheel to wheel," "Never had such prodigality": Murray, *2nd Battalion*, 115.

191   The plan was to seize the entire ridge: Gilbert, *Somme*, 144. "Haig to Foch that, once the line Pozières-Morva-Sally-Saillisel had been reached, the combined Anglo-French army could strike northward."

191   "render whatever assistance the Australians might require": Murray, *2nd Battalion*, 118.

192   "before undertaking any offensive operations": Gilbert, *Somme*, 173.

192   "thrilled," "We were on the offensive," "terrific bombardment": Clarke, "Warfare," 63.

192   German shells falling: Murray, *2nd Battalion*, 118.

192   "the way to victory": Gilbert, *Somme*, 145.

192   "The Army was obviously going forward": Murray, *2nd Battalion*, 115.

193   "one of the greatest tragedies," "top brass held men's lives": Clarke, "Warfare," 64.

193   the battle was killing: Gilbert, *Somme*, 160.

194   "the most terrible days of my life": Ibid., 155.

194   "surpassed in horror all my previous experiences": Ibid., 165.

194   "self-contained": Murray, *2nd Battalion*, 120.

195   "One hears far less criticism": Watson, *Enduring*, 167.

195   "cut off," "We were not sentimentally inclined": Clarke, "Warfare," 65.

196   "creeping barrage": Keegan, *First World War*, 314 and 315.

196–197 "went too fast": Rawling, *Surviving Trench Warfare*, 27.

197 "a new idea for attacks": Clarke, "Warfare," 65.

197 "all hell was let loose": Clarke, "Warfare," 65.

198 In theory: Keegan, *First World War*, 314.

198 "Casualties were heavy": Murray, *2nd Battalion*, 124.

198 "German forage caps," "thickly," "The leveled rifles spat a vicious stream," "worming their way forward on their stomachs": Ibid., 125.

198 "Go on, boys": Ibid.

199 "Major McLaughlin Dead," *Toronto Star*, October 7, 1916.

199 "bravest thing that I ever saw": "Lieut. Pringle Charges German Machine Gun," *Grande Prairie Herald*, October 10, 1916.

199 Henry Cuthbert Stuart, McLaughlin radio message: Murray, *2nd Battalion*, 128.

200 "My party never threw a bomb," "six lovely German Dress Helmets," "Did you happen to realize that there's a war on?" "just wilted away," "very lonely job," "I felt the heat of it," "Fred Tyo," weeping soldier: Clarke, "Warfare," 65 and 66.

202 "Good God": Ibid., 67.

202 "I'm glad to see you," "They are all gone": Ibid., 68.

POZIÈRES RIDGE

203 William Nichols: Nichols attestation papers and military personnel file, Collections Canada. Nichols's attestation papers state that he was born in Sunderland, Brock, Ontario, on May 21, 1891, and he was listed as a farmer at the time of his enlistment in Winnipeg, Manitoba.

204   Leo Clarke's detail to billeting party: Ibid., 61.

204   La Panne: Identified now as De Panne, but denoted as "in the vicinity of" La Panne in Second Battalion War Diary, August 12, 1916. Collections Canada.

204   Leo Clarke billet in La Panne: Clarke, "Incidents," 27. "We march and out comes the girl and runs and throws her arms around that brother of mine's neck, and cries out his name in a loud voice, was his face red." This account is also included on page 61 of Clarke's "Warfare."

205   Leo Clarke's squad: Murray, *2nd Battalion*, 126. According to Murray, the scouts included "Ptes Ranger and Johnston," and the machine gunner was Lance Corporal James Staback.

205   "out ranged them," "temporary barricade," "Turning tail, they fled": Ibid.

206–207 Leo Clarke's battle on the left flank of Pozières Ridge: Ibid., 126–28. Details of this battle are recorded in Leo Clarke's Victoria Cross citation, and elaborated upon in *2nd Battalion*. These accounts state that Leo Clarke at one point picked up a rifle from the trench floor and fired it on the squad of attacking Germans he was single-handedly defending against.

Before his death, Leo Clarke told his brother, Charles, that this interpretation was incorrect. His only weapon in this battle was his Colt handgun. Charles Clarke describes this discrepancy in his postwar account *One Man's Warfare*, and communicated this information years later in conversations with his son, Leo Clarke Jr. Charles Clarke also described these events in an interview appearing in CBC Radio "Morning Comment," November 11, 1964. The official account may have included a rifle because the Colt handgun Leo Clarke used was a non-regulation weapon.

PINE STREET

209   The communication trench Luxton Avenue: William Fisher Luxton (1844–1907), Winnipeg's first school-teacher, co-founder of the Manitoba *Free Press*, member of Manitoba's Legislative Assembly, and a candidate in the city's first election for mayor.

210   "Lieut. Pringle Charges German Machine Gun": *Grande Prairie Herald*, Oct. 10, 1916.

211   "four Canadian divisions": "Canadians in Victory at Somme," Winnipeg *Tribune*, September 11, 1916, 1.

211   "We have allowed men": McClung, *Next of Kin*, Foreword.

212   Harriet Waugh: Jim Blanchard, *Winnipeg's Great War*, 149.

213   "Mother Receives Victoria Cross," Manitoba *Free Press*, August 26, 1915, 16.

213   Mary Hall's appeal to Marie Steele: Harry Hall to Gail Burton, June 17, 1979. Private collection.

215   Jim Foley: Ibid., June 9, 1979. Private collection.

215   "black from gangrene," "'If you had gone to a lesser hospital you would have one arm now'": Ibid., July 15, 1979. Private collection.

215   "didn't think it would do any good": Ibid., July 17, 1979. Private collection.

218   Details of returned Winnipeg wounded: "They Have Done Their Bit for the Empire," Winnipeg *Tribune*, November 22, 1915, 1.

218   "That was just like him. He never thought of himself. He did not fear anything": "Mother Receives Victoria Cross," Manitoba *Free Press*, August 26, 1915, 16.

SWINGING THE LEAD

219   "Gazing to the rear," "turn this position into a cauldron again": Murray, *2nd Battalion*, 131.

219–220 "section by section": Ibid., 132.

220   "everything that was asked of them": Ibid., 131.

220   "we dragged our feet": Clarke, "Warfare," 69.

221   "bare uplands," "flash of guns": Urquhart, *Sixteenth Battalion*, 161.

222   "quiet, decisive way": Ibid., 136.

222   "big impressive man": Clarke, "Warfare," 70.

222   Currie's speech to Bombers at Rozel: Charlie Clarke relates this speech in two postwar accounts: "One Man's Warfare," pages 69 and 70, and "Leo Clarke, V.C.," chapter 11, page 1. All but the last sentence is derived from "Leo Clarke." I have added the final sentence—"and live up to the good name you have made for yourselves"—from his quote in "Warfare" (page 70).

223   "something mysterious": Clarke, "Warfare," 70.

223   "Mastodons," tank in Fler: MacDonald, *Somme*, 275 and 282.

223   Haig quote "tanks have done marvels": Haig, *War Diaries*, 230.

224   "the same as if I was making logs": Cook, *Sharp End*, 450.

224 mustered in Harponville: Second Battalion War Diary, September 16, 1916. Collections Canada.

224 "sullen, wet skies": "Interlude," chapter by General A.E. Swift in Murray, *2nd Battalion*, 142.

224 "deluged the area": Ibid., 134.

224 "synonym for all the destruction": Ibid.

225 "Tipped crazily to one side and straddling the trench": Clarke, "Warfare," 71.

225 "long weary road": Clarke, "Leo Clarke," 2.

225 "blue shoulder straps," "lost all interest": Ibid., 1.

226 was still a Bomber at heart, and braved a "poisonous" war zone: Murray, *2nd Battalion*, 134. "In the language of the troops, this place was utterly 'poisonous.'"

226 "big Dixie of tea still piping hot," "It was all above and beyond the call of duty": Clarke, "Warfare," 72.

226 "sad tale of how he had lost his way": Clarke, "Leo Clarke," 2.

226 Again, Hoey drew his gun: Ibid. "Lieut. Hoey was furious, and ordered Bill to take charge of the outpost down on the sunken road, on the other side of the village, again his gun came out."

226 He chose "a good man," a Bomber veteran steady under fire: Ibid.

227 "kamerad": Clarke, "Warfare," 73.

227 "One minute there were men": Ibid., 74.

227 "Sometimes, it didn't take much shelling": Clarke, "Leo Clarke," 3.

228 "canned fruit, fancy biscuits": Clarke, "Warfare," 75.

228 "I had to shoot some of the men": Clarke, "Warfare," 76. "I had to shoot some of the men that were surrendered," Leo had confessed to Charlie. "He had to keep shooting," Charlie realized, and he told Leo so.

229 "gloom and death": Scott, *The Great War*, 139.

229 "casualties had been mounting": Clarke, "Warfare," 75.

229 "took stock of myself": Clarke, "Leo Clarke," 5.

230 "consider him a coward": Ibid. "swinging the lead," "I'm going with you this time": Clarke, "Warfare," 78 and 79.

UNBURIED DEAD

231 "getting to be an obsession": Clarke, "Leo Clarke," 5.

232 "freight trains": Ibid.

232 "been over in England": Clarke, "Warfare," 79.

232 "Their skin was all wizened up," he would later reflect, "and I thought how like monkeys they looked": Clarke, "Leo Clarke," 5.

233 "I'm dead, I'm dead": Clarke, "Warfare," 68.

233 "his first and only victim of the whole war," "I had fired thousands of grenades back at Wulverghem": Ibid.

234 "chafed under the delay": Ibid., "Leo Clarke," 5.

234 "stretcher-bearers would come by": Ibid.

234 "Go to a dressing station": Ibid., 6.

235 bolstered the men: Ibid.

235 "extra rations": Clarke, "Warfare," 80.

235 "badly needed rest": Ibid.

236   "fairly quiet," "brisk artillery duel": Second Battalion War Diary, October 13, 1916, Collections Canada.

236   Most of the shelling seemed to come from the Allied side: Second Battalion War Diary, October 13, 1916. Collections Canada.

236   A "fine" morning had broken: Ibid., October 14, 1916. Collections Canada.

236   "commotion," "with red tabs on their shoulders": Clarke, "Leo Clarke," 6.

236   Watson profile, "dashing, charming ... self-promoter," "plumb job": Brennan, "Byng's and Currie's Commanders," 8.

236   Aitken's eagle-eye watch on the German line included suspicions that an enemy dressing station protected by "at least two M.G. [Machine Gun] positions" was in fact a "Strong Point": Fourth Canadian Division, INTELLIGENCE REPORT No. 1., October 14, 1916. Collections Canada.

237   "full view of the Germans," "filthy looks": Clarke, "Warfare," 80. "I took it upon myself to remind them that they were in full view of the Germans. I just got some filthy looks."

238   "a direct hit": Ibid.

238   Hoey scrambling towards Murray Avenue: In both "One Man's Warfare" (page 80) and "Leo Clarke, V.C.," Chapter 11 (page 1), Charlie Clarke describes "Our Bombing Officer running down the trench" ("Warfare") and "Mr. Hoey was running away" ("Leo Clarke"). No further details are given apart from stating in "Leo Clarke," "he [Hoey] turned partly and said ..." Hoey may have been running away on the far side of the collapsed trench where Leo Clarke was buried, but it is more likely he was running down the communication trench, Murray Avenue.

238   Dialogue between Hoey and C. Clarke: Clarke, "Leo Clarke," chap. 11, 1.

238   "eyes staring in shock": Clarke, "Warfare," 80.

239   "like fury": Clarke, "Leo Clarke," chap. 11, 1.

240   Assessment of Leo Clarke's wounds: Ibid. "Leo, on whom I could see no wound, was paralyzed from the waist down but still conscious, and as the shock had not yet warn off, was not yet in pain."

240   "how boyish": Clarke, "Warfare," 81. "How boyish this face seemed, this older brother of mine."

240   "spend his money": Ibid.

240   "biggest and best": Ibid.

240   Account of Leo Clarke's wounding: Ibid., 79, 80, 81; Clarke, "Leo Clarke," 6, Ibid., chap. 11, 1, and 2. Also briefly noted in Murray, *2nd Battalion*, 139.

THE LAST PARADE

241   "kept close to our own part": Clarke, "Warfare," 82.

241   "We were tired and still numb": Ibid.

242   leaving the line: Ibid.

242   The statue of Albert, "in a despairing gesture": Fussell, *Great War*, 164.

242   In fact, British commanders, determined that the war not end under any conditions other than their own, ordered

army engineers to fasten the relic to the church: Cook, *Sharp End*, 424.

242   "when the smoke cleared": Fussell, *Great War*, 163 and 164.

242   Second Battalion casualty figures: Murray, *2nd Battalion*, 140.

242   "It was a sad journey": Clarke, "Leo Clarke," 2.

243   A. E. Swift remarks: Murray, *2nd Battalion*, 142.

243   "We tried to be proud": Clarke, "Warfare," 82.

243   "missing faces": Clarke, "Leo Clarke," 2.

244   Le Meillard, Barly: Second Battalion War Diary. General Swift spells Le Meillard "Mailard" and Barly "Barley."

244   "Didn't I say": Clarke, "Warfare," 82.

PASSCHENDAELE

246   "War, that merciless revealer": Atkinson, *The Guns at Last Light*, 389.

247   Lt.-Col. Robert MacDonald Thomson funeral at the Somme: Gordon, *Postscript*, 252.

248   "enemy is faltering": Keegan, *First World War*, 393.

248   "there was to be no retreat": Scott, *The Great War*, 242.

249   "precise, school master's mind": Keegan, *First World War*, 394.

249   "filthy oozing mud," "It was mud, mud everywhere": Arthur, *Forgotten Voices*, 235. Quotes from J. W. Palmer, Twenty-Sixth Brigade, Royal Field Artillery.

249   Worst spate of rain in thirty years: Rawling, *Surviving Trench Warfare*, 144.

250   "give the infantry a fighting chance": Cook, *Shock Troops*, 325.

250–251 German strategy at Passchendaele: Rawling, *Surviving Trench Warfare*, 144. *See also* Cook, *Shock Troops*, 329–335; Keegan, *First World War*, 392.

251   "still, gray, humped raccoons": Wheeler, *No Man's Land*, 166.

252   "Men advanced with such practiced skill," "a polyphony of carefully orchestrated sounds": Ibid., 167

252   "very awfulness of the situation": "Captain Robert Shankland, V.C., D.C.M." by C. Cornell, Winnipeg *Tribune*, December 21, 1918, 51.

254   Shankland knew enough about poker: "Ayr's V.C. Holder Pays Brief Visit," July 10, 1964, *Ayrshire Post*, Postscripts section. Shankland was a good enough card player to seize on this advantage. He knew that his "Poker hand"—the size of his force—was only as strong as the Germans feared it to be. Shankland suggested in a newspaper interview forty-eight years after the battle of Passchendaele that bluffing the size and strength of his force may have been part of his tactics. When asked by a reporter for the *Ayrshire Post* how he had triumphed at Passchendaele, Shankland said: "I played poker with the Hun. That's a game of bluff."

255   "The worst show we had had," "Shankland converted what looked like a bad day into victory": "Captain Robert Shankland, V.C., D.C.M." by C. Cornell, Winnipeg *Tribune*, December 21, 1918, 51.

257   According to the *Official History of the Canadian Army in the First World War*, O'Kelly and his fighters worked "southward" and engaged the bunkers one at a time, laying down

a "diversion with their rifle grenades and Lewis guns" while a handful of soldiers circled around behind and cleared each stone hut with grenades; "bitter fighting": Nicholson, *Official History*, 318–320.

257   "rebuke for Sanctuary Wood": Bennett, 4th Mounted Rifles, 89.

258   Tommy Holmes, who looked younger than his 19 years and "wore a perpetual grin on his face." Bishop, "Passchendaele Nine Plus One," *Legion Magazine*, May 1, 2005. http://legion magazine.com/en/2005/05/the-passchendaele-nine-plus-one

258   15,634 casualty figure: Keegan, *First World War*, 394.

259   One veteran called it "the most ghastly attack in which I ever participated": Joliffe, "Interview," Library and Archives Canada.

259   "It was undoubtedly Shankland's good work that won the day": "Captain Robert Shankland, V.C., D.C.M." by C. Cornell, Winnipeg *Tribune*, December 21, 1918, 51.

260   Shankland VC citation: "Lieut. Shankland Gets Army's Highest Honor," Manitoba *Free Press*, December 22, 1917, 8.

261   "glistening" insignia, "Whistles shrieked, bells jangled, and thousands cheered," "cold rain," "I wouldn't give a hoot if it was hailing brickbats": "City Goes Wild Over Own Units," Winnipeg *Evening Tribune*, March 24, 1919, 1 and 2.

261   "Women laughed hysterically, and tears coursed down their faces as they embraced their dear ones and held them tightly, as if afraid that they would be torn from them again." In the first moments after the men and their families were re-joined, "a strange quiet settled down over the station": "Soldiers' Kin First To Welcome Them," Winnipeg *Tribune*, March 24, 1919, 1.

HOME

263   Charles Clarke's arrival to Winnipeg: Clarke, "Leo Clarke," 5. "I got off the train at the Winnipeg station of the C.P.R. … just six weeks less than four years from the time I had marched down Main St. to the C.N.R. to go overseas."

264   L. Clarke's condition at No. 1 General Hospital: L. Clarke military attestation papers and military personnel file, Collections Canada.

265   "I felt that this was the end": Clarke, "Warfare," 81.

265   the news was a "shock": Clarke, "Leo Clarke," 3.

265   "If I march with the Bombers": Ibid.

266   "There was nothing else I could do": Ibid.

267   Freddie Harrison: James Frederick Harrison, who was born in Cheshire County (Cheshire), England on September 9, 1892, and died at Passchendaele on November 6, 1917. He was a farmer in Portage la Prairie at the time of enlistment. He was a member of the Scouts and Snipers and was killed by a German shell. According to a letter by Private J. R. Shelton, which was mailed to his mother Mary Harrison, living in Washington state, "he was killed by a German shell." His body was never found. He is listed on the Menin Gate at Ypres, panel 10-26-28.

267   "We then went down the road": Clarke, "Warfare," 85.

268   Charlie even instructed: Ibid., 91.

268   "the war was to go on": Ibid.

268–269   fine baths we had: Ibid., "Vignettes of Vimy."

269   Bombers' Christmas dinner: Clarke, "Warfare," 90, 91, 94.

270   He was not home long: Ibid., "Incidents," 5

271   "Some men": Ibid., "Warfare," 93.

271   Doug "Dolly" Ledgerwood died on July 29, 1917.

272   "all of these men": "70,000 Men Have Gone From Winnipeg Since Aug 1," Winnipeg *Tribune*, July 27, 1918, 1.

272   "Major, I dinna grudge my boy": Gordon, *Postscript*, 230.

273   St. Patrick's Anglican held its first service in 1912 in a church building on the corner of Pine and Ellice Streets, but was moved to the corner of Spruce and Riddle Street in 1915. In 1927, the church returned to Pine Street, which was then called Valour Road. The church closed due to dwindling attendance in 2006. The plaque and accompanied scroll currently resides with the Museum of the Royal Winnipeg Rifles, Minto Amoury, Winnipeg.

273   "soldiers' relatives," "happy informality," "seems to wave good-bye to his loved ones" : Blanchard, *Winnipeg's Great War*, 261.

274   1914 population: the 1911 census recorded Canada's population at 7,206,643. The 1921 national census: 8,787,949.

EPILOGUE

276   "Winnipeg": Blanchard, *Winnipeg's Great War*, 260.

277   Duncan Cross, Hector McIvor: Records obtained through Collections Canada indicate that Duncan Cross of the Tenth Battalion, born on Dec. 18, 1885, in Rosshire, Scotland, died on April 9, 1917. No military death record could be found for an individual named Hector McIvor. In a letter to his granddaughter, Gail Burton, dated July 8, 1979, Harry Hall wrote: "You asked about Duncan and Hector. They were both killed at Vimy Ridge in 1917. I didn't know for a

long time, but will tell you later how I found out and corresponded with Duncan earlier."

278 Ayr Town Council bestows "Freedom" on Shankland: Wade, "Lieutenant Robert Shankland." In early 1918, Bob returned home to be presented with the title Freedom of the Burgh of Ayr.

278 In 1920, he returned home to marry Anne Haining: "Wedding of Ayr V.C.," *Ayrshire Post*, April 23, 1920, 6.

278 "I played poker with the Hun": "Ayr's V.C. Holder Pays Brief Visit," Ibid., July 10, 1964, postcripts section.

280 "There was a very happy buzz the night of his visit." Richard Clarke to author, September 30, 2013.

281 "Dad's outstanding accomplishments," "with the rest of his Comrades": Clarke, "Warfare," prologue, written by Leo Clarke Jr.

283 "As I read the list of names": Clarke, "Omands Creek," 4.

BIBLIOGRAPHY

ARCHIVES AND DATABASES

Ancestor Seekers of Kenora. *Kenora Great War Project.* http://askgen.
ning.com/group/kenora-great-war-project.

Attestation papers. Library and Archives Canada, Collections Canada.
Ottawa. http://www.bac-lac.gc.ca/eng/discover/military-heritage/
first-world-war/first-world-war-1914-1918-cef/Pages/search.
aspx.

Canadian Expedionary Force War Diaries for Second, Eighth, Tenth,
Forty-Third Battalions. Library and Archives Canada, Collections
Canada. Ottawa. www.collectionscanada.gc.ca.

Canadian Great War Project. http://www.canadiangreatwarproject.
com.

Canadian Virtual War Memorial. Veterans Affairs Canada. Ottawa.
http://www.veterans.gc.ca/eng/remembrance/memorials/
canadian-virtual-war-memorial.

Joliffe, W. H., Fourth Battalion. "Interview." Library and Archives Canada. Ottawa. http://www.collectionscanada.gc.ca/first-world-war/interviews/025015-1620-e.html.

1901 and 1911 British and Canadian census material accessed through www.ancestry.ca and http://automatedgenealogy.com/census11/.

Queen's University Online Archives. http://archives.queensu.ca/databases.html.

Savage, Henry Charles, Fifth CMRs Battalion. Post-War Memoir, Library and Archives Canada, Collections Canada. Ottawa.

ARTICLES

Bishop, Arthur. "The Passchendaele Nine Plus One: Part 9 of 18." *Legion Magazine*, (2005). http://legionmagazine.com/en/2005/05/the-passchendaele-nine-plus-one/.

Brennan, Patrick. "Byng's and Currie's Commanders: A Still Untold Story of the Canadian Corps." *Canadian Military History 11*, no. 1 (2012).

Oxford, J. S., and A. Sefton. "Early Herald Wave Outbreaks of Influenza in 1916 prior to the Pandemic of 1918." *International Congress Series* 1219 (2001): 155–161.

Smith, Paul. "Paul Fussell's *The Great War and Modern Memory*: Twenty-five Years." *History and Theory 40*, no. 2 (2001): 241–260. http://www.jstor.org/discover/10.2307/2678033?uid=3738216&uid=2&uid=4&sid=21103821588571.

Winnipeg, City of. "The Bank of Commerce Went Up on Main Street." *Winnipeg Historical Buildings Committee Report* (1980): 2. http://www.winnipeg.ca/ppd/historic/pdf-consv/Smith256-long.pdf.

BOOKS

Aitken, E. Melville, ed. *In Memoriam Rev. John Pringle, D.D., Lt. D., 1852–1935: For Sixty Years a Preacher of the Gospel: Pioneer, Padre, and Pastor.* Sydney, NS: printed by Don MacKinnon, 1935.

Arthur, Max. *Forgotten Voices of the Great War: A New History of World War I in the Words of the Men and Women Who Were There.* London: Ebury Press, 2002.

Atkinson, Rick. *The Guns at Last Light: War in Western Europe, 1944–1945.* London: Little, Brown, 2013.

Beckett, Ian F. W. *Ypres: The First Battle 1914.* Oxford: Routledge, 2013.

Bennett, S. G. *The 4th Canadian Mounted Rifles, 1914–1919.* Toronto: Murray Printing Company, 1926.

Berton, Pierre. *Vimy.* Toronto: Anchor Canada, 2001.

Bird, Will R. *Ghosts Have Warm Hands: A Memoir of the Great War 1916–1919.* Ottawa: CEF Books, 1997.

Blanchard, Jim. *Winnipeg 1912.* Winnipeg: University of Manitoba Press, 2005.

———. *Winnipeg's Great War: A City Comes of Age.* Winnipeg: University of Manitoba Press, 2010.

Borden, Robert Laird. *Robert Laird Borden: His Memoirs.* 2 vols. Montreal and Kingston: McGill-Queen's University Press, 1969.

Cassar, George H. *Hell In Flanders Fields: Canadians at the Second Battle of Ypres.* Toronto: Dundurn Press, 2010.

Chandler, David, ed. *The Oxford History of the British Army.* Oxford: Oxford University Press, 2003.

Christie, Norm. *The Canadians at Ypres, 22nd–26th April 1915: A Social History and Battlefield Tour.* For King and Empire: The

Canadians in the First World War. vol. 1. Ottawa: CEF Books, 1999.

Cook, Tim. *At the Sharp End: Canadians Fighting the Great War 1914–1916.* Vol. 1. Toronto: Viking Canada, 2007.

———. *Shock Troops: Canadians Fighting the Great War, 1917–1918.* Vol. 2. Toronto: Viking Canada, 2008.

Crankshaw, Edward. *The Fall of the House of Habsburg.* London: Papermac, 1981.

Crerar, Duff. *Padres in No Man's Land: Canadian Chaplains and the Great War.* Montreal and Kingston: McGill-Queen's University Press, 1995.

Cruttwell, Charles R. M. F. *The War Service of the 1/4 Royal Berkshire Regiment.* Oxford: Blackwell, 1922.

Currie, J. A. *"The Red Watch": With the First Canadian Division in Flanders.* Reprint of the 1916 Toronto edition, Project Gutenberg, 2009. http://www.gutenberg.org/cache/epub/28116/pg28116.txt.

Curry, Frederick C. *From the St. Lawrence to the Yser: With the 1st Canadian Brigade.* Reprint of the 1916 Toronto edition, Project Gutenberg, 2009. http://www.gutenberg.org/files/29045/29045-h/29045-h.htm.

Douglas, J. Harvey. *Captured: Sixteen Months as a Prisoner of War.* New York: George H. Doran Company, 1918.

Ferguson, Niall. *The Pity of War, 1914–1918.* New York: Basic Books, 1999.

Fetherstonhaugh, R. C. *The 13th Battalion Royal Highlanders of Canada 1914–1919.* Canada: Published by Royal Highlanders of Canada, 1925.

Ferris, Lieut. J. R. *Bombers' Training: and Application of Same in Trench Warfare.* Toronto: William Briggs, 1916.

Fraser, Donald. *The Journal of Private Fraser*. Edited by Reginald Roy. Ottawa: CEF Books, 1998.

Friesen, Gerald. *The Canadian Prairies: A History*. Toronto: University of Toronto Press, 1987.

Fussell, Paul. *Great War and Modern Memory*. New York: Sterling Publishing, 2009.

Gass, Clare. *The War Diary of Clare Gass 1915–1918*. Edited by Susan Mann. Montreal and Kingston: McGill-Queen's University Press, 2000.

Gilbert, Martin. *Somme: The Heroism and Horror of War*. London: John Murray, 2000.

Gordon, Charles. *Postscript to Adventure: The Autobiography of Ralph Connor*. London: Hodder and Stoughton, 1938.

Granatstein, J. L. *Hell's Corner: An Illustrated History of Canada's Great War, 1914–1918*. Vancouver: Douglas & McIntyre, 2004.

Grant, Maurice. *The Lion of the Covenant*. Darlington, UK: EP Books, 1997.

Graves, Dianne. *A Crown of Life: The World of John McCrae*. Staplehurst, UK: Spellmount, 1997.

Graves, Robert. *Goodbye to All That*. London: Penguin Books, 1985.

Great Britain, Historical Section of the Committee of Imperial Defence. *Official History of the Great War, Military Operations France & Belgium, 1915*. Vol. 2. Compiled by Brig-General Sir James Edmonds. Sussex: The Naval & Military Press, 1928.

Great Britain, War Office. *Statistics of the Military Effort of the British Empire During the Great War, 1914–1920*. London: His Majesty's Stationery Office, 1922.

Haig, Douglas. *War Diaries and Letters 1914–1918*. Edited by Gary Sheffield and John Bourne. London: Weidenfeld & Nicolson, 2005.

Holland, J. A. *The Story of the Tenth Canadian Battalion 1914–1917*. London, 1918. https://archive.org/details/storyoftenthbatt00holl.

Humphries, Mark. *The Selected Papers of Sir Arthur Currie: Diaries, Letters, and Report to the Ministry, 1917–1933*. Waterloo, ON: Wilfrid Laurier University Press, 2008.

Inglis, John M. *The Steadfast Way: Ayr Battalion, The Boys's Brigade 1886–2011*. Scotland: Printed by 2nd Prestwick Company, 2011.

Jenkins, Roy. *Churchill*. London: Pan Books, 2002.

Junger, Ernst. *Storm of Steel*. Translated by Michael Hoffman. London: Penguin, 2003.

Keegan, John. *The First World War*. London: Random House, 1999.

———. *A History of Warfare*. London: Random House, 1994.

Lee, John. *The Gas Attacks at Ypres 1915, Campaign Chronicles*. Barnsley, UK: Pen & Sword Military, 2009.

MacDonald, Lyn. *1915: The Death of Innocence*. London: Headline Book Publishing, 1993.

MacPherson, Donald Stuart. *A Soldier's Diary*. St. Catharines: Vanwell Publishing, 2001.

McClung, Nellie. *In Times Like These*. Reprint of the 1915 Toronto edition, Project Gutenberg, 2009. http://www.gutenberg.org/files/29861/29861-h/29861-h.htm.

———. *The Next of Kin: Those Who Wait and Wonder*. Reprint of the 1917 Toronto edition, Project Gutenberg, 2005. http://www.gutenberg.org/files/16552/16552-h/16552-h.htm.

————, and Mervin Simmons. *Three Times and Out*. Reprint of the 1918 Toronto edition, Project Gutenberg, 2004. http://www. gutenberg.org/ebooks/12880?msg=welcome_stranger.

Metaxas, Eric. *Bonhoeffer: Pastor, Martyr, Prophet, Spy*. Nashville: Thomas Nelson, 2010.

Morton, Desmond, and J. L. Granatstein. *Marching to Armageddon: Canadians and the Great War 1914–1919*. Toronto: Lester and Orpen Dennys, 1989.

Murray, William Waldie. *Five Nines and Whiz Bangs: "The Orderly Sergeant."* Ottawa: Legionary Library, 1937.

————. *History of the 2nd Battalion (East. Ontario Regiment): Canadian Expeditionary Force in the Great War, 1914–1918*. Ottawa: Historical Committee, 2nd Battalion, C.E.F., 1947.

Nicholson, G. W. L. *Official History of the Canadian Army in the First World War: Canadian Expeditionary Force, 1914–1919*. Ottawa: Queen's Printer, 1962.

Otter, Rev. William. *The Life and Remains of Edward Daniel Clarke: Professor of Mineralogy in the University of Cambridge*. New York, 1827. https://archive.org/details/liferemainsofedw01otte.

Purdom, C. B., ed. *Everyman at War: Sixty Personal Narratives of the War*. London: J. M. Dent, 1930.

Rawling, Bill. *Surviving Trench Warfare: Technology and the Canadian Corps, 1914–1918*. Toronto: University of Toronto Press, 1992.

Reed, John. *War in Eastern Europe: Travels through the Balkans in 1915*. London: Orion Books, 1995.

Reid, Brian A. *Named by the Enemy: A History of the Royal Winnipeg Rifles*. Winnipeg: The Royal Winnipeg Rifles, 2010.

Scott, Frederick. *The Great War As I Saw It*. Toronto: F. D. Goodchild, 1922.

Sinclair, J. D., ed. *The Queen's Own Cameron Highlanders of Canada, 25th Anniversary Souvenir.* N.p.: 1935.

Urquhart, Hugh. *The History of the Sixteenth Battalion.* Toronto, 1932. http://catalog.hathitrust.org/Record/000445747.

Vance, Jonathan. *Death So Noble: Memory, Meaning, and the First World War.* Vancouver: UBC Press, 1997.

Watson, Alexander. *Enduring the Great War: Combat, Morale, and Collapse in the German and British Armies, 1914–1918.* Cambridge: Cambridge University Press, 2008.

Wheatcroft, Andrew. *The Hapsburgs: Embodying Empire.* London: Viking, 1995.

Wheeler, Victor W. *The 50th Battalion in No Man's Land. 50th Canadian Infantry Battalion (Alberta Regiment) Canadian Expeditionary Force 1915–1919.* Ottawa: CEF Books, 2000.

UNPUBLISHED AND SELF-PUBLISHED MATERIAL

Clarke, Amelia Birnie. "Autobiography" (unpublished manuscript, undated), handwritten pages.

Clarke, Arthur. Letter to Harry Clarke, May 11, 1916.

Clarke, Charles. "Autobiography by Charles E. Clarke, 1895–1974" (unpublished manuscript, undated), typewritten pages.

———. "Incidents & Anecdotes: Trench Life in Flanders Fields with the Red Patch, 1914–1918" (unpublished manuscript, undated), typewritten pages.

———. "Leo Clarke" (unpublished manuscript, undated).

———. "One Man's Warfare" (unpublished manuscript, undated).

———. "Vignettes of Vimy" (unpublished manuscript, undated), typewritten pages.

————. "Weekend Review, Omands Creek" (unpublished manuscript, undated), typewritten pages.

Hall, Henry Cecil "Harry." "Correspondence with Gail Burton" (private collection).

Thirty-Second Battalion Association. "Members of the 32nd Battalion Association C.E.F. Association Directory and List of Members" (*circa* 1940), scanned pages.

Wade, George. "Lieutenant Robert Shankland: Ayr's Supreme Hero" (unpublished manuscript).

INDEX